W9-AJO-240

PRO/CON VOLUME 6

MEDIA

Fluvanna County High School
3717 Central Plains Road
Palmyra, VA 22963

Published 2002 by Grolier Educational
Sherman Turnpike
Danbury, Connecticut 06816

© 2002 Brown Partworks Limited

Library of Congress Cataloging-in-Publication Data

Pro/con
p. cm
Includes bibliographical references and index.
Contents: v. 1. The individual and society – v. 2. Government – v. 3. Economics – v.
4. Environment – v. 5. Science – v. 6. Media,
ISBN 0-7172-5638-3 (set : alk. paper) – ISBN 0-7172-5639-1 (vol. 1 : alk. paper) –
ISBN 0-7172-5640-5 (vol. 2 : alk. paper) – ISBN 0-7172-5641-3 (vol. 3 : alk. paper) –
ISBN 0-7172-5642-1 (vol. 4 : alk. paper) – ISBN 0-7172-5643-X (vol. 5 : alk. paper) –
ISBN 0-7172-5644-8 (vol. 6 : alk. paper)
1. Social problems. I. Grolier Educational (Firm)

HN17.5 P756 2002
361.1–dc21

2001053234

Printed and bound in Singapore

SET ISBN 0-7172-5638-3
VOLUME ISBN 0-7172-5644-8

For Brown Partworks Limited
Project Editors: Aruna Vasudevan, Fiona Plowman
Editors: Sally McFall, Dawn Titmus, Matt Turner, Ben Hoare
Consultant Editors: James Shanahan,
Department of Communication, Cornell University
Fritz Messere, Associate Professor, Communication Studies, SUNY Oswego
Designer: Sarah Williams
Picture Researcher: Clare Newman
Set Index: Kay Ollerenshaw

Managing Editor: Tim Cooke
Design Manager: Lynne Ross
Production Manager: Matt Weyland

GENERAL PREFACE

"All that is necessary for evil to triumph is for good men to do nothing."
—Edmund Burke, 18th-century British political philosopher

Decisions

Life is full of choices and decisions. Some are more important than others. Some affect only your daily life—the route you take to school, for example, or what you prefer to eat for supper— while others are more abstract and concern questions of right and wrong rather than practicality. That does not mean that your choice of presidential candidate or your views on abortion are necessarily more important than your answers to purely personal questions. But it is likely that those wider questions are more complex and subtle and that you therefore will need to know more information about the subject before you can try to answer them. They are also likely to be questions about which you might have to justify your views to other people. In order to do that, you need to be able to make informed decisions, be able to analyze every fact at your disposal, and evaluate them in an unbiased manner.

What is *Pro/Con*?

Pro/Con is a collection of debates that presents conflicting views on some of the more complex and general issues facing Americans today. By bringing together extracts from a wide range of sources—mainstream newspapers and magazines, books, famous speeches, legal judgments, religious tracts, government surveys—the set reflects current informed attitudes toward dilemmas that range from the best way to feed the world's growing population to gay rights, and from the connection between political freedom and capitalism to the fate of Napster.

The people whose arguments make up the set are all acknowledged experts in their fields, and that makes the vast differences in their points of view even more remarkable. The arguments are presented in the form of debates for and against various propositions, such as "Does Global Warming Threaten Humankind?" or "Should the Media Be Subject to Censorship?" This question format reflects the way in which ideas often occur in daily life: in the classroom, on TV shows, in business meetings, or even in state or federal politics.

The contents

The subjects of the six volumes of the set—*Individual and Society, Government, Economics, Environment, Science*, and *Media*—are issues on which it is preferable that people's opinions are based on information rather than simply on personal bias.

Special boxes throughout *Pro/Con* comment on the debates as you are reading them, pointing out facts or analyzing arguments to help you think about what is being said.

Introductions and summaries also provide background information that might help you reach your own conclusions. There are also comments and tips about how to structure an argument that you can apply on an every day basis to any debate or conversation, learning how to present your point of view as effectively and persuasively as possible.

3

VOLUME PREFACE
Media

The word "media" comes from the Latin word for middle—*medius*—and originally referred to the connection between news or information and people. That connection has grown in the last century, so much so that the media are one of the most important influences on society today, shaping every aspect of our lives from our thoughts and the way we dress to the way we perceive ourselves and others.

Why are media important?

Over the years society has come to recognize the influence and power of the media on society. While at the beginning of the 20th century the average person got information from reading newspapers, magazines, and books, radio and movies changed that within decades. The influence of television on U.S. culture from the 1960s, the power of Hollywood, and the emergence of the Internet at the end of the century have all increased the range and influence of the media today.

Although there are many different views on the role played by the mass media—newspapers, magazines, radio, television, movies, the Internet—many scholars believe that it is just as important to understand a popular culture product, such as a film like *The Matrix*—one of many films currently studied in media studies departments around the world— precisely because millions of people will go to see it, and it thus has the power to potentially influence their thoughts and behavior. By comparison, academic culture may potentially influence a much smaller audience and have less effect on society.

Influence on society

The relationship between the media and society—for example, the influence of movie and TV violence on behavior in society—has been the subject of many recent studies. The power of media to influence individual and group behavior has led critics to question whether the media should be monitored in some way. In liberal democracies, such as the United States, however, any talk of media regulation immediately leads to concerns about censorship and possible restrictions on the individual's right to free speech.

The increased importance and growth in information technology in the global economy have made the issue of regulation increasingly important. Easy access to the Internet has meant that everyone has the opportunity to tap into a wide range of information literally at the click of a button. But because anyone can post material on the World Wide Web, information there can range from quotation and dictionary sites to those featuring child pornography, racist literature, or instructions on how to make a bomb.

Media regulation is just one of many issues discussed in this volume. It is important to understand the effect that the media have on your behavior and opinions. This volume will help you do that by discussing important issues currently under debate in this area.

HOW TO USE THIS BOOK

Each volume of *Pro/Con* is divided into sections, each of which has an introduction that examines its theme. Within each section are a series of debates that present arguments for and against a proposition, such as whether or not the death penalty should be abolished. An introduction to each debate puts it into its wider context, and a summary and key map (see below) highlight the main points of the debate clearly and concisely. Each debate has marginal boxes that focus on particular points, give tips on how to present an argument, or help question the writer's case. The summaries to the debates have supplementary material to help you do further research.

Boxes and other materials provide additional background information. There are also special materials on how to improve your debating and report-writing skills. At the end of each book is a glossary that provides brief explanations of key words in the volume. The index covers all six books, so it will help you trace topics throughout the set.

background information
Frequent text boxes provide background information on important concepts and key individuals or events.

summary boxes
Summary boxes are useful reminders of both sides of the argument.

further information
Further Reading lists for each debate direct you to related books, articles, and websites so you can do your own research.

other articles in the Pro/Con series,
See Also boxes list related debates throughout the Pro/Con series.

marginal boxes
Margin boxes highlight key points in the argument, give extra information, or help you question the author's meaning.

key map
Key maps provide a graphic representation of the central points of the debate.

CONTENTS

PART 1
MEDIA AND SOCIETY

The word "media" derives from the Latin *medius*, meaning middle, and reflects the original role of the various media as the connection between news or information and people. The media tell people not only what is happening, but also in many cases how to perceive it. It is because of the power of this role that the media have often been the subject of controversy. Those who disseminate information have the potential power to control it.

Although the role of the media has often been the subject of debate, it became a particular issue during the 20th century. Technological developments increased the range of the media, the speed at which they worked, and the masses of people they could reach. The power of the mass media—newspapers, magazines, radio, television, movies, the Internet—grew, and so did a corresponding suspicion.

At the beginning of the century newspapers, magazines, and books dominated the information diet of the average citizen. Within decades, however, the emergence and popularity of the radio on one hand and movies on the other both fascinated and horrified audiences and social critics. The dominance of television from the 1960s and the emergence of the Internet at the end of the century provoked the same mixture of excitement and nervousness. The questions people ask about the media—Do violent images provoke violence in viewers? What effect does it have on the imagination and emotions of children?—are often the same that were asked in the late 1920s by studies into the effects of film on audiences.

Media and society

The relationship between society and the media is highly complex. At its heart lies a contradictory tension. On the one hand, people generally support a philosophy of free speech, as enshrined in the First Amendment, and therefore of free media. On the other, however, there is continual anxiety about the possible effects of the media.

Common sense seems to suggest, for example, that if the media show violent images, that might have the social effect of making violence more acceptable. In dealing with such questions, a socially liberal approach that advocates media freedom often comes into conflict with research that suggests the negative effects of the media. Why protect the freedom of media that have manifestly negative effects? One possible answer is that a simple cause-and-effect relationship between the media and behavior is very difficult to test and remains unproven. In such a situation many people seem to feel that the negative effects of the media are a price worth paying for its positive effects as a source of information, entertainment, and so on.

Censorship

Topic 1 Should the Media Be Subject to Censorship? examines the arguments surrounding this central issue. Although world media have moved away from government control toward a more market-oriented system—but often not during wartime—censorship of various types still remains an issue. The market censors viewpoints by limiting access for those with fewer economic resources. The self-censorship of an entertainment society, content to focus on sitcoms, sports, and sensational news, also troubles some observers.

watching too much television. This subject is examined in *Topic 3 Do People Watch Too Much Television?* Behind the issue lies a moral concern that someone sitting in front of a television/video screen could be doing something more "productive."

This concern is part of a wider debate about the effect of television, film, and music on behavior. That concern led to the development of technology such as the V-chip in the United States, which is supposed to help parents control children's exposure to certain television programs.

"Our liberty depends on the freedom of the press and that cannot be limited without being lost."

—THOMAS JEFFERSON, THIRD U.S. PRESIDENT

Celebrity v. privacy

Topic 2 Do Newsmakers Have a Right to Privacy? looks at celebrities and the media, and raises some interesting questions. By virtue of becoming "public figures," do celebrities relinquish their rights to privacy? Does the public's right to information about a public figure outweigh that figure's right to privacy? Should we have unrestricted access to information about our politicians, even extending to very graphic and detailed information about their private lives?

TV, the V-chip, and violence

Television has attracted much research and media attention since it became the most popular of the media in the 1960s. Early educators were concerned that people, in particular children, were

This subject is examined in *Topic 4 Does the V-chip Work?* The broader relationship between violence in the media and the individuals who watch it is discussed in *Topic 5 Does Movie and Television Violence Cause Social Violence?*

Body images

Finally, *Topic 6 Do the Media Encourage a Distorted Body Image?* and the article on *Eating Disorders* on pages 84–85 discuss the possible effects of media exposure on personal health. Given that the media increasingly tend to focus on difficult-to-attain body ideals—absurdly thin women or highly muscular and "macho" men—does exposure to such images have a connection to the occurrence of eating disorders among young people?

Topic 1

SHOULD THE MEDIA BE SUBJECT TO CENSORSHIP?

YES

"THE MATTER OF THE PLAGUE/DIE SACHE MIT DER LEICHENPEST"
FROM *DAS EHERNE HERZ,* MUNICH, 1943
JOSEF GOEBBELS

NO

"FREEDOM OF EXPRESSION IN THE ARTS AND THE MEDIA"
ACLU REPORT 14, 1997
AMERICAN CIVIL LIBERTIES UNION

INTRODUCTION

The media are subject to many types of censorship of varying degrees of stringency. In the U.S. the government exerts very direct controls on the media in terms of both content and structure. The Federal Communication Commission (FCC) controls access to the airwaves through licensing and exerts influence on program content through its licensing activities, through rule making in areas such as political communication, and through regulations dealing with areas such as obscenity, equal employment, and fairness in the media.

Courts do generally hold that so-called "prior restraint" of the media is objectionable. Instances of prior restraint are not uncommon, however, especially in times of crisis. During wartime, as the first article on this topic reveals, governments take an even more direct role in censorship, directly limiting or revising material that might be detrimental to a nation's war effort.

Are such activities in keeping with a society that places great emphasis on free communication? Or do a nation's war aims override the importance of the free flow of information?

In World War II the German minister of propaganda, Josef Goebbels, took total control of the news media and punished by imprisonment or death anyone seeking an alternative view to his own. In the recent history of the United States the Vietnam War is generally considered to have presented a defining moment for press coverage of a war and a nation's war aims. The pressure placed on the government during the waning years of the Vietnam War was seen to have emerged largely from the power of television in conveying two aspects of the war: the deadly carnage and the lack of clarity in American policy. Taken together, they created a situation that George Bush, Sr., would later dub the "Vietnam syndrome": a nation paralyzed by fear of public opposition to American blood being shed, leading to an ineffective conduct of the war. The Bush administration and the Pentagon thus pursued what became a very successful policy of information control. They allowed only a few reporters access to the scenes of battle during the Gulf War and subjected reporters to direct supervision from military aides, who could literally censor material after it left the sites.

"Whenever books are burned, men also in the end are burned."

—HEINRICH HEINE, WRITER

Such restraint was widely accepted by the U.S. public, which rated Bush very highly as a president throughout the war. The campaign of yellow ribbons to "support the troops" tended to mask opposition to the war as well as public awareness of the censorship that was taking place. Even *Saturday Night Live* helped out by lampooning reporters who sought information about key battle plans as sabotaging war aims. Veteran reporter Peter Arnett was criticized for reporting from what some considered to be an Iraqi perspective.

War presents perhaps the toughest test case for our views on media censorship. On the one hand, a nation is never more focused than when it is at war; this is the time for information to flow freely and quickly to fuel debate and develop policy. On the other hand, the consequences of unrestricted

access to information are highest during wartime: Unfettered reporting could endanger lives or even the nation itself.

Who decides how far the government can go in censoring news? During recent conflicts the government has operated with relative freedom. Not since the Vietnam War has there been a major public debate about its role in controlling information during wartime.

The following articles present two views on the issue. In the first article Josef Goebbels underlines his view that during wartime only the government is in full possession of the facts and can judge what is best for the people to know or not to know. Further, he contends, anyone seeking information from any source other than governmental agencies is a traitor and should be subject to the full rigors of the law. In the second article the American Civil Liberties Union takes the unequivocal view that censorship of any kind is a direct affront to our First Amendment rights. No one— certainly not government—has any right to make decisions about what we can or cannot watch, listen to, or read, it says. The ACLU argues that any form of censorship, no matter how minimal, would be the beginning of the end for free speech—and for freedom itself.

Should the United States become involved in another war, it seems likely that the Gulf War experience will provide the touchstone for how we approach public access to information. Moreover, the experience sheds light on wider questions of how the media inform the U.S. people. Research suggests that journalists went along with the government's management of the news, supporting the war from the outset. But what does this say about an independent press?

THE MATTER OF THE PLAGUE
Josef Goebbels

YES

In the interests of the war, German news policy was forced into silence, which naturally led to a certain nervousness on the part of the German people. English and Bolshevist propaganda thought that their hour had come. They could speak, we could not. All the nonsense from London and Moscow over the past weeks would take a long time to discuss. It is also unnecessary to repeat any of it. It is already trash, tossed aside by the fiery storm of earth-shaking military operations whose long-term effects we still cannot entirely foresee. Silence was worth it.

In all their chattering and boasting, the Bolshevists and the English entirely forgot to pay attention. They thought our reluctance to answer their simple and ridiculous lies was the result of weakness, so one day Budenny and his five armies found themselves in our trap. We won a battle that will go down in history as a classic battle of annihilation. Now all the uproar is on the other side.

Illusionary successes and false predictions
We have often seen similar things during the war. They always follow the same plan, and one should assume that our opponents have learned something. There is no evidence that they have. They run into the mousetrap as soon as they smell the cheese, with the result that their premature shouts of victory lead to a moral defeat as well.

If only they could shut up and wait! But no, they take their illusionary successes seriously and keep talking big. If we had made even a small percentage of the mistakes they have made, not even a dog would take a piece of bread from us. It began with Poland and continues in the Soviet Union. They have always made false predictions. They still have the gall to present themselves to the world as pure and incorruptible fanatics for truth who present things as they are, while we, they claim, abolish freedom of the press, send lie after lie into the world, and lie so much that even we do not know the truth any longer.

It is true that we have made some mistakes during the war. We do not hesitate to admit it. By and large, however, we have told the truth. In contrast to England, we have correctly

The term "Bolshevist" refers to the Bolshevik (or Communist) Party that took power in Russia in 1917. The word is often used in a derogatory sense to describe any radical party or person that advocates revolution or anarchy.

Semyen Mikhailovich Budenny was in command of Soviet military forces defeated by the Germans.

Goebbels claims that the Allies have accused Germany of manipulating the truth about the war. It has been said that truth is always the first casualty of war. Why might this be the case?

estimated the military, economic, and psychological strengths of the warring powers. We do not need to be embarrassed when one reminds us of our speeches and articles from 1939 or 1940. Can Mr. Churchill say the same? He missed the bus just before the Norwegian campaign. Then there was the unbreakable Maginot Line, the Ruppel Pass that could be held forever, the Island of Crete that England would defend as dearly as its own life, or the Stalin Line, which was to be defended to the last man, but then suddenly never even existed. All swindles and lies!

Winston Churchill was British prime minister and wartime leader from 1940 until the war's end in 1945.

The power of propaganda

One ought to be able to assume that English news policy has lost all credibility with neutral nations. To the contrary! Swedish and Swiss newspapers cite their lies every day with general satisfaction, printing our facts only when they can no longer be denied. There are even some unteachable people among us who cannot resist turning secretly and quietly, behind closed doors, to Radio London in order to enrich their political and military knowledge with English swindles. Two recent death sentences and a series of prison terms proves that. What are they doing wrong? Their behavior is not only criminal, it is tremendously stupid. They can hardly seriously maintain that the plutocrats in London are producing expensive German-language programming to keep Herr Bramsig and Frau Knöterich informed about the political and military situation. They openly admit that they are doing it to throw our people into uncertainty and sow dissension between the leadership and the nation. Their news is directed entirely toward this goal, and serves only this purpose. Herr Bramsig and Frau Knöterich volunteer, with no compulsion, to hear such nonsense. Do they gain anything? Hardly! First, they run the risk of ending up in jail as traitors, and secondly, even if that does not happen, they wind up with new worries and sleepless nights, since they have no way to separate right from wrong and truth from falsehood.

"Propaganda" is the deliberate spreading of ideas, information, half-truths, or rumors to boost the standing of one's own position or to undermine the position of one's opponent or enemy.

Bramsig and Knöterich are Goebbels' stereotypes of foolish Germans taken in by British propaganda.

The manipulation of statistics

The English for example estimated our casualties at three million during the weeks we were silent. That naturally was utter nonsense. First, the English are in no position to estimate our losses, and second they do not want to, since they want to cause unrest in the German population through their enormously exaggerated figures. We cannot reply to their lies since we want to provide only accurate figures, which simply are not available at the moment. We therefore

Here Goebbels points out what he considers to be the dangers of listening to an enemy's version of events. Do you think that propaganda is an effective weapon of war, and why? Should propaganda be called a form of censorship?

Josef Goebbels, the minister of propaganda in Adolf Hitler's regime, seen here speaking in 1940. Goebbels controlled all aspects of the media in Nazi Germany during World War II.

have to restrict ourselves to saying that our losses are at the expected levels, which we can say in good conscience given the facts available to us. The prison-deserving listeners to Radio London run around for three or four weeks with a casualty total of three million, whispering it to others, only to learn one day that although our losses are painful to those directly involved, they are not even 10 percent of the English figures.

In Nazi Germany during World War II it was an offense punishable by death or imprisonment to listen to enemy radio broadcasts.

The silence of the German media

Aside from the criminal nature of such behavior, does it really pay to listen to the English? We have to listen to them for professional reasons. Cross our hearts, we would be delighted if we were free from this unpleasant duty. It is so boring and stupid that it gradually revolts us. Remember too that we know how things really stand, and thus can separate truth from swindle, something Herr Bramsig and Frau Knöterich cannot do. No one gives them speeches about the real state of things. If our radio and press are silent, it usually means operations of truly gigantic scope are being prepared. It is the duty of each German to wait with confidence—a confidence, by the way, that is justified by countless historical successes. When [people] secretly listen to Radio London, they are being played for fools by our most bitter enemies.

Here Goebbels tries to justify the fact that his totalitarian government does not keep the German people informed about the progress of the war. What are the benefits and dangers of this policy of media silence?

That is not only criminal, it is absolutely unfair. The Führer and his military and political staff are working day and night, and not for themselves, but for the people that mean everything to them. Just before the great successes, they often hold their breaths, wondering if everything will work … if perhaps somewhere unforeseen problems will surface. Then they are delighted to once again announce a great victory to the people, compensating them for the long period of silence. Our soldiers march day and night through dust and rain, destroying bunkers and fortifications, wading through streams and swimming across raging rivers, having only one thought: to close the pocket at the right time and to seal the enemy within an unbreakable wall.

The Führer was Germany's wartime leader, Adolf Hitler.

Learning the lessons of the past

Meanwhile, Herr Bramsig and Frau Knöterich sit at the radio listening to Mr. Churchill. That is thankless, contemptible and vile….We know well enough the terrible consequences British propaganda had for us in the World War. We do not want to run the risk of that danger a second time. If we had had someone then able to stand up to London's lies, this war probably would not have been necessary. This time, we have learned our lesson thoroughly and forever more.

The world war referred to here is World War I, which took place in the years 1914–1918. Germany and its allies were defeated by the United States, Britain, and France, among others.

15

FREEDOM OF EXPRESSION IN THE ARTS AND THE MEDIA
American Civil Liberties Union

NO

In the late 1980s, state prosecutors brought a criminal obscenity charge against the owner of a record store for selling an album by the rap group, 2 Live Crew. Although this was the first time that obscenity charges had ever been brought against song lyrics, the 2 Live Crew case focused the nation's attention on an old question: should the government ever have the authority to dictate to its citizens what they may or may not listen to, read, or watch?

Censorship and the First Amendment

American society has always been deeply ambivalent about this question. On the one hand, our history is filled with examples of overt government censorship, from the 1873 Comstock Law to the 1996 Communications Decency Act. Anthony Comstock, head of the Society for the Suppression of Vice, boasted 194,000 "questionable pictures" and 134,000 pounds of books of "improper character" were destroyed under the Comstock Law—in the first year alone. The Communications Decency Act imposed an unconstitutional censorship scheme on the Internet, accurately described by a federal judge as "the most participatory form of mass speech yet developed."

On the other hand, the commitment to freedom of imagination and expression is deeply embedded in our national psyche, buttressed by the First Amendment, and supported by a long line of Supreme Court decisions. Provocative and controversial art and in-your-face entertainment put our commitment to free speech to the test. Why should we oppose censorship when scenes of murder and mayhem dominate the TV screen, when works of art can be seen as a direct insult to peoples' religious beliefs, and when much sexually explicit material can be seen as degrading to women? Why not let the majority's morality and taste dictate what others can look at or listen to?

The answer is simple, and timeless: a free society is based on the principle that each and every individual has the right to decide what art or entertainment he or she wants—or does not want—to receive or create. Once you allow the government to censor someone else, you cede to it the power to censor you, or something you like. Censorship is like poison gas: a powerful weapon that can harm you when the wind shifts. Freedom of expression for ourselves requires freedom of expression for others. It is at the very heart of our democracy.

Sexual speech

Sex in art and entertainment is the most frequent target of censorship crusades. Many examples come to mind. A painting of the classical statue of Venus de Milo was removed from a store because the managers of the shopping mall found its semi-nudity "too shocking." Hundreds of works of literature, from Maya Angelou's *I Know Why the Caged Bird Sings* to John Steinbeck's *Grapes of Wrath*, have been banned from public schools based on their sexual content. A museum director was charged with a crime for including sexually explicit photographs by Robert Mapplethorpe [1946-1989] in an exhibit.

American law is, on the whole, the most speech-protective in the world—but sexual expression is treated as a second-class citizen. No causal link between exposure to sexually explicit material and anti-social or violent behavior has ever been scientifically established, in spite of many efforts to do so. Rather, the Supreme Court has allowed censorship of sexual speech on moral grounds—a remnant of our nation's Puritan heritage.

This does not mean that all sexual expression can be censored, however. Only a narrow range of "obscene" material can be suppressed; a term like "pornography" has no legal meaning. Nevertheless, even the relatively narrow obscenity exception serves as a vehicle for abuse by government authorities as well as pressure groups who want to impose their personal moral views on other people.

What does artistic freedom include?

The Supreme Court has interpreted the First Amendment's protection of artistic expression very broadly. It extends not only to books, theatrical works and paintings, but also to posters, television, music videos and comic books—whatever the human creative impulse produces. Two fundamental principles come into play whenever a court must decide a case involving freedom of expression. The first is "content neutrality"—the government cannot limit expression just because any listener, or even the majority of a community, is

Should works of art that were created centuries ago in different times and cultures be judged by the prevailing moral codes of the present day? Do we have the right to impose a form of retrospective censorship on the creative efforts of a bygone age?

COMMENTARY: Challenged books

Even before the invention of printing in the the 15th century people have sought to ban or suppress certain books for ideological reasons. In 1933 in Nazi Germany, for example, students, academics, and Nazis publicly burned books that they considered to be "un-German." Such books had been written by left-wing, pacifist, and Jewish authors. The right to freedom of expression is enshrined in the U.S. Constitution, yet even today there are people who seek to ban certain books. Every year the American Library Association's Office for Intellectual Freedom releases its list of the "10 Most Challenged Books" of the year. In 1999 J.K. Rowling's books featuring Harry Potter were the most frequently challenged of the year and among the 100 most frequently challenged books of the decade. For most people who have read *Harry Potter*, the books create a magical world. Yet for the people who protest about them, the books are evil because they are about witchcraft. The main reason for challenging any book, however, is that it is too sexually explicit. Judy Blume, one of the most popular of contemporary young people's writers, appears on the Top 100 list five times, more than any other author. Some of her books deal with issues such as puberty and sexual awakening. Similarly Michael Willhoite's book *Daddy's Roommate* was said to promote homosexuality. Both Willhoite and Blume say their books aim to help young people cope with important issues in their lives. The following list indicates why certain books have been challenged.

Top 10 most challenged books from 1990 to 1999

1. *Scary Stories* by Alvin Schwartz—said to be scary, violent, and to deal with the occult.
2. *Daddy's Roommate* by Michael Willhoite—said to promote homosexuality and be inappropriate for age group.
3. *I Know Why the Caged Bird Sings* by Maya Angelou—seen as sexually explicit.
4. *The Chocolate War* by Robert Cormier—said to contain offensive language and be sexually explicit.
5. *The Adventures of Huckleberry Finn* by Mark Twain—said to have offensive language and be racist.
6. *Of Mice and Men* by John Steinbeck—thought to contain offensive language.
7. *Forever* by Judy Blume—thought to be sexually explicit, contain profanity, and challenge morality (premarital sex).
8. *Bridge to Terabithia* by Katherine Paterson—said to contain offensive language and promote fantasy (references to witchcraft).
9. *Heather Has Two Mommies* by Leslea Newman—said to promote homosexuality and be inappropriate for age group.
10. *The Catcher in the Rye* by J. D. Salinger—thought to contain offensive language and be sexually explicit.

offended by its content. In the context of art and entertainment, this means tolerating some works that we might find offensive, insulting, outrageous—or just plain bad. The second principle is that expression may be restricted only if it will clearly cause direct and imminent harm to an important societal interest. The classic example is falsely shouting fire in a crowded theater and causing a stampede. Even then, the speech may be silenced or punished only if there is no other way to avert the harm.…

Do you agree that with freedom of expression comes a responsibility to ensure that no other person or group is harmed in the process? How important is the concept of self-regulation in a free society?

Which media violence would you ban?

A pro-censorship member of Congress once attacked the following shows for being too violent: *The Miracle Worker*, *Civil War Journal*, *Star Trek 9*, *The Untouchables*, and *Teenage Mutant Ninja Turtles*. What would be left if all these kinds of programs were purged from the airwaves? Is there good violence and bad violence? If so, who decides? Sports and the news are at least as violent as fiction, from the fights that erupt during every televised hockey game, to the videotaped beating of Rodney King by the LA Police Department, shown over and over again on prime time TV. If we accept censorship of violence in the media, we will have to censor sports and news programs.

The Independent Media Center is a collective of media organizations and journalists. It describes itself as a "democratic media outlet for the creation of radical, accurate, and passionate tellings of truth." See www.indy media.org.

Individual rights, individual decisions

The First Amendment is based upon the belief that in a free and democratic society, individual adults must be free to decide for themselves what to read, write, paint, draw, see and hear. If we are disturbed by images of violence or sex, we can change the channel, turn off the TV, and decline to go to certain movies or museum exhibits. We can also exercise our own free speech rights by voicing our objections to forms of expression that we don't like. Justice Louis Brandeis' advice that the remedy for messages we disagree with or dislike in art, entertainment or politics is "more speech, not enforced silence," is as true today as it was when given in 1927.

Louis Dembitz Brandeis (1856– 1941) was a progressive liberal who became the first Jewish member of the Supreme Court in 1916.

Conclusion

[W]e can exercise our prerogative as parents without resorting to censorship. Devices now exist that make it possible to block access to specific TV programs and internet sites. Periodicals that review books, recordings, and films can help parents determine what they feel is appropriate for their youngsters. Viewing decisions can, and should, be made at home, without government interference.

Summary

Should the media be subject to censorship? Even in the case of military conflicts in which lives are at stake, there are public rights to information. Journalists will battle for access to information, while information managers and politicians attempt to spin things (propagandize) for their own benefit. Corporations, universities, and the military recognize the importance of public understanding and public opinion.

The first article by Josef Goebbels, the minister for propaganda in Adolf Hitler's Third Reich, made the case for government control of information in wartime. He argued that it is the Nazi government that knows best what the people should and should not be told about the progress of the war. He strongly disapproved of those citizens who seek an alternative source of news in Allied radio broadcasts, which he dismissed as enemy propaganda. His desire to gain and keep control of the news agenda reached to the imprisonment or execution of any German citizen who sought an unapproved version of the truth.

In the second article the American Civil Liberties Union argues for complete freedom of expression in the arts and the media. The concept of censorship, it says, is not compatible with the First Amendment, and the government should have no place in deciding what art or entertainment a citizen can or cannot consume. The ACLU recognizes only very limited restraints on the freedom of the individual, and in the case of material deemed harmful to children, it espouses parental guidance over governmental interference. A central theme of the article is that any form of censorship, no matter how small, would merely be the beginning of a downward spiral that would see the concepts of morality and decency twisted by those with ulterior motives, inexorably leading to the death of free speech and of freedom itself.

FURTHER INFORMATION:

Books:

Foerstel, Herbert N., *Banned in the Media*. Westport, CT: Greenwood Press, 1998.

Heins, Marjorie, *Not in Front of the Children: Indecency, Censorship, and the Innocence of Youth*. New York: Hill & Wang Publishers, 2001.

Shaw, Colin, *Deciding What We Watch: Taste, Decency, and Media Ethics in the U.K. and the USA*. Oxford, U.K.: Clarendon Press, 1999.

Useful websites:

www.freedomforum.org
The Freedom Forum website, dedicated to free speech.

The following debates in the Pro/Con series may also be of interest:

In this volume:
Censorship in the Media, pages 22–23

Topic 4 Does the V-chip work?

Topic 12 Should the Internet be policed?

SHOULD THE MEDIA BE SUBJECT TO CENSORSHIP?

YES: Giving people free access to military information could jeopardize the outcome and endanger lives. The banning of foreign propaganda is necessary to prevent the undermining of national morale.

YES: Young people are vulnerable and lack the judgment of adults. Therefore they need to be protected from certain harmful media.

WARTIME
Is it appropriate to censor news during wartime?

YOUTH
Should certain media items be censored for teenagers?

NO: Military information is inevitably sensitive, but the public has a right to know what the government is doing on its behalf in wartime

NO: Parents have the right to monitor what their own children watch, read, or listen to. The government has no mandate to decide what information, art, or entertainment can or cannot be consumed.

SHOULD THE MEDIA BE SUBJECT TO CENSORSHIP? KEY POINTS

YES: Cries for freedom of speech ignore the fact that certain members of society, especially children, are vulnerable to harmful media

YES: Harmful items, such as child pornography, and sensitive information, such as in wartime, should be subject to censorship

FREEDOM OF EXPRESSION
Is censorship compatible with our rights to free speech?

NO: Censorship of any kind is a direct affront to our First Amendment rights

NO: Any attempt at censorship is ideologically based and should always be resisted

Topic 2
DO NEWSMAKERS HAVE A RIGHT TO PRIVACY?

YES
"THE MEDIA: SINKING EVER DEEPER"
THE WASHINGTON POST, DECEMBER 2, 1998
JUDY MANN

NO
"IF IT'S *OK!* FOR STARS TO CASH IN ON WEDDINGS ... THEN THEY
MUST ACCEPT IT IS *HELLO!* TO LOSS OF PRIVACY"
"OPINION AND LETTERS," *THE GUARDIAN*, DECEMBER 23, 2000
MARK LAWSON

INTRODUCTION

Newsmakers often complain about the stories that circulate about them in the media. They feel that they should be known for their work rather than their private lives, and that they are entitled to privacy like any other citizen. Following the news of the breakdown of their marriage, film actors Tom Cruise and Nicole Kidman appealed to the media to leave them to sort out their problems in private. However, the media produced numerous stories about the breakup of Hollywood's golden couple, including ones that speculated about Cruise's sexuality and Kidman's fidelity.

The media, on the other hand, respond that the public has a right to know about the lives of public figures. If some celebrities court publicity to enhance their careers, then they should accept any bad publicity along with the good. But if a person is in the media spotlight, should they have to accept the risk of being hounded by reporters and having the intimate details of their lives made public, often in sordid detail?

In this topic the authors examine some recent events to determine how far the normally accepted privilege of privacy extends in a media world. Most people want, like Greta Garbo, to be "left alone," a right that in 1890 American judge Louis Brandeis declared was the most important right. At least two classes of people have come under increasing scrutiny in today's society: the celebrity and the politician.

The 1990s presented several cases that illustrate how the media can intrude on individual privacy. The story of Diana, Princess of Wales, shows how celebrities can engage in a bizarre love/hate relationship with the media when it comes to privacy—using the media for desired publicity and criticizing them when they feel they are portrayed in a negative light. As soon as Diana became connected with the Prince of Wales, her photogenic image was rarely absent from the pages of the world's press. While she frequently complained about the media attention, Diana also dealt directly with the media, releasing details that she felt would be beneficial to her reputation, particularly after the breakdown of her marriage. After her death in a high-speed car chase with the paparazzi in 1997, Diana's brother claimed that the tabloid media had actually killed her.

Former President Bill Clinton made ill-advised decisions when it came to the issue of his sexual involvement with former White House intern Monica Lewinsky (see *Government* volume, *The Case of President Clinton*, pages 200–201). Even if we accept that Clinton's judgment was poor, was it right that his private affair should be opened up to public scrutiny? The independent counsel pursuing the case, Kenneth Starr, seemed to think that such indiscretions were a matter of the public record for a "public figure."

Ordinary Americans, however, disagreed in two ways. First, they continued to support Clinton during the ordeal, paradoxically raising their support for him as he came under further attack. Also, in public opinion polls Americans consistently argued that the media were paying too much attention to the scandal. However, they belied this concern in one important way: They watched and read all news about the scandal. The ratings for news programs that dealt with the scandal were never higher. So what was the truth: Had Americans really had enough of the scandal, or should we believe the audience ratings?

In the first article a U.S. journalist argues that a line must be drawn somewhere on this issue. Coverage of the former U.S. first daughter, Chelsea Clinton, had been off-limits for some time when some tabloids focused on her alleged disapproval of her father's behavior. Most mainstream journalists disagreed with this, accepting the unwritten rule that presidential offspring should be off-limits.

> *"The most important service rendered by the press and the magazines is that of educating people to approach printed matter with distrust."*
>
> —SAMUEL BUTLER,
> ENGLISH AUTHOR

Judy Mann links this case to that of Jack Kevorkian, the Michigan doctor who was imprisoned for helping terminally ill people end their lives, to argue that certain things should simply remain off-limits.

An opposing view is taken in the second article in this section, which suggests that celebrities give up their rights to privacy when they enter the public arena. Britain, arguably, has the most intrusive press, and the article looks at the issue from a British perspective, where celebrities wage a continuing battle with the press over just how much of their private lives should be front-page material. The article does not sympathize much with celebrities, who, the author argues, have made a bargain of sorts with the devil.

THE MEDIA: SINKING EVER DEEPER
Judy Mann

Just when you think the media has hit bottom, something happens to let us know that we haven't yet excavated the last layer of pointless excess. Not by a long shot.

This observation comes courtesy of two stories that burst onto the national scene last week. The stories have little in common, except that in both, a human being's privacy was shredded.

I saw the first instance at the supermarket checkout. There was a time when all I did was read the tabloid headlines, not daring to pick up a copy lest someone I knew should see me reading it. "Look but don't touch" was my supermarket tabloid policy.

Then the tabs started breaking major stories from the dark edge of the cultural abyss. I started breaking my rule: If a headline grabs me, I'll pick up the tab and hastily try to find the story, cursing the editors for not having an index so I can read the story before I have to unload my groceries.

So there I was last week, in line with my Thanksgiving supplies when I saw the headlines about Chelsea Clinton in the *National Enquirer* and the *Star*. The *Enquirer* story, which I had time to skim, reported that Chelsea had had a screaming match with her father, President Clinton, and that her health was suffering as a result of the stress of the Lewinsky scandal.

The "Lewinsky scandal" refers to President Clinton's affair with a young intern at the White House, Monica Lewinsky.

Well, this was news to me, but hardly surprising, if it indeed happened. I can't imagine what my 19-year-old daughter would say to her stepfather if he had an affair, but I know it would be loud and it wouldn't be pretty. It also would not be public. We are not a public family.

The first daughter becomes fair game

The Clintons, however, are the most public family in America. They have done a wonderful job of raising their daughter, and the media have been unusually responsible in going along with their request that she be allowed to grow up out of the spotlight. But the tabloids have now decided that the 18-year-old Stanford sophomore is fair game. The rationale offered is that she's grown up and that she's being used as part of the White House spin machine, which makes her part of the story.

Chelsea Clinton, daughter of Hillary and Bill Clinton, during a visit to Ireland in 2000.

Star Editor Phil Bunton put it this way in an interview with *The Washington Post*:"She's getting more mature. She's inevitably been dragged into a peacemaking role between her mother and father and the fallout from the whole Monicagate thing. We felt, within some boundaries, it was all right to investigate her."

"Once a newspaper touches a story, the facts are lost forever, even to the protagonists."
—NORMAN MAILER, U.S. NOVELIST

What's wrong with this statement? For one thing, I cannot imagine President and Mrs. Clinton dragging their daughter into a marital mess as a peacekeeper. That burden should not be placed on any child's shoulders, no matter how old she is. Bunton's next loony notion is to "investigate her." For what? Bad grades? Is he going to dispatch a squad of bottom-feeding reporters to interrogate Chelsea's friends, teachers, the dorm mother? "Investigate" is a term usually associated with an inquiry into wrongdoing. You don't "investigate" a feature story on, say, Chelsea's roommate.

Pure exploitation

Where's the humanity in this? This has got to be the most difficult period of Chelsea Clinton's life. Most of us can think back on our sophomore year in college, and it wasn't easy. We had hard classes, and we were trying to grow up—and we weren't trying to do this under the watchful eye of the Secret Service while our father was in the political fight of his life. Chelsea doesn't need buzzards from the media swooping down on her. Turning her into fair game is nothing but pure exploitation. And whether the tabs do it or the mainstream press, given how murky the lines have become, it gives all of us a blooming black eye. If mainstream media organizations follow this predatory course, and we sink even further in the public's esteem, we've only ourselves to blame. Nobody else is driving this story.

Which brings us to the *60 Minutes* broadcast of Jack Kevorkian's [Dr. Death's] latest stunt. In this instance, the retired pathologist and tireless campaigner for euthanasia, or assisted suicide, is driving the story. He says he wants to obtain a legal resolution to the issue of euthanasia. To

Do you agree that the children of people in the public eye should be off-limits to journalists?

For a debate on euthanasia see Topic 5 Should a doctor be able to assist in euthanasia?, pages 64–75, in the Science volume.

this end, he personally injected a lethal dose of potassium chloride into Thomas Youk, who suffered from Lou Gehrig's disease [amyotrophic lateral sclerosis, or ALS, a disease that causes muscle wasting and paralysis and eventually death].

Death on TV

Kevorkian had Youk's consent and that of his wife. And the event, including Youk's death, was recorded with a home video camera. Kevorkian then turned the tape over to *60 Minutes*, which showed the doctor administering the fatal injection and Youk's death on its Nov. 22 broadcast. "Turn it off if you don't like it" was correspondent Mike Wallace's sanctimonious response to the torrent of criticism.

One of the most devastating indictments of the broadcast came from Stephen Smith, editor of *U.S. News & World Report*, who said, in part: "I don't think CBS can plausibly claim that the debate over euthanasia requires a snuff film to get going. That's just bogus. I just couldn't believe my eyes."

Death is an intensely private event. We learn about it as we lose our parents and friends; we learn to fear it less as we sit by bedsides of dying loved ones. We learn about it from books. We don't need to watch someone dying on television to learn about death or turn up the decibels on the euthanasia debate. "Death is always and under all circumstances a tragedy," wrote Theodore Roosevelt, "for if it is not, then it means that life itself has become one."

Do you agree with the author's point that a person's death should never be televised, even if it is to support the case for euthanasia?

For terminally ill patients, that is often the case, and that is why we are having the assisted-suicide debate. But it's the debate that should be public, not the deaths. Death is the most profound loss there is, and we are at our most human when we are with it. It belongs in a sacred family circle that should not be violated.

IF IT'S *OK!* FOR STARS TO CASH IN ON WEDDINGS ... THEN THEY MUST ACCEPT IT IS *HELLO!* TO LOSS OF PRIVACY
Mark Lawson

Opening with an anecdote can be an effective way to gain the attention of your audience.

Some years ago, during one of those tours of the stars' homes advertised on the streets of Los Angeles (I was present, you understand, for journalistic purposes), the bus pulled up outside a strawberry-walled mansion said to belong to Barbra Streisand. It should be pointed out that our inspection of the celebrity addresses was entirely external. Indeed, the exercise should strictly have been called "Peering down the drives of the stars' homes."

As our guide-driver pointed out, some of those big in what he called "the business" had now taken to constructing high walls to thwart such tours. Barbra was one. "How dare she?" roared a fan from the rear of our van. "I paid for that house! I bought it for her! And now I've come to see it!"

Do you agree that fans have a stake in a celebrity's fame because they have paid for their records or to see their movies?

There was a chilling logic to this view. Barbra was able to live in her big Barbie castle because people such as the lady in the van had handed over their dollars for records and cinema tickets. A shareholder in the star's fame, she had now come to claim her dividend. Stalkers lethally apply the same reasoning.

The British press

But, while the view that you get visiting rights by buying a couple of CDs may seem an extreme one, this has essentially been the position of the British press for several years. Celebrities who allow the media into their lives for the purposes of publicity for their work are subsequently assumed to have admitted photographers and journalists to every aspect of their lives.

Hello! and OK! are British magazines that contain articles about popular celebrities.

More understandably, there is a particular lack of sympathy for those who sell exclusive rights to aspects of their lives to *Hello!* or *OK!* magazine. Although journalists and their readers often have very different opinions, the view is widely shared that you can't be a peacock on your wedding day and an ostrich when something goes wrong: what is known as the Posh–Becks Position. This is what makes so extraordinary

Thursday's court of appeal ruling that, in Lord Justice Sedley's words, "the law recognizes and will appropriately protect a right of personal privacy."

The right to privacy

Instead, the rebuke to media intrusion follows from the anger of Michael Douglas and Catherine Zeta-Jones that their exclusive deal with *OK!* magazine for wedding pictures was breached by the rival *Hello!*. The judges seem even to have accepted a vain part of the claim: that the unauthorized images had not been vetted and retouched in the way the couple wanted. And so there is now legal precedent not only for a right of privacy, and a right to surrender that privacy to the bidder you choose, but also apparently a right to enhance the image of you which the public sees.

"Posh" and "Becks" are celebrity couple Victoria (Posh Spice) Adams, a pop singer, and David Beckham, a soccer player. In 1999 the pair sold the rights to their wedding photographs to OK! magazine for $1.6 million.

> *"In the old days men had the rack. Now they have the Press."*
>
> —OSCAR WILDE, IRISH NOVELIST, PLAYWRIGHT, AND WIT

Senior British judges can almost certainly be relied on not to know who [popstar] Madonna and [film director] Guy Ritchie [who married in December 2000] are but it is strangely perfect timing that the judgment should have been handed down on the eve of another wedding made in magazine heaven: one which overshadows even the trans-atlantic match of Douglas and Zeta-Jones.

The event at which Ms Ciccone [Madonna] becomes Mrs Ritchie indicates in several ways the nature of the age. It shows that—as the spacing of the Windsor generations leaves the British media in a long gap without a royal wedding— celebrities have indeed become the new kings and queens. And, like one of those tactical marriages between the great royal houses of Europe, this unlikely union in a Scottish castle seems designed to give Britain a share of celebrity and America a little of the class system.

"The Windsor generations" refers to the British royal family.

But the Madonna marriage also shows the complicated games of access which stars play. A star whose career has consisted of theatrical reinventions constructs a wedding—

ancient castle, choir of pop legends, celebrity guests—which seems as geared to public viewing as most movies. A woman known to all by the Virgin Mary's name weds about as close to Christmas Day as is legally possible. And yet she announces that the ceremony will be private, with images released later at the couple's discretion. However, in a scrap to fans, the Christening of the couple's child will take place in public. This, in an essence, is the *Hello!/OK!* culture: now you see me, now you don't.

Admittedly, stars on this scale can be excused a little illogic, so horrible are their lives. The general contempt aimed, for example, at David Beckham and Victoria Adams fails to acknowledge the unprecedented unpleasantness of modern celebrity: always fearing the long lens, the phone tap, even ultimately the gun.

Lawson acknowledges that loss of privacy can be highly unpleasant for celebrities.

Privacy and publicity

There's another image I remember from that gawper's morning in Los Angeles: the terrified eyes of the elderly wife of a veteran American comic as she drew her curtains at the sight of our van at the end of her drive. Now the courts have helped stars to pull across their shades in a more formal way. It might be a sensible reaction to a world of paparazzi and stalkers but celebrities are going to have to adjust their behavior. It can't be striptease one minute and dark glasses the next. There's a difference between a right to privacy and a right to choose which media high-bidder you'll expose yourself to. If these hypocrisies are not acknowledged, then fans and tabloid editors will understandably shout, like the Streisandite outside the star's house: We paid for that! We paid for that!

The author is saying that celebrities who seek publicity when it suits them give up their right to privacy to some degree. Do you agree with him?

COMMENTARY: Publicity v. privacy

Michael Douglas and his wife Catherine Zeta-Jones, May 29, 2001.

Film stars Michael Douglas and Catherine Zeta-Jones got more than they bargained for when they married in November 2000 in New York. They had signed an exclusive deal with the British magazine *OK!* for $1.6 million to take and publish photographs of the wedding. Guests were warned not to bring cameras, and everyone working at the wedding had to sign a strict contract promising not to take photos or be subject to legal action if they disobeyed. However, rival magazine *Hello!* sneaked in some hidden cameras and published photos of the wedding three days before *OK!* went on sale. *OK!* magazine went to court to attempt, unsuccessfully, to stop *Hello!* from publishing the photos. The couple themselves wanted to sue *Hello!* for damages for invading their privacy. At first, Douglas and Zeta-Jones won an injunction to prevent *Hello!* printing further copies of the magazine after 15,750 copies had already been put on sale. The English Court of Appeal then overturned this injunction, saying that it did not feel an injunction could protect the couple's privacy. Some people argued that the pair had sold their right to privacy by allowing the wedding to be photographed and the results published. Lord Justice Sedley in the appeal court disagreed. He said that because they announced their desire to retain editorial control over the pictures to be published, any pictures published other than those they had personally chosen were an invasion of their privacy. The appeal court decided that the couple were likely to succeed if they claimed damages against *Hello!* for breach of privacy.

This was the first time that an English court ruled that there is a privacy law to protect individuals. This is due to the incorporation of the European Human Rights Act into British law. Article 8 says, "Everyone has the right to respect for his private and family life." However, Article 10 guarantees the freedom of expression and the freedom of the press. When the media want to publish something about someone's private life, there is bound to be tension between the two principles. Judges will have to perform a delicate balancing act when deciding whether someone's privacy has been invaded or whether to uphold the freedom of the press.

Summary

Some people are desperate for celebrity. Celebrity is, by definition, the abnegation of some rights to privacy. In the first article Mann argues that the media has hit rock bottom in its reporting of two stories. Political figures in particular are more likely to be under the public eye while they are in the spotlight. The first concerns a story in the tabloids the *National Enquirer* and the *Star* that Chelsea Clinton had argued with her father, President Clinton, and that her health was suffering because of the stress of the Lewinsky scandal. Mann argues that it is pure exploitation and even inhumane to report on the first daughter at this difficult time in her life. She then goes on to link this story with the broadcast on *60 Minutes* of Thomas Youk's death by lethal injection. The injection was administered to Youk, who was terminally ill, by Jack Kevorkian, the campaigner for euthanasia. Mann argues that death is an intensely private affair and that it's the debate about euthanasia that should be public, not the deaths. She argues that in both of these stories a human being's right to privacy has been shredded.

In the second article Lawson takes a very different viewpoint, arguing that by virtue of seeking fame, celebrities give up their right to privacy. He takes as an example the case of Michael Douglas and Catherine Zeta-Jones suing *Hello!* magazine for invading their privacy by publishing photographs of their wedding without their permission. Lawson's position is that celebrities cannot have it both ways, seeking publicity when everything's going well and it suits them and shunning it when things go wrong. The main elements of this debate are summarized in the diagram opposite.

FURTHER INFORMATION:

Books:

Smith, Robert Ellis, *Celebrities and Privacy*. Providence, RI: Privacy Journal, 1985.

Wacks, Raymond, *Privacy and Press Freedom*. London: Blackstone Press, 1995.

Articles:

Andrews, James, "Celebrities for Privacy." *U.S. News and World Report*, vol. 129, issue 13.

Nordhaus, Jamie E., "Celebrities' Right to Privacy: How Far Should the Paparazzi Be Allowed to Go?" *The Review of Litigation*, Spring 1999.

Useful websites:

www.medialit.org
Organization for media literacy.

www.britannica.com/magazine/article?content_id+31316
&query=celebrities%20privacy
Article in the wake of Diana, Princess of Wales' death, in *Christian Science Monitor*, September 4, 1997.

www.law.cornell.edu/topics/publicity.html
Overview of the right to publicity and privacy in U.S. law.

www.britannica.com/magazine/article?content_id=57740
&query=celebrity%20privacy
Christian Science Monitor 1998 article on the paparazzi.

The following debates in the Pro/Con series may also be of interest:

In this volume:
Topic 1 Should the media be subject to censorship?

DO NEWSMAKERS HAVE A RIGHT TO PRIVACY?

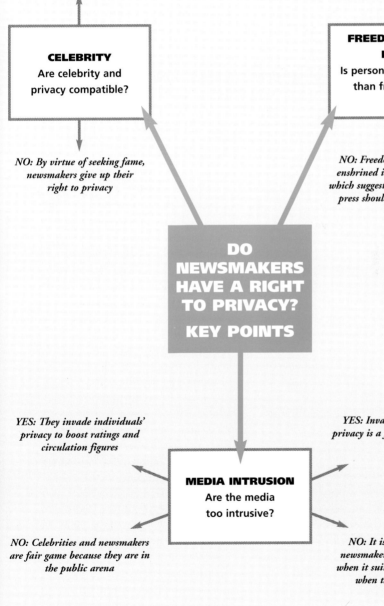

YES: Everyone has the right to privacy in their personal life, even if they are famous

YES: A person's right to privacy must be balanced against what is in the public interest

CELEBRITY
Are celebrity and privacy compatible?

FREEDOM OF THE PRESS
Is personal privacy more than freedom of the press?

NO: By virtue of seeking fame, newsmakers give up their right to privacy

NO: Freedom of expression is enshrined in the Constitution, which suggests that freedom of the press should also be protected

DO NEWSMAKERS HAVE A RIGHT TO PRIVACY? KEY POINTS

YES: They invade individuals' privacy to boost ratings and circulation figures

YES: Invading newsmakers' privacy is a form of exploitation

MEDIA INTRUSION
Are the media too intrusive?

NO: Celebrities and newsmakers are fair game because they are in the public arena

NO: It is hypocritical for newsmakers to seek publicity when it suits them and shun it when things go wrong

Topic 3
DO PEOPLE WATCH TOO MUCH TELEVISION?

YES
"WARNING: TOO MUCH TV IS HAZARDOUS TO YOUR HEALTH"
WWW.TV TURNOFF.ORG/HAZARDOUS.PDF
TV TURNOFF NETWORK NEWSLETTER

NO
"TELEVISION HEALS"
FROM *WHY VIEWERS WATCH: A REAPPRAISAL OF TELEVISION'S EFFECTS*
JIB FOWLES

INTRODUCTION

Virtually everyone in developed and developing countries owns a television, and many people spend a significant portion of their day watching it. Depending on what estimate one uses, the average American watches around four hours of television a day. In fact, viewing television has been shown to be the most popular use of leisure time. Because we watch so much TV, it's not surprising that some people are critical of the habit, even seeing it as the root of such problems as violence and consumerism. It is also criticized for being a waste of time. Bill McKibben, in *The Age of Missing Information* (1992), watched hundreds of hours of cable television, then compared it to spending a day in the Adirondacks. He argued that watching television fundamentally disconnects people from a natural experience of the world.

However, the reason many people spend so much time watching TV suggests that they enjoy the activity.

TV programs clearly entertain many people. The experience of watching television can feed people's fundamental need for fantasy and need to escape the sometimes mundane routines of everyday life. But television can also serve an educational purpose, for example, with documentaries and wildlife programs, by informing people about issues that are important and about how the world around us works. While critics believe that excessive TV watching can disrupt family life, discourage communication, and promote violence and materialism in viewers, it is important to make a distinction between the issue of the time spent watching TV and the question of the actual program content.

So if TV attracts a great deal of criticism, does it deserve it? A number of studies on the amount of television use do show effects that should be of concern. The American Medical Association has linked inactivity due to

TV viewing to obesity. Other studies have shown links between television viewing and reduced academic achievement. A whole research literature exists showing that television viewing contributes significantly to perceptions of social reality. And finally, as discussed in Topic 5, there is the question of whether exposure to televised violence might be related to levels of social violence.

"TV is chewing gum for the eyes."

—FRANK LLOYD WRIGHT,

U.S. ARCHITECT

Considering that most people watch significant amounts every day, however, can the situation be all that bad? The two articles in this section provide two viewpoints. First is a summary from the TV Turnoff organization detailing why we should spend less time with television and how to do it. TV Turnoff sponsors an annual week in which families are asked simply not to watch television. Those who do are often surprised at the results. After initial feelings of boredom new paths of communication and family interaction can open up. The amount of time spent reading can increase. Time spent simply talking with one another increases.

But can it be possible that TV is actually good for us? Although this seems to go against the grain of everything our teachers and parents have traditionally told us, some critics argue that TV is fundamentally good. Jib

Fowles thinks that TV viewing simply serves a basically natural function: entertainment, diversion, and eventually catharsis. By "catharsis" Fowles is referring to the possible positive effect that can be derived from viewers being exposed to fictional tragedy and disaster. This idea originated with the ancient Greek writer Aristotle (see page 44). Aristotle believed that when people see horrific situations depicted in a fictional situation, such as in a play, the experience of watching them can cleanse them of any repressed desires by bringing them to consciousness. As a result they are then probably less likely to act on any dangerous and taboo feelings in real life.

Fowles argues that "TV Prigs" miss the fact that everyone watches TV and that they must do so for good reasons— escapism, entertainment, personal regeneration. Research on the catharsis hypothesis has not been widely accepted, but Fowles develops an argument that says it's OK to watch television; he even hints that it's all right to watch a lot. Though his argument goes against the mainstream critical position, it is well formulated.

This position, that we have always been fascinated by stories of violence, fantasy, and horror, finds confirmation in the history of literature. From the Bible onward the compelling narrative has been a staple of the human experience. The new dimension that TV introduces is time: 24-hour-a-day access to such stories, with commercial sponsorship. Does this yield effects that are different? People can draw on their personal experience to tell them whether TV is contributing meaningfully to their lives. A host of research results, discussed here and in Topic 5, also shed light on the question.

WARNING: TOO MUCH TV IS HAZARDOUS TO YOUR HEALTH
TV Turnoff Network Newsletter

YES

More than four hours a day: that's how much television Americans watch on average. Watching TV is our most popular pastime, and it seems that we spend about as much time talking about it as we do watching. But what we don't talk about so much is how all that time in front of the television affects us as individuals and as a society.

As an abundance of evidence makes clear, our television habit has serious, negative consequences. To top the list, excessive TV-watching cuts into family time, harms our kids' ability to read and perform well in school, encourages violence, and promotes sedentary lifestyles and obesity.

Keep a TV diary for a week to see how much you and your friends watch TV every day. How does it compare with this estimate?

Fast facts
- Americans watch an average of more than four hours of TV a day, or two full months of TV a year.
- Forty percent of families always or often watch TV while eating dinner.
- Only 14 percent of 12th-graders who watch TV six hours a day or more achieve proficiency on reading tests, whereas 52 percent of students who watch an hour or less do.
- By age 18, American children will have seen an average of more than 200,000 acts of violence, including 16,000 murders on TV.
- Virtually all 3,500 research studies over 40 years show a link between watching media violence and committing acts of real violence.
- The proportion of overweight children has doubled since 1980 due, in part, to sedentary leisure time activities such as watching TV.

TV undermines family time
Many people feel that they do not have enough time to spend with their families. In fact, according to a *Newsweek* poll, even 73 percent of teens think that their parents do not spend enough time with them.

Although often overlooked, television plays a crucial role. In the average American household, the TV is on for seven hours and 40 minutes a day, and 40 percent of Americans [surveyed in 1999] report always or often watching television while eating dinner.

What's more, most family members watch different programs in separate rooms. Families who watch little or no television, on the other hand, often find that they have more time to spend with one another in more engaging and interactive activities.

TV harms reading and academic performance

Excessive television-watching harms reading skills both by displacing them from our daily lives and, according to some experts, by affecting the physical structure of the brain. Researcher Susan B. Neuman of the University of Lowell put it succinctly more than a decade ago: "Reading scores diminished sharply for those students watching more than four hours a day," and today's data continue to support her conclusion.

"Children whose movements are limited because they're spending their time in front of computers or televisions … are at risk of never fulfilling their potential."

—PETE EGOSCUE, EXERCISE PHYSIOLOGIST

In 1998, 52 percent of 12th-graders who watched an hour or less of TV a day achieved proficiency on reading tests, whereas only 14 percent of those who watched more than six hours did. Only 27 percent of those who watched four to five hours read proficiently. Moreover, researchers such as Jane Healy of Harvard argue that watching TV instead of reading may actually influence the physical structure of the brain as it develops, making learning and working in the schoolroom environment difficult.

For a discussion on violence in the media see Topic 5 Does Movie and Television Violence Cause Social Violence? *pages 60–71.*

TV encourages violence

The evidence is overwhelming: violence on TV promotes violent behavior in real life. Of more than 3,500 research studies on the effects of media violence over the past 40 years, 99.5 percent have shown a positive correlation between watching violence on TV and committing acts of real-life violence Watching glorified and consequence-free violence time and time again on television influences behavior, especially among children.

Television's lesson is an enduring one. According to Dr. Leonard D. Eron's 32-year study, watching television violence at age eight was the strongest predictor of aggression later in life, stronger even than violent behavior as children. The more violent television the subjects watched at age eight, the more serious was their aggressive behavior 22 years later, at age 30.

Some people argue that TV news reports are a good way to show people what real violence is like. Do you agree?

In addition to promoting violence, TV also desensitizes viewers to real-life violence and distorts viewers' perceptions of how dangerous the world really is. Television violence dulls the emotional response to violence and its victims.

TV promotes sedentary lifestyles and obesity

Americans, by and large, do not get enough physical exercise. We spend most of our free time watching television, which promotes obesity and its related illnesses. According to Dr. William Dietz, Director of the Division of Nutrition and Physical Activity at the Centers for Disease Control, "The easiest way to reduce inactivity is to turn off the TV set. Almost anything else uses more energy than watching TV."

The prevalence of obesity among adults and children is increasing. The Centers for Disease Control report that 27 percent of adults are obese nationwide and that obesity and its attendant health risks account for an estimated 300,000 deaths a year. The proportion of young children who are obese jumped from just over 4 percent in 1965 to over 11 percent in 1994. Childhood obesity is a leading factor in the unprecedented rise of Type II ("adult-onset") diabetes among adolescents. What's more, sedentary children risk suffering from other ailments later in life, including chronic pain, heart disease, falls from dizziness, and migraines.

TV-Turnoff tips

How would these steps change life in your family?

- Move your television to a less prominent location.
- Keep the TV off during meals.
- Designate certain days of the week as TV-free days.
- Do not use television as a reward.
- Listen to music or the radio for background noise.
- Cancel your cable subscription and [buy] books.
- Don't worry if children claim to be bored. Boredom passes and often leads to creativity.

Three children watching three different small televisions on the living room floor. Concerns about watching television frequently center on how much and what children watch.

TELEVISION HEALS
Jib Fowles

NO

For the Athenians and for Americans, for all peoples in between, for those who came before and for those who will come after, a yearning for fantasy lies at the core of human existence. Fantasy may well be the best redemption for the arduousness of the real world, the saving grace of human life. In summary, this is how fantasy serves:

The need for fantasy

Since Homo sapiens first appeared, the human brain has always allocated most of its energy and ability to negotiation with reality. In fact, the condition of "consciousness"— something that continues to trouble the philosophers and psychologists who ponder it—can be seen as nothing more than the operating mode of the brain when it is dealing with or reflecting upon the real world. During periods of conscious awareness (which generally describes the workday), the brain remains alert and poised. If this wondrous organ was not attentive to what surrounded it, and did not promote prudent behavior, then individuals would have failed in the economic and social realms where success, and thus survival, must be had. But for most humans most of their lives, the mind has permitted enduring instead of subsiding, swimming instead of sinking, and as a result society overall has not gone under.

A build-up of tension

The author starts to build the case for the beneficial effects of TV by describing the presence of tension in everyday life.

For all the brain has accomplished in aligning individuals to the real world and keeping each one a functioning member of society, there have always been costs. Just being alert entails a certain degree of tenseness, and the tension does mount up. Most societies, now and in history, offer little opportunity to get rid of this tension during the course of a day, and little chance to discharge the retaliatory feelings that can form in response to the onrush of real-world stimuli. These impulses must be held in check, and so must the urges that well up from more primal regions of the brain. Much of the time human beings have to do what Archie Bunker tried to get Edith to do—they must stifle themselves.

Archie Bunker was a central character in the TV program All in the Family.

The brain is an exceedingly complex center whose workings even at this late date are still the subject of various interpretations and some controversy. But one thing that's clear is that the brain has always had the capability of holding back the impulses and drives that might be damaging to the individual or his reputation, or to the fabric of his society. Inappropriate energy can be repressed for a time, sentenced to a holding tank located as far beneath the level of consciousness as possible. Later, when in repose, the brain will produce a stream of fantasies that spurt from the unconscious and, in effect, reduce the pressure there.

The author is saying here that dreaming is a kind of safety valve for the brain.

"Television has raised writing to a new low."
—SAMUEL GOLDWYN,
U.S. FILM PRODUCER

If individuals are not allowed to dream or daydream—an effect modern experimenters can accomplish by taking readings of brain waves and bringing subjects back to full consciousness whenever fantasizing begins—then they soon become uncomfortable and, in time, disoriented. The opposite is true too: If individuals are denied real-world stimulation, as when they are placed in a tank of saline water with blindfolds on for a sensory-deprivation experiment, then they also become confused and disoriented after a time. What the human brain seems to demand is a balance of reality and fantasy. Both have always been needed for good mental health.

Fowles connects classic Greek tragedy, such as the satyr plays and Heracles' 12 labors, with modern TV shows like Alex Haley's slavery epic Roots and the legal comedy Night Court to show that certain dramatic content has always drawn audiences since ancient times.

Popular narratives

Fantasizing, and the playing-out of deep-lying mental pressures, has been enhanced throughout history by fantasies that are not formed within the individual's mind but are supplied from outside. Through the ages people have flocked to story-tellers for the narrations that had the effect of soothing troubled brains. To judge by the enormity of the audience for Heracles's 12 labors and for *Roots*, for satyr-plays and for *Night Court*, these supplemental fantasies have had an appeal above and beyond private fantasies. This is because they can more artfully stimulate and more thoroughly discharge repressed emotions. When all goes perfectly, members of the audience will experience the mental purging that Aristotle identified to his fellow Athenians as catharsis. The Athenians received their therapeutic dose of fantasy

Aristotle (384– 322 B.C.) wrote of the purging, or cathartic, effect of drama, whereby feelings of fear and pity are discharged.

productions—whose tastefulness ranged from the most refined to the most vulgar—in the Theater of Dionysius, and Americans get the same thing from their television sets. Before their eyes every evening there unreel the fictions and phantoms that are the antidote for daytime strains. To elicit the discharge of reined-in drives, television presents, instead of a rendition of the real world which is much to blame for these repressions, a sort of half-world where violence exists but not pain, sex but not lovelornness, humor but not misery, youth but not age, heroics but not passivity, comradeship but not loneliness, gain but not loss. By being distorted in these ways, televised fantasies can provide after-hours redress for the shortcomings of the real world.

Sex and violence on TV

Let's take just sex and violence. TV Prigs serve their interests well by focussing on these, for they are the two essences of television entertainment. In situation comedies … they are cloaked in humor, while in action/adventure shows they are frequently undisguised. The reason these two themes are so prominent in televised fantasies is that they are so prominent in the subconscious repressions of viewers, as indicated by the fact that they are frequent components of dreams. The real world does not provide all the opportunities people desire for aggressive retribution or sexual contact, but dramatized fantasies offer a setting to carry out these drives vicariously and without repercussions. Individuals need this harmless outlet and would suffer if it were denied them. Gerhardt Wiebe stated in terms of his explanatory scheme:

Gerhardt Wiebe was a media scholar at Boston University.

> *Because the very essence of restorative messages is their token retaliation against the establishment, the likely effect of well-intentioned attempts by proponents of high standards to "improve" popular restorative content is clear. Let's take out the violence, they say, and substitute a theme of cooperative problem solving. The restorative essence is removed and directive content is substituted. The psychological utility of the message is altered and its popularity is correspondingly reduced.*

By having television entertainment with adequate sex and violence, Americans are nightly able to empty their subconscious; aggressive fantasies produce tranquil minds. Writing a column for the *Wall Street Journal* [in 1980], Daniel Henninger observed:

Most people use television to relax. They use it to relax because the medium produces restfulness—the mind is made blank, one stares, and in fact the eyes defocus slightly. Indeed the condition of watching television very much resembles the dyhanas, *or stages, of Buddhist meditation, whose purpose is to achieve a state of equanimity by drawing one's mind away from earthly concerns. One text indicates that during dyhana one might meditate by concentrating on a colored patch. The events that occur between the time we get up and Prime Time are our earthly concerns. Television is our colored patch. Viewing television induces something resembling the pleasant, trance-like qualities of meditation. This is why we watch so much of it.*

Almost all Americans experience television as life-maintaining, ridding the mind of toxic stress and animosity. Of all possible ways to compensate for the strains of modern life, televised fantasies are what most people, most of the time, have found to be the most congenial means. We shouldn't forget that television serves other purposes too—daytime serials add rather than subtract from minds, as does informational programming—but the greatest part by far of the television experience consists of the evening and weekend fantasies that roll through minds and clean out the mental debris. Viewers are more receptive by far to this "cleaning-out" function than to any "stuffing-in" attempts. Edmund Carpenter note: "Although TV showed these things, many believe that Kennedy lived on as a vegetable, and that the moon landings did not transpire. TV is fictive in essence."

Do you agree that watching TV is similar to meditation? How might critics of violence on TV respond to this argument?

Is it getting easier or more difficult to believe what appears on the television?

Summary

Two very different viewpoints are put forward here as to whether people watch too much television. In the first article the TV Turnoff Network lists a number of effects of watching too much television, which include creating sedentary lifestyles and obesity, adversely affecting reading standards and the ability to learn in the classroom, eating into the time families spend together, and encouraging violence in everyday life as well as desensitizing viewers to violence in real life. The article cites a number of studies that show that obesity in children and adults is increasing in the U.S. and links this to the sedentary lifestyle that watching TV can lead to. It also cites evidence that children who watch several hours of TV a week score poorly on reading tests compared to those who watch less. Although no absolute causal link has been found between watching violence in the media and violence in real life, the article states that most studies demonstrate a "positive correlation between watching violence on television and committing acts of real-life violence." *Topic 5 Does Movie and Television Violence Cause Social Violence?* discusses this issue in more length.

The opposing case is taken by Jib Fowles. He argues in "Television Heals" that TV provides a necessary cathartic effect. By watching televised fantasies, including violent ones, he says, we are able to discharge tension and repressed emotion. He also quotes an article that suggests that watching TV is a form of meditation, ridding the mind of toxic stress. The main elements of this debate are summarized in the diagram opposite.

FURTHER INFORMATION:

Books:

Mander, G., *4 Arguments for the Elimination of Television*. New York: Quill, 1978.

McKibben, B., *The Age of Missing Information*. New York: Random House, 1992.

Shanahan, J. and M. Morgan, *Television and Its Viewers*. Cambridge, England: Cambridge University Press, 1999.

Articles:

Woodward, Will, "Viewers Admit Their Guilt at Watching Too Much TV." *The Guardian*, April 30, 1999.

Useful websites:

www.tv-turnoff.org
Website for the TV Turnoff Network.
www.whitedot.org
Website for an international campaign against television.

www.aces.edu/dept/extcomm/newspaper/april19d01.html
For article "Too Much TV Can Have Negative Impact on Children."

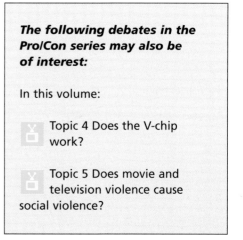

The following debates in the Pro/Con series may also be of interest:

In this volume:

Topic 4 Does the V-chip work?

Topic 5 Does movie and television violence cause social violence?

DO PEOPLE WATCH TOO MUCH TELEVISION?

YES: It promotes sedentary lifestyles and obesity

YES: It harms reading skills and may influence the brain's structure to make learning more difficult

HEALTH
Is watching TV harmful to health?

ACADEMIC PERFORMANCE
Does watching TV affect academic performance?

NO: It delivers a therapeutic dose of fantasy, a way of discharging tension and repressed emotion

NO: Watching TV is a form of meditation, ridding the mind of toxic stress

DO PEOPLE WATCH TOO MUCH TELEVISION?
KEY POINTS

YES: Most research shows a link between watching media violence and committing acts of real violence

YES: TV desensitizes viewers to real-life violence, dulling the emotional response to violence and its victims

VIOLENCE
Does watching violence on TV encourage social violence?

NO: Televised violence offers a way for people to carry out aggressive drives vicariously and without repercussions

NO: People need the harmless outlet of watching violence on TV and would suffer if it were denied them

Topic 4
DOES THE V-CHIP WORK?

YES
"THE V-CHIP: WHERE DO WE GO FROM HERE?:
THE REALITY OF TELEVISION RATINGS IN THE UNITED STATES"
CHILDREN NOW

NO
"'V' IS FOR VIRTUALLY IGNORED: FEW AMERICANS HAVE BOTHERED
TO LEARN HOW TO USE THE CHILD-PROTECTING V-CHIP"
THE KANSAS CITY STAR, APRIL 27, 2000
AARON BARNHAART

INTRODUCTION

The issue of how much violence and sexual explicitness should be allowed on television has been a matter of public debate since 1952, when Congress first held hearings on the subject. Parents and other concerned members of society have always been quick to ask how they can stop children and other impressionable people from viewing material that might be deemed unsuitable.

Similarly, critics have questioned both the influence of violence on TV on consumers, and also whether it is possible to monitor the amount of questionable images seen on screen. The V-chip or Violence Chip is one such method. Invented by Canadian engineer Tim Collings, this electronic chip works in conjunction with the television and allows the user to select an "appropriate" rating level for the audience concerned.

Advocates, such as former president Bill Clinton, claim that the chip enables parents to block inappropriate programs and thus control what their children view. However, opponents, such as the civil rights organization the ACLU, state that the V-chip is little more than censorship under another name.

For a long time broadcasters fought against the idea that television had any influence on the behavior of its viewers. However, in the last 20 years or so that opinion has been challenged time and time again.

In 1993 Senator Paul Simon arranged a conference with broadcasters to discuss the issue of media violence. For the first time some industry leaders acknowledged that there could be a reason for concern, and both the broadcast and cable industry agreed to examine the amount of violence shown in their programs. UCLA monitored broadcast television, while a nonprofit research and policy organization, Mediascope, did the same for the cable industry. The resulting reports declared that the level of broadcast violence was far too high and was therefore inappropriate for youth audiences.

Bill Clinton focused on TV violence and its effect on U.S. society during his second election campaign, urging Congress to pass legislation that would require blocking equipment in new television sets. In 1996 this was put into law as part of the Telecommunications Act, which required manufacturers. after January 1, 2000, to install V-chips in every new television with a screen over 13 inches.

In order for the V-chip to work, a ratings system must be broadcast with the television signal or video. If the program or video's rating exceeds the rating set by the adult of the household, the chip blocks the material.

> *"[The V-chip is] a technology which is likely to prove at least as important for television as the seatbelt has been for the automobile."*
>
> —ED MARKEY,
> CONGRESSMAN, MASSACHUSETTS

There are an estimated 250 million television sets in the United States. However, the Henry J. Kaiser Family Foundation, a California based public health group, released a report arguing that V-chip use is low in the United States. Using a sample of about 800 parents, it estimated that some 40 percent of U.S. families own a set with a V-chip installed. But the survey showed that more than half of them did not even know that the V-chip existed, and of those that did only about a third had ever used it. The Foundation concluded that 7 percent of all parents were actually using the V-chip, although most parents remained concerned about the viewing habits of their children.

Part of the reason for this could be that U.S. television viewers are probably only marginally aware of the rating system that is now in place for most TV programs. Ratings such as TV-Y (All Children), TV-Y7 (Directed to Older Children), TV-G (General Audience), TV-PG (Parental Guidance Suggested), TV-14 (Parents Strongly Cautioned), and TV-MA (Mature Audience Only) are not widely understood by viewers.

Some scholars have even suggested that the ratings themselves actually promote inappropriate programs to children, giving them the credence of "forbidden-fruit." However, advocates argue that the benefits of the V-chip outweigh the disadvantages.

The following articles examine the arguments in this debate. The first is excerpted from a conference held by the organization Children Now. The speakers compare reaction to the V-chip to that of seatbelts when they were first introduced when they were actively opposed by the automobile industry. Now, of course, they are an accepted part of life. This, they argue, will happen with the V-chip. Conversely, the second article by Aaron Barnhaart asserts that the V-chip simply does not work and that the technology is irrelevant without the ratings system. He asserts that it will most probably be forgotten in years to come.

THE V-CHIP:
WHERE DO WE GO FROM HERE?
Children Now-sponsored panel discussion

YES

Vicki Rideout (Children Now): Tony Cox is executive vice president of Viacom International and has been one of the leaders of the cable industry's anti violence effort.

Cox: To go to your question about why the broadcast networks are in such strong opposition to V-chip. No matter what else may be said, it's fundamentally economics. I think there is a legitimate concern that shows that get rated will lose advertising. And then you jeopardize the whole system of broadcasting, at least over the air television in this country. And so if we can solve that economic issue, I think the objections essentially would go away ...

If we do it right, we could get to the point where having ratings is considered a good thing by the advertisers and not having ratings is considered a bad thing ... It's entirely possible that a rating system would turn that all around and make it so that the shows that are rated are those where the advertisers will go ...

My analogy is to the automobile industry where ten years ago you never saw advertising ... about automobile safety ... Today you don't see an automobile ad that doesn't start off with and end with the safety features of the car ... So maybe the automobile industry has learned that automobile safety mattered to their viewers ... I think that violent content on television is an important issue to our customers, to our viewers. And to ignore it, to do nothing about it, I think is to potentially cause a loss of customer loyalty ...

Rideout: Let me ask if any of our panelists have information on public opinion on the issue of ratings and the V-chip. Kathryn Montgomery is president of the Center for Media Education, an organization that has done a lot of public policy work on media issues.

Montgomery: Well, there have been, as everybody in this room knows, a number of public opinion polls recently that have been fairly consistent in showing that there's a broad, a widespread dissatisfaction among the American public with the quality of a lot of the programming on the electronic media. We did a poll a few months ago that identified that 82 percent of Americans believe there is not enough educational programming on children's television, and a large percentage were very concerned about levels of violence in that programming.

When you look at children's programming we do have a real problem with TV violence, and the industry has refused to acknowledge for the most part that kids' TV programs have any real violence or that it really makes any difference at all. They refuse to put their own warnings about violent programming on any of the kids' programming and basically exempted that. But we also have an opportunity here with the Children's Television Act to make sure that we have more of the good stuff on. If educational TV were labeled, and if there were a commitment on the part of advertisers to say we want to support this kind of educational programming, and we want you parents to know it's here, and a commitment on the part of the industry to really make that programming as high profile and as good quality as it could be, we'd see a great improvement.

Revised rules to the Children's Television Act mean that major stations must broadcast a minimum of three hours of core educational programming a week.

Chris Wright (deputy general counsel, FCC): I want to just make the response … that I think the free speech interests are on the V-chip side here, not on the broadcaster side. The most analogous Supreme Court decision is a case called *Meese v. Keene*, which also involved a labeling requirement. It was labeling on films. Films had to be labeled as being produced by foreign governments under a law that termed them political propaganda. The court upheld it, and mentioned three times that the First Amendment interests were on the statute side there. The court said, quote, "This kind of disclosure serves rather than deserves the First Amendment," unquote, and indeed went on to call paternalistic the views in that case that not providing additional information was a good thing. And there are many aspects of this case that in my view make the very cautious bill that's currently pending easy to defend. But I just wanted to make the point first that properly understood as explicated by the Supreme Court, the First Amendment interests would be on the government side in that case. Economic interest would be on the industry side …

This speaker is making the point that disclosing information relating to content is in keeping with the First Amendment, that is, the right to free speech.

Rideout: Martine Vallee is the director of social issues for the Canadian Radio-television and Telecommunications

The Federal Communications Commission (FCC) is an independent government agency that regulates interstate and international communications by radio, television, wire, satellite, and cable.

Commission, the CRTC, which is the Canadian equivalent of our FCC. Martine, can you tell us a little bit about what kind of a system you have in place now in Canada?

Vallee: We don't actually have a rating system in place right now. And what we've done is we've just gone through a whole series of public consultations on what measures should be taken on the violence issue. We have been involved in the issue for a number of years, and right now, broadcasters have a code which gives guidelines on what programming should and should not be broadcast with respect to violent content.

Rideout: You actually regulate the content? In Canada the government actually is regulating the content of what can be shown on TV, which is a far cry from what we're talking about here.

Vallee: Well, they're industry codes, they were developed by the industry but approved by the commission; they're sort of regulated with a soft hand. But they're put on adherence to the code and it's part of a condition of broadcasters' license. So what we have right now is broadcasters have to adhere to provisions with respect to what programming would be suitable for children. There's a ban on the broadcast of any sort of glamorized and gratuitous violence. Programming with scenes of violence intended for adult audiences can only be shown after nine o'clock and it has to have advisories and so on.

What we did recently is we went into the second phase of our effort on violence, and we held a series of regional consultations across the country to look at how we can provide the tools for parents so that parents can decide for themselves what programming they want their children to watch. And within this we looked at what a classification system should look like, what sort of parental control technologies are most appropriate to use.

Now at the same time the industry has been doing quite a lot of work in the area and the cable industry is going to what will be now their third round of trials on the V-chip. They did two rounds last year. One was in one city, in Edmonton. And with that they used a nine-level rating system with four different categories, including intended audience, violent language, and sexual content. They found the nine levels were too much. They had a second round last summer in two cities, and with that they used a six-level rating system. Again, with the four categories.

Rideout: I'm sorry, can you say the four categories again?

Vallee: Intended audience, that's an age category and that's similar to the motion picture categories that are used. Then we have a violence category, language, and a sex/nudity category. And within that there's six levels. In February they're going to be doing another round of V-chip testing in four cities. They're going to be starting anytime now and they will probably be collapsing the number of levels to five. And the reason for that is because it would fit better with what I understand are the standards that are being set from the electronic industry's association for the V-chip …

Rideout: And the way that works is you can sort of set a dial on your TV set—for example, setting it at 4 for violence, 2 for sex, 3 for language, and then the chip will block anything that's rated above that?

Vallee: Yes and if something exceeds that, then on the TV screen you get a graph showing what levels you had set and what the program is rated at.

Rideout: Do consumers like that?

Vallee: Apparently with the second round of tests over 70 percent of the participants in the trials really liked it. The first time they tested it they were rating individual scenes within a program instead of entire programs. Consumers did not like that, they found it too confusing.

Myers (Television Production Partners): This appears through that research to be a commercially viable product. If we accept that that the V-chip is practical and that it does work, then I would suggest that the marketplace forces are working here, and that some form of V-chip may, in fact, be a commercially viable product. If consumers want it then the marketplace forces will bring it to the consumers. And perhaps we may have competitive rating systems offered by various organizations, whether it be commercial manufacturers or private interest groups like the church. Perhaps rating systems may be developed by software manufacturers and by other interest groups to support this technological development in the marketplace. And perhaps we can envision a system in the future where there will be multiple choices available to consumers as opposed to a single governmentally and network dictated system.

The U.S. TV ratings system uses five categories: violence, sexual situations, coarse or crude indecent language, suggestive dialogue, and fantasy violence.

This speaker is suggesting that an open ratings system may be possible in the future in which different interest groups take part in setting ratings. Why do you think some people would consider this a good idea?

"V" IS FOR VIRTUALLY IGNORED
Aaron Barnhaart

NO

Ushered into the world in 1996 by an act of Congress, it was immediately hailed by a host of pro-family advocates and Vice-President Al Gore. Behold, they said, a $3 gizmo that will let parents block any TV shows that exceed their personal thresholds for sex, violence, and adult language. Set it once and walk away—the V-chip does the rest.

Not everyone was overjoyed by this technical miracle mandated by Uncle Sam. Hollywood cried censorship, while the makers of TVs grumbled about having to install something that actually prevented people from watching TV.

For a discussion about media and censorship see Topic 1 Should the media be subject to censorship? pages 10–21

Ignored and overlooked
Now, four years later, it looks like the naysayers are having their way. Somehow, the V-chip has become the red-headed stepchild of the television business, ignored and overlooked despite being built into every new TV set sold in the U.S.

Here's the latest sign of the V-chip's identity crisis: Nearly two out of five parents don't even know what it is. That's the finding of a study published earlier this month by the Menlo Park, California-based Kaiser Family Foundation, a leading proponent of V-chip use.

V-chip awareness campaign
To counter that, the Odyssey Network (which is part-owned by Hallmark Entertainment), RCA, and Circuit City stores announced a V-chip awareness campaign earlier this month. The companies will reissue 720,000 copies of a booklet, printed last year by the Kaiser Foundation and the Center for Media Education, telling parents about the device and how to use it. The booklets bear the image of Kermit the Frog, the campaign's "V-chip spokesfrog."

The government's "V-chip czar" is Gloria Tristiani, the FCC commissioner.

Meanwhile, the government's "V-chip czar"—who wields only slightly more power than a "spokesfrog"—fired off a memo to the TV networks April 4, pleading with them to "recommit themselves to educating parents about the V-chip."

That seems unlikely. Nothing would please the networks more than to see the demise of the V-chip. Having lost much of their audience to cable, the notion of losing millions more potential viewers to an electronic nanny would have their ad sales staffs reaching for the Maalox. One "bad" rating (an "adults only," for example) and a program could be instantly wiped off the TV screen in millions of homes.

Networks give little publicity to the chip

It's no surprise, then, to learn that in the first three months of 2000, the four networks aired announcements about the V-chip exactly 59 times, or roughly 90 seconds' worth per week, according to numbers released by the Federal Communications Commission. Of those 59 spots, CBS aired 54; NBC, ABC, and Fox combined aired five.

"The impact felt from the [new ratings] system and the chip will be virtually nothing for five years."
—ROD PERTH, FORMER ENTERTAINMENT CHIEF AT USA NETWORKS, INC., 1998

As of January 2000 all TV manufacturers in the United States are required to include a V-chip in sets that are 13 inches or larger.

For those of you with new TV sets (and who weren't watching CBS), you'll find the V-chip controls through the same menu system you use to adjust the picture, captioning, and other settings on your TV. Menus vary, but most refer to V-chip settings as "parental controls." I've used them, and they're a snap to set up. I've also hauled a TV out to speaking engagements and handed the remote to audience members. They've figured it out, too.

In the United States the TV rating system, or TV Parental Guidelines, rates programs by content and age-appropriateness. It is a voluntary system, and not all broadcasters use it.

The TV ratings

But figuring out the V-chip and putting it to good use are two different things. The technology is useless without the "TV ratings" you see on-screen every 30 minutes or so. The rating is encoded into the TV signal, enabling the V-chip to check its own settings against the rating.

For example, if the parent has set the threshold at "TV-PG," and a show comes in with a "TV-14" rating, it's blocked. Only someone who knows the password to the TV set can watch that show. There are also content-based ratings for sex (S), racy dialogue (D), violence (the "V" in V-chip), and so on.

Broadcasters began voluntarily airing the ratings in 1997, though not without a fight. The cable industry, which is supported mainly by subscriber fees, has been more supportive of TV ratings and the V-chip.

Problems with the ratings

Currently, though, the ratings system is so glitch-riddled as to be almost unusable. Two studies in the last two years found that the vast majority of shows with sexual and violent content weren't being tagged as such.

The Henry J. Kaiser Family Foundation's website is at www.kff.org.

Even if ratings were more accurate, it's unclear parents would notice: Just four percent of those surveyed a year ago by the Kaiser Foundation knew that the "FV" rating stood for fantasy violence—the only rating for violent content approved for use in children's shows.

Then there's the problem of cable companies that garble the ratings-encoded part of the signal. A college professor in Wisconsin recently found her V-chip wasn't blocking *South Park*, the potty-mouthed cartoon on Comedy Central, because somewhere in the transmission the show's "TV-MA" (adults only) rating had been lost.

Do you think that the standards for newcasts should be any different to those set for movies or drama?

Parents also may be surprised to learn that newscasts are exempt from ratings. You can solve that problem by programming your set to simply block all unrated shows— but that will knock out sporting events, too.

The chip's biggest drawback

Perhaps the V-chip's biggest drawback is that it is hard-wired into TV sets and thus into history. Other parental controls, such as those offered by cable companies and satellite-dish systems, are software-driven, which means a future software designer could improve them, then download the new program to subscribers. For instance, HBO and Showtime, in addition to the standard TV ratings, have extra codes that distinguish between mild and graphic violence. The V-chip doesn't recognize them and never will.

Breaking the rules of retail sales

And because the V-chip is a single standard imposed across all TV models, it breaks a cardinal rule of retail sales: Always have a feature the other guy doesn't—or, if you've both got the feature, make yours better. In my visits to showrooms, I've found that salespeople can go on all day about the virtues of various TV models. But few of them know much about "parental controls" and none of them ever brings it up. In its current design, the V-chip seems unpromotable.

That's not stopping Gloria Tristiani, the aforementioned "V-chip czar" and FCC commissioner. When I spoke with her last year, she pointed to surveys showing that three-quarters of parents would use the TV controls if they were offered.

"But I can't expect people are going to buy a set because there's a V-chip," Tristiani said. "We need time to gauge what the acceptance level is, and by time I mean years."

Years? That sounds like a timetable devised by enemies of the V-chip, not its chief proponent.

At that rate, it may not be long before "parental controls" joins brightness and contrast as yet another ubiquitous, little-used and mostly forgotten setting on the TV set.

Summary

The first article contains excerpts from a panel discussion sponsored by the organization Children Now. The full discussion contained contributions from a variety of people working in the television industry, but nobody from the networks or the National Association of Broadcasters chose to accept the invitation to attend. One speaker suggested that introducing V-chips could be compared to equipping cars with seat belts and other safety measures. Another speaker argued that the Children's Television Act, which requires stations to broadcast three hours of core educational programming a week, was a good opportunity to improve the quality of children's programming in the United States. The extent of that improvement would depend on educational TV being labeled as such by the stations and advertisers supporting educational programming. Traditionally, the First Amendment has pushed broadcast policy toward less restrictive options when dealing with program content. But a speaker from the FCC cited a legal case regarding the labeling of foreign films to support his view that the interests of free speech were on the side of the V-chip. A speaker from the Canadian equivalent of the FCC described tests that had been undertaken in that country. More than 70 percent of the parents who took part rated the chip favorably.

Barnhaart's article, on the other hand, presents a number of reasons why he thinks the V-chip does not, and cannot, work. These reasons include parental ignorance of the ratings system and of the existence of the chip, the networks' reluctance to support a system that could potentially alienate their advertisers, inaccurate or nonexistent rating of certain programs that contain sex and violence, and the fact that the chip is hardwired into TV sets and not software-driven, which would allow improvements to be made.

FURTHER INFORMATION:

Books:

Price, Monroe E. (editor), *The V-Chip Debate: Content Filtering from Television to the Internet*. Mahwah, NJ: Lawrence Erlbaum Associates, 1998.

Useful websites:

www.vchipeducation.org
"A Parent's Guide to the TV Ratings and V-chip," on the Kaiser Family Foundation/Center for Media Education site.
www. childrennow.org
Children Now's website.
www.fcc.gov/vchip
Federal Communications website about the V-chip.
www.tvguidelines. org
The parental TV guidelines monitoring board's website.

www.cep.org/vchip.html
Site focusing on the moral and political implications of using the V-chip.

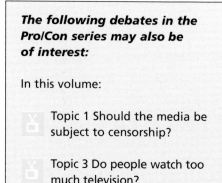

The following debates in the Pro/Con series may also be of interest:

In this volume:

Topic 1 Should the media be subject to censorship?

Topic 3 Do people watch too much television?

DOES THE V-CHIP WORK?

YES: Advertisers will want to be associated with shows that have been rated, not with those that have not

YES: The chip allows parents easily to regulate what their children see on TV

THE MARKETPLACE
Is the chip economically viable for the networks?

SEX AND VIOLENCE
Will the chip prevent children from seeing inappropriate programs?

NO: A "bad" rating could wipe a program off millions of TV screens, losing the networks substantial sums in advertising revenue

NO: Programs often are inaccurately rated or not rated at all, such as news broadcasts

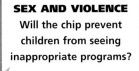

DOES THE V-CHIP WORK? KEY POINTS

YES: Although it is a voluntary code of practice, most broadcasters have adopted the system

YES: Advertisers will not want to be associated with "bad" ratings, so controversial shows will receive less backing

YES: It's a feature that will become as important to the television industry as seat belts are to the automobile industry

TV RATINGS
Is the TV ratings system effective?

CENSORSHIP
Does the V-chip work to censor content?

NO: Many parents are ignorant of the system and do not even know about the V-chip

NO: Broadcasters are reluctant to implement it accurately because it could alienate their advertisers

NO: The V-chip allows network programmers to make the shows they want by allowing the viewer to decide what he or she wants to see

Topic 5
DOES MOVIE AND TELEVISION VIOLENCE CAUSE SOCIAL VIOLENCE?

YES
"IMPACT OF TELEVISED VIOLENCE"
WWW.KSU.EDU/HUMEC/IMPACT.HTM
JOHN P. MURRAY

NO
"TEN THINGS WRONG WITH THE 'EFFECTS MODEL'"
FROM *APPROACHES TO AUDIENCES: A READER*
DAVID GAUNTLETT

INTRODUCTION

In 1998 the National Center for Education Statistics published a report called "Violence and Discipline in U.S. Public Schools, 1996–1997." The report found that 10 percent of all public schools had experienced one or more serious violent crimes (including murder), and that there had been around 7,000 incidents of rape/sexual battery, 11,000 incidents of physical assault with a weapon, and 190,000 incidents of assault/fights without weapons in that school year. Such high levels of violent crime in schools, and indeed in society at large, have created much concern over the causes. While studies have shown that children are affected by violent family backgrounds, academics, educators, and other concerned people have been quick to lay the blame for U.S. society's seemingly escalating violence at the door of the media. Television violence has caused particularly vociferous arguments, and politicians often turn to

the media when seeking reasons for episodes of social violence that cannot otherwise be easily explained. Similarly, as long ago as 1917, for example, the U.K. government tried to ban children from seeing certain films because they believed they encouraged juvenile delinquency. But can television and movie violence really have such a great influence on social violence?

Since the 1950s hundreds of studies have been carried out on this subject. Most social scientists agree that the evidence shown in them supports a relationship between exposure to media violence and actually being violent in "real life." However, these surveys often fall short of demonstrating true causality. Furthermore, the point of many of the studies has often been obscured by sensational media attention to specific acts of outrageous/copycat media-inspired violence, although cases of people committing violent crimes directly inspired by the media are quite rare. Also, critics argue that it is to the criminals' advantage to blame the media for their actions rather than take full responsibility for the crime themselves.

Within this context studies on media violence can often seem to be strident or overworried. Most of us feel immune from any media effects (this is called the "third person effect"—people assume that the media only affect other people) and thus might tend to see warnings about media violence as prudish or ill advised.

> *"Seeing a murder on television can ... help work off one's antagonisms."*
> —ALFRED HITCHCOCK,
> FILM DIRECTOR

Critics of media effects studies have pointed out that studies carried out in artificial laboratory settings have little bearing on viewers in the real world and often find rather weak relationships between media violence and actual violence. Often the researchers have not had the time and money to conduct studies in a valid environment and have instigated tests that are conspicuously out of context, and which may then be viewed by the participants as a game. Moreover, critics of these studies argue that almost everyone watches significant amounts of television without becoming extremely violent. In fact, if we are to believe that the amount of violence watched on TV is proportional to its effect on the viewer, then it would be TV and film censors, who see more media violence than any other members of the public, who would be society's killers and rapists. In the 1960s increasing levels of social violence started to worry policy-makers. As society seemed to be fraying at its edges, some politicians thought that media violence might be playing a role. The U.S. Surgeon General compiled research on whether exposure to media violence played any causal role in social violence. The studies did indeed find relationships between the two; they were also updated 10 years later. In a 2001 report on youth violence the Surgeon General reported that:

> *A substantial body of research now indicates that exposure to media violence increases children's physically and verbally aggressive behavior in the short term ... [it] also increases aggressive attitudes and emotions, which are theoretically linked to aggressive and violent behavior.*

Another complication in the debate is determining what kind of media violence has an effect on social violence. Most studies examine fictional violence in cartoons, films, and television shows. But what about the real violence shown in news reports and factual programs? Does it affect the viewer differently?

The following two articles examine some of the arguments in this debate. Murray argues that there is a relationship between the two. But Gauntlett states that the studies are flawed and that the researchers assume an indefensible moral high ground over their subjects.

IMPACT OF TELEVISED VIOLENCE
John P. Murray

Questions about the effects of television violence have existed since the earliest days of this medium. Indeed, the first expression of formal concern can be found in Congressional hearings in the early 1950s. For example, the United States Senate Committee on the Judiciary, Subcommittee to Investigate Juvenile Delinquency held a series of hearings during 1954-55 on the impact of television programs on juvenile crime. These hearings set the stage for continuing congressional investigations by this committee and others in the House and Senate from the 1950s to the present.

Concern over media violence became a major issue in the United States in 1992-1993. The debate was partly fueled by the publication in 1992 of Michael Medved's book Hollywood vs. America: Popular Culture and the War on Traditional Values.

Despite decades of research, there is a perception that the research evidence on TV violence is unclear or contradictory. This perception is incorrect and this review will address the following issues: What do we know about the impact of television violence? What are some of the major research findings that form the basis for concern?

The Gerbner studies

The most extensive analyses of the incidence of violence on television are the studies conducted by Gerbner and his colleagues on the nature of American television programs. The results of these yearly analyses of the level of violence on American television for the 22-year period 1967-89 indicate a consistently high level of violence ... According to Gerbner's initial analysis eight out of every ten plays broadcast during the survey period [beginning] in 1969 contained some form of violence, and eight episodes of violence occurred during each hour of broadcast time. Furthermore, programs especially designed for children, such as cartoons, are the most violent of all programming ... Overall, the levels of violence in prime-time programming have averaged about five acts per hour and children's Saturday morning programs have averaged about 20 to 25 violent acts per hour.

What are the effects of ... exposure to these levels of televised violence? What do we know about the influence of TV violence from the broad range of correlational, experimental, and field studies that have been conducted over the past 40 years? The weight of evidence from correlational studies is fairly consistent: viewing and/or preference for violent television is related to aggressive attitudes, values, and behaviors. This result was true for the studies conducted when television was new, and the measures of children's aggression were teachers' ratings. It is still true for more recent studies when the measures of aggressiveness have become more sophisticated.

Early studies of televised violence

The major initial experimental studies of the cause and effect relation between television/film violence and aggressive behavior were conducted by Bandura and his colleagues working with young children, and by Berkowitz and his associates who studied adolescents. In a typical early study conducted by Bandura (1963), a young child was presented with a film, back-projected on a television screen, of a model who kicked and punished an inflated plastic doll. The child was then placed in a playroom setting and the incidence of aggressive behavior was recorded. The results of these early studies indicated that children who had viewed the aggressive film were more aggressive in the playroom than those children who had not observed the aggressive model. These early studies were criticized on the grounds that the aggressive behavior was not meaningful within the social context and that the stimulus materials were not representative of available television programming. Subsequent studies have used more typical television programs and more realistic measures of aggression, but basically Bandura's early findings still stand.

Studies of preschool children

One early field-experiment was a study conducted by Stein and Friedrich (1972) for the Surgeon General's project. These investigators presented 97 preschool children with a diet of either "antisocial," "prosocial," or "neutral" television programs during a four-week viewing period. The antisocial diet consisted of twelve half-hour episodes of *Batman* and *Superman* cartoons. The prosocial diet was composed of twelve episodes of *Mister Roger's Neighborhood* (a program that stresses such themes as sharing possessions and cooperative play). The neutral diet consisted of children's programming which was neither violent nor prosocial. The children were observed through a nine-week period, which consisted of three weeks of pre-viewing baseline, four weeks of television exposure, and two weeks of post-viewing follow-up. All observations were conducted in a naturalistic setting while the children were engaged in daily school activities. The

Some studies contradict the author's claim that watching violent TV is related to aggressive attitudes, values, and behaviors. For one such study see news1.thdo.bbc.co.u.k./low/english/despatches/newid_47000/47792.stm.

Another criticism of this study is that it failed to differentiate between punishing the doll and real violence. That is, there may have been an element of play in the children's behavior that was not acknowledged by the researchers.

observers recorded various forms of behavior that could be regarded as prosocial (i.e. helping, sharing, cooperative play) or antisocial (i.e. pushing, arguing, breaking toys). The overall results indicated that children who were judged to be initially somewhat aggressive became significantly more so as a result of viewing the *Batman* and *Superman* cartoons. Moreover, the children who had viewed the prosocial diet of *Mister Roger's Neighborhood* were less aggressive, more cooperative, and more willing to share with other children ... In another field-experiment, Parke and his colleagues (1977) found similar heightened aggression among both American and Belgian teenage boys following exposure to aggressive films

Longitudinal studies

The long-term influence of television has not been extensively investigated but we do have indications from several major studies. In an initial longitudinal study Lefkowitz and his colleagues (1972) were able to demonstrate long-term effects in a group of children followed up over a ten-year period. In this instance, Eron (1963) had previously demonstrated a relationship between preference for violent media and the aggressive behavior of these children at the age of eight. One question now posed was, would this relationship hold at later ages? To answer this question, the investigators obtained peer-rated measures of aggressive behavior and preferences for various kinds of television, radio, and comic books when the children were eight years old. Ten years later, when the members of the group were eighteen years old, the investigators again obtained measures of aggressive behavior and television program preferences. The results for boys indicated that preference for television violence at age eight was significantly related to aggression at age eight, but that preference for television violence at age eighteen was not related to aggression at age eighteen. A second question posed was, could this adolescent aggressiveness be predicted from our knowledge of their viewing habits in early childhood? And, the answer seems to be yes. The important finding here is the significant relationship, for boys, between preference for violent media at age eight and aggressive behavior at age eighteen. Equally important is the lack of relationship in the reverse direction; that is, preference for violent television programs at age eighteen was not produced by their aggressive behavior in early childhood. The most plausible interpretation of this pattern of correlations is that early preference for violent television programming and other media is one factor in the production of aggressive and

The statement that the 18-year-olds who preferred TV violence were not rated as aggressive appears to contradict the author's claim that there is a correlation between watching media violence and real-life aggression.

antisocial behavior when the young boy becomes a young man. Finally, the 22-year longitudinal study (Huesmann, Eron, Lefkowitz & Walder, 1984)—a follow-up to the earlier Lefkowitz et al. (1972) study—has found significant causal-correlations between violence viewing at age eight and serious interpersonal criminal behavior at age 30.

Summary

In summarizing the extent of the effects, we agree with Comstock that there are multiple ways in which television and film violence influence the viewer. Comstock suggests four dimensions: Efficacy relates to whether the violence on the screen is rewarded or punished; Normativeness refers to whether the screen violence is justified or lacks any consequences; Pertinence describes the extent to which the screen violence has some similarity to the viewer's social context; and Suggestibility concerns the predisposing factors of arousal or frustration.

Here Murray refers to an important book by G. Comstock and H. Paik, Television and the American Child, published in 1991.

Drawing on these four dimensions, Comstock suggests situations for which we have experimental evidence of the effects of film or television violence:

1. Rewarding or lack of punishment for those who act aggressively.
2. If the aggressive behavior is seen as justified.
3. There are cues in the portrayed violence which have similarity to those in real life.
4. There is similarity between the aggressor and the viewer.
5. Strong identification with the aggressor, such as imagining being in their place.
6. Behavior that is motivated to inflict harm or injury.
7. Violence in which the consequences are lowered, such as no pain, sorrow, or remorse.
8. Violence that is portrayed more realistically or seen as a real event.
9. Violence which is not subjected to critical commentary.
10. Portrayals which seem to please the viewer.
11. Portrayals of violence that are unrelieved by other events.
12. Violence that includes physical abuse in addition to or compared to verbal aggression.
13. Violence that leaves the viewer in a state or arousal.
14. When viewers are predisposed to act aggressively.
15. Individuals who are in a state of frustration after they view violence, either from an external source or from the viewing itself.

The author clarifies his argument by listing some of the main points he would like to emphasize at the end of his article.

TEN THINGS WRONG WITH THE "EFFECTS MODEL"
David Gauntlett

NO

It has become something of a cliché to observe that despite many decades of research and hundreds of studies, the connections between people's consumption of the mass media and their subsequent behavior have remained persistently elusive. Indeed, researchers have enjoyed an unusual degree of patience from both their scholarly and more public audiences. But the time comes when we must take a step back from this murky lack of consensus and ask—why? Why are there no clear answers on media effects?

This author states his case in the introduction: that the results of media effects studies are inconclusive.

1. Tackles social problems "backwards"

To explain the problem of violence in society, researchers should begin with that social violence and seek to explain it with reference, quite obviously, to those who engage in it: their identity, background, character, and so on. The "media effects" approach, in this sense, comes at the problem backwards, by starting with the media and then trying to lasso connections from there on to social beings …

2. Treats children as inadequate

Gauntlett is saying here that researchers assume middle-class and adult values when studying children.

In psychology … children are often considered not so much in terms of what they can do, as what they (apparently) cannot. Negatively defined as non-adults, the research subjects are regarded as the "other," a strange breed whose failure to match generally middle-class adult norms must be charted and discussed. Most laboratory studies of children and the media presume, for example, that their findings apply only to children, but fail to run parallel studies with adult groups to confirm this. We might speculate that this is because if adults were found to respond to laboratory pressures in the same way as children, the "common sense" validity of the experiments would be undermined.

3. Assumptions are characterized by barely concealed conservative ideology

The condemnation of generalized screen "violence" by conservative critics … can often be traced to concerns such as "disrespect for authority" and "anti-patriotic sentiments"…. Programs which do not necessarily contain any greater quantity of violent, sexual, or other controversial depictions than others can be seen to be objected to because they take a more challenging sociopolitical stance. This was illustrated by a study of over 2,200 complaints about British TV and radio … [which] showed a relatively narrow range of most complained-of programs were taken by complainants to characterize a much broader decline in the morals of both broadcasting in particular and the nation in general.

4. Inadequately defines its own objects of study

Effects studies have generally taken for granted the definitions of media material, such as "antisocial" and "prosocial" programming, as well as characterizations of behavior in the real world, such as "antisocial" and "prosocial" action….These can be ideological value judgments; throwing down a book in disgust, smashing a nuclear missile, or—to use a Beavis and Butt-Head example—sabotaging activities at one's burger-bar workplace will always be interpreted in effects studies as "antisocial," not "prosocial."

5. Often based on artificial studies

Since careful sociological studies of media effects require amounts of time and money which limit their abundance, they are heavily outnumbered by simpler studies which are usually characterized by elements of artificiality. Such studies typically take place in a laboratory, or in a "natural" setting such as a classroom but where a researcher has conspicuously shown up and instigated activities, neither of which are typical environments. Instead of a full and naturally viewed television diet, research subjects are likely to be shown selected or specially recorded clips which lack the narrative meaning inherent in everyday TV productions. They may then be observed in simulations of real life presented to them as a game, in relation to inanimate objects … or as they respond to questionnaires, all of which are unlike interpersonal interaction, cannot be equated with it, and are likely to be associated with the previous viewing experience in the mind of the subject, rendering the study invalid.

6. Often based on studies with misapplied methodology

Many of the studies which do not rely on an experimental method, and so may evade the flaws mentioned in the previous section, fall down instead by applying a

The author is saying that condemnation of TV violence is often mixed up with conservative ideology concerning respect for authority and patriotism. What other ideological values do you think influence the effects model?

This point is similar to the one above: that some actions in the effects model are judged with an ideological bias.

The point being made here is that simple studies are invalid because they do not replicate real-life situations. What arguments would you use to counter this point?

methodological procedure wrongly, or by drawing inappropriate conclusions from particular methods. The widely cited longitudinal panel study by Huesmann, Eron, and colleagues, for example, has been less famously slated for failing to keep to the procedures, such as assessing aggressivity or TV viewing with the same measures at different points in time, which are necessary for their statistical findings to have any validity.

Murray, the author of the opposing article, also cites this longitudinal panel study.

The same researchers have also failed to adequately account for why the findings of this study and those of another of their own studies absolutely contradict each other, with the former concluding that the media has a marginal effect on boys but no effect on girls, and the latter arguing the exact opposite (no effect on boys, but a small effect for girls).

7. Selective in its criticisms of media depictions of violence

In addition to the point that "antisocial" acts are ideologically defined in effects studies, we can also note that the media depictions of "violence" which the effects model typically condemns are limited to fictional productions. The acts of violence which appear on a daily basis on news and serious factual programs are seen as somehow exempt. The point here is not that depictions of violence in the news should necessarily be condemned in just the same, blinkered way, but rather to draw attention to another philosophical inconsistency which the model cannot account for. If the antisocial acts shown in drama series and films are expected to have an effect on the behavior of viewers, even though such acts are almost always ultimately punished or have other negative consequences for the perpetrator, there is no obvious reason why the antisocial activities which are always in the news, and which frequently do not have such apparent consequences for their agents, should not have similar effects.

Why do you think that news and serious factual programs are seen as "somehow exempt" in the effects model?

8. Assumes superiority to the masses

Surveys typically show that whilst a certain proportion of the public feel that the media may cause other people to engage in antisocial behavior, almost no one ever says that they have been affected in that way themselves. This view is taken to extremes by researchers and campaigners whose work brings them into regular contact with the supposedly corrupting material, but who are unconcerned for their own well-being as they implicitly "know" that the effects will only be on "other people." Insofar as these others are defined as children or "unstable" individuals, their approach may seem not

This phenomenon is known as the "third person effect," as noted in the introduction to this topic.

unreasonable; it is fair enough that such questions should be explored. Nonetheless, the idea that it is unruly "others" who will be affected—the uneducated? the working class?—remains at the heart of the effects paradigm, and is reflected in its texts (as well, presumably, as in the researchers' overenthusiastic interpretation of weak or flawed data).

The author is reiterating his earlier point that the effects model is based on conservative political assumptions.

9. Makes no attempt to understand meanings of the media

A further fundamental flaw, hinted at in points three and four above, is that the effects model necessarily rests on a base of reductive assumptions and unjustified stereotypes regarding media content. To assert that, say, "media violence" will bring negative consequences is not only to presume that depictions of violence in the media will always be promoting antisocial behavior, and that such a category exists and makes sense, as noted above, but also assumes that the medium holds a singular message which will be carried unproblematically to the audience. The effects model therefore performs the double deception of presuming (a) that the media presents a singular and clear-cut "message," and (b) that the proponents of the effects model are in a position to identify what that message is.

The point the author is making here is that not all media violence conveys the same message. For instance, while some programs might promote violence as being glamorous, others show violence as being a pitiful activity that leads only to punishment and imprisonment. What other meanings might be read from media violence?

10. Not grounded in theory

Finally, and underlying many of the points made above, is the fundamental problem that the entire argument of the "effects model" is substantiated with no theoretical reasoning beyond the bald assertions that particular kinds of effects will be produced by the media. The basic question of why the media should induce people to imitate its content has never been adequately tackled, beyond the simple idea that particular actions are "glamorized." (Obviously, antisocial actions are shown really positively so infrequently that this is an inadequate explanation.) Similarly, the question of how merely seeing an activity in the media would be translated into an actual motive which would prompt an individual to behave in a particular way is just as unresolved.

So what future for research on media influences?

The effects model, we have seen, has remarkably little going for it as an explanation of human behavior, or of the media in society. Whilst any challenging or apparently illogical theory or model reserves the right to demonstrate its validity through empirical data, the effects model has failed also in that respect. Its continued survival is indefensible and unfortunate.

Summary

In the first article Murray states his case that watching media violence has a clear and unambiguous effect on subsequent behavior. That is, that media violence leads to aggressive and antisocial behavior in viewers, particularly young ones. This theory is known as the "media effects" model. He acknowledges that the general perception is that research evidence is unclear and contradictory, and puts forward his contention that this perception is incorrect. In doing so, he cites a number of research studies that have been conducted since the 1960s that purport to demonstrate this effect.

Gauntlett, in the second article, argues that the media effects model is useless and should be abandoned because it has failed to conclusively demonstrate any connection between people's consumption of mass media and their subsequent behavior. He goes on to cite 10 reasons why the model has failed to deliver any results. They include the unstated assumptions, values, and ideological bias of the researchers, particularly the conservative political ideology that underlies the research. The fundamental problem for him is that the model does not tackle the basic question of why the media should induce people to imitate its content.

FURTHER INFORMATION:

Books:

Barker, Martin (editor), *The Video Nasties: Freedom and Censorship in the Media*. London: Pluto, 1984.

Comstock, G. & H. Paik, *Television and the American Child*. San Diego, CA: Academic Press, 1991.

Gauntlett, D., *Moving Experiences: Understanding Television's Influences and Effects*. London: John Libbey, 1995.

Levine, Madeline, *See No Evil: A Guide to Protecting Our Children from Media Violence*. San Francisco: Jossey-Bass, 1998.

Medved, Michael, *Hollywood vs. America*. London: HarperCollins, 1992.

Articles:

"Some Effects of Violent and Nonviolent Movies on the Behavior of Juvenile Delinquents," in *Advances in Experimental Psychology, 10* by L. Berkowitz (editor). New York: Academic Press, 1977.

Useful websites:

www.apa.org/pubinfo/violence.html
American Psychological Association's site.

www.lionlamb.org
The Lion and Lamb project's site: information about the effects of violent entertainment, toys, and games on children's behavior.

www.nctv.org
The site for the National Coalition on TV Violence.

The following debates in the Pro/Con series may also be of interest:

In this volume:

Topic 1 Should the media be subject to censorship?

Topic 3 Do people watch too much television?

Topic 4 Does the V-chip work?

DOES MOVIE AND TELEVISION VIOLENCE CAUSE SOCIAL VIOLENCE?

YES: Because many viewers, especially young ones, have had no experience of real violence, this is the only depiction of violence they know

YES: Several studies indicate a direct link between watching violence on the media and subsequent aggressive behavior

FICTION AND REALISM
Do viewers believe what they see on the screen is real?

CLEAR CAUSALITY
Have the effects of media violence been firmly established?

NO: Viewers, even very young ones, are able to distinguish between fictional violence and violent acts in the real world

NO: Media effects studies are flawed in a number of fundamental ways and present no clear conclusions

DOES MOVIE AND TELEVISION VIOLENCE CAUSE SOCIAL VIOLENCE?

KEY POINTS

YES: Violence is antisocial, shows a disrespect for authority, and can lead to criminal behavior

YES: There would not be so many research studies into the effects of media violence if society as a whole was not concerned about it

DEFINING VIOLENCE
Is media violence always bad?

NO: Much of the media effects research is based on a conservative ideology that defines all violence as antisocial

NO: Viewers can read many different meanings into media violence, such as that it is glamorous or sad or terrifying— not just one

Topic 6
DO THE MEDIA ENCOURAGE A DISTORTED BODY IMAGE?

YES
"BODY IMAGE AND ADVERTISING"
ISSUE BRIEFS, APRIL 25, 2000
MEDIASCOPE PRESS

NO
"WEIGHTY MATTERS: THE BRITISH GOVERNMENT PLANS TO TAKE ON
HEROIN CHIC IN A BODY IMAGE SUMMIT THIS MONTH"
SALON.COM, JUNE 7, 2000
WILLIAM UNDERHILL

INTRODUCTION

A common accusation against the media is that they pedal a glamorous view of life and encourage people to emulate an unrealistic lifestyle they can never achieve. This criticism has been leveled against a range of Hollywood movies and TV shows, but is particularly directed against advertising. One of the ways in which TV or print advertising campaigns work, critics allege, is by showing people idealized images—a happy family occasion, say, a perfect designer house, or an office where all the workers are attractive, honest, and witty. These images encourage consumers to believe that by buying a particular product, they somehow buy in to the lifestyle portrayed. Advertisers, on the other hand, acknowledge that they create appealing images, but argue that consumers are sophisticated enough to distinguish fact from fantasy.

The debate becomes particularly heated when it comes to fashion. Critics allege that designers, photographers, stylists, magazine editors, and models are all part of a process that encourages people to be dissatisfied with their bodies. Fashion magazines and advertising campaigns for designers such as Ralph Lauren portray a world of physically "perfect" men and women. "Perfect" means, in this case, slim and well muscled for men and tall and skinny for women.

Critics point out that there is a fundamental problem with these images: Most people simply do not fit. The majority of women are not shaped like models such as Jodie Kidd, who is extremely thin. The media, they argue, are setting an ideal of beauty that is unattainable for most people. The danger is that such images may encourage some people to be dissatisifed with their shape. This might lead to shyness and inhibition in overweight people, for example, or to an unhealthy interest in dieting and exercise. But it might also have far more serious effects, such as encouraging eating disorders, including anorexia nervosa and bulimia, which affect mainly women. Notorious fashion pictures that appeared in reputable magazines in the late 1990s featured models so painfully thin that critics wondered if they might even be drug addicts. There was even a term for the look: "heroin chic."

> *"Models are becoming thinner at a time when women are becoming heavier, and the gap between the ideal body shape and the reality is wider than ever."*
> —BRITISH MEDICAL ASSOCIATION

The fashion industry insists that the images it creates are intended to make women feel good about themselves, not bad. Most models are thin only because they show off clothes better. The media do not shape society's concept of beauty, the argument continues, but simply reflect it. The popularity of ultra-thin models is a passing vogue. When fuller female shapes become fashionable again, as they were, for example, in the 1950s, then the fashion industry will adopt them in turn.

Beyond fashion there are further examples of the media creating unhealthy physical role models. Actresses such as Calista Flockhart (*Ally McBeal*) and the female stars of the comedy show *Friends* were suspected of themselves suffering from eating disorders. Some academic studies seem to confirm that consumption of media is related to higher incidences of body image problems.

On the other hand, the media may prove the most powerful means to demolish common stereotypes of beauty and attractiveness. Many TV shows and movies manage—deliberately or otherwise—to portray people with ordinary looks or bodies as attractive and desirable. Many books and press articles expose for readers the ways in which Madison Avenue sets out to exploit them. Some advertising campaigns even mock advertising conventions for comic effect, showing an impossibly handsome man as being equally stupid, for example.

The following articles show two different attitudes to reports on media and self-image. The contribution from Mediascope provides a straightforward summary of research and findings on the issue and identifies certain problems, but it does not offer any solutions. William Underhill's article takes an openly cynical tone as he attacks British governmental attempts to address the issue; whether he offers any solutions is open to debate.

BODY IMAGE AND ADVERTISING
Mediascope Press

Advertisers often emphasize sexuality and the importance of physical attractiveness in an attempt to sell products, but researchers are concerned that this places undue pressure on women and men to focus on their appearance. In a recent survey by *Teen People* magazine, 27 percent of the girls felt that the media pressure them to have a perfect body, and a poll conducted in 1996 by … Saatchi and Saatchi found that ads made women fear being unattractive or old. Researchers suggest advertising media may adversely impact women's body image, which can lead to unhealthy behavior as women and girls strive for the ultrathin body idealized by the media. Advertising has also been recently accused of setting unrealistic ideals for males.

The 27 percent statistic in the first paragraph is relatively low. Does this weaken the report's impact?

The beautiful message

The average woman sees 400 to 600 advertisements per day, and by the time she is 17 years old, she has received over 250,000 commercial messages through the media. Only 9 percent of commercials have a direct statement about beauty, but many more implicitly emphasize its importance—particularly those that target women and girls. One study of Saturday morning toy commercials found that 50 percent of commercials aimed at girls spoke about physical attractiveness, while none of the commercials aimed at boys referred to appearance. Other studies found 50 percent of advertisements in teen girl magazines and 56 percent of television commercials aimed at female viewers used beauty as a product appeal. This constant exposure to female-oriented advertisements may influence girls to become self-conscious about their bodies and to obsess over their physical appearance as a measure of their worth.

Do you think there are too many commercials in the media?

Advertisements emphasize thinness as a standard for female beauty, and the bodies idealized in the media are frequently atypical of normal, healthy women. In fact, today's fashion models weigh 23 percent less than the average female, and a young woman between the ages of 18 and 34 has a 1 percent chance of being as thin as a supermodel. However, 69 percent of girls in one study said that magazine models influence their idea of the perfect body shape.

Do you agree that girls are brought up to be more conscious of their appearance than boys?

Some researchers believe that advertisers purposely normalize unrealistically thin bodies in order to create an unattainable desire that can drive product consumption. "The media markets desire. And by reproducing ideals that are absurdly out of line with what real bodies really do look like … the media perpetuates a market for frustration and disappointment. Its customers will never disappear," writes Paul Hamburg, an assistant professor of Psychiatry at Harvard Medical School. Considering that the diet industry alone generates $33 billion in revenue, advertisers have been successful with their marketing strategy.

Support your argument by quoting from an authoritative source such as an academic.

The effects of advertising

Women frequently compare their bodies to those they see around them, and researchers have found that exposure to idealized body images lowers women's satisfaction with their own attractiveness. People shown slides of thin models had lower self-evaluations than people who had seen average and oversized models, and girls reported that "very thin" models made them feel insecure. In a sample of Stanford undergraduate and graduate students, 68 percent felt worse about their own appearance after looking through women's magazines. Many health professionals are also concerned by the prevalence of distorted body image among women, which may be fostered by their constant self-comparison to extremely thin figures promoted in the media. Seventy-five percent of "normal"-weight women think they are overweight and 90 percent of women overestimate their body size.

"Guys do seem to wonder how a man can deal with a big, powerful woman."
—EMME, 180-POUND AMERICAN SUPERMODEL

Dissatisfaction with their bodies causes many women and girls to strive for the thin ideal. The number-one wish for girls ages 11 to 17 is to be thinner, and girls as young as five have expressed fears of getting fat. Eighty percent of 10-year-old girls have dieted, and at any one time 50 percent of American women are currently dieting. Some researchers suggest depicting thin models may lead girls into unhealthy weight-control habits, because the ideal they seek to emulate is unattainable for many and unhealthy for most. One study

Does this figure surprise you? How does it fit in with your own experience?

COMMENTARY: Celebrities in the spotlight

"One can never," said Wallis Simpson, duchess of Windsor, "be too rich or too thin." Though she lived to the age of 89, the relentless pursuit of a slender profile has brought illness or even death to many other celebrities.

In 1983 eating disorders were suddenly in the spotlight when the singer Karen Carpenter died from cardiac arrest brought on by the anorexia nervosa she had been fighting since the late 1970s. A more recent casualty was Lena Zavaroni, a one-time British child star who developed eating disorders by the age of 13. In 1999, aged 35, she underwent brain surgery, a last-ditch attempt at curing her depression and anorexia, but she developed bronchial pneumonia during the operation and died.

The actress Jane Fonda was more fortunate. At about the time that Karen Carpenter was wasting away, Fonda addressed her own long battle with bulimia, and from her binge-and-purge routine she turned to a healthy diet and a fitness regime that helped her recovery. Elton John checked into a clinic with bulimia in the 1980s. The late Diana, Princess of Wales, reportedly began to suffer from bulimia soon after her marriage in 1981. By 1987 she appeared emaciated on TV and in the press, but toward the end of her life was beginning to manage the problem. Comedienne Joan Rivers recovered from eating disorders that developed after the suicide of her husband, Edgar Rosenberg.

In denial or naturally slim?

While society usually sympathizes with such casualties, it is less tolerant of those who publicly slim down to skeletal dimensions and yet assert that they are simply in good shape as a result of a rigorous fitness regime or a special diet. The stars of *Ally McBeal* have been regular media targets. The show's star, Calista Flockhart, has staunchly denied being anorexic, instead attributing any loss to hard work and abstention from junk food. Her costars Portia de Rossi and Courtney Thorne-Smith faced similar media attention, and the fierce competition to stay slim drove the latter to leave the show. She confessed, "I started undereating, overexercising, pushing myself way too hard. The amount of time I spent thinking about food and being upset about my body was insane." Sarah Michelle Geller of *Buffy the Vampire Slayer*, who visibly slimmed down across several episodes, has acknowledged, "Everyone says I'm too skinny—but this is Hollywood."

Such female celebrities, colloquially called "lollipop ladies," face a dilemma. On top of the pressure to slim there is an implicit duty toward fans, some of whom may have eating disorders but, unlike their idols, cannot check into rehab. The media feed at random off this relationship. In Flockhart's words, "[Media] exploitation of human beings is astonishing. Why? Is it because we, the public … want the gossip? I believe we do, but is it also because that's what they're feeding us? What came first?"

found that 47 percent of the girls were influenced by magazine pictures to want to lose weight, but only 29 percent were actually overweight. Stringent dieting to achieve an ideal figure can play a key role in triggering eating disorders. Other researchers believe depicting thin models appears not to have long-term effects on most adolescent women, but they do agree it affects girls who already have body-image problems. Girls who were already dissatisfied with their bodies showed more dieting, anxiety, and bulimic symptoms after prolonged exposure to fashion and advertising images in a teen girl magazine. Studies also show that a third of U.S. women in their teens and twenties begin smoking cigarettes in order to help control their appetite.

The National Institute of Health defines overweight as a body mass index (BMI) of 25–29.9kg/m². A person's BMI is calculated by dividing weight in kilograms by height in meters squared.

Boys and body image

Although distorted body image has widely been known to affect women and girls, there is growing awareness regarding the pressure men and boys are under to appear muscular. Many males are becoming insecure about their physical appearance as advertising and other media images raise the standard and idealize well-built men. Researchers are concerned about how this impacts men and boys, and have seen an alarming increase in obsessive weight training and the use of anabolic steroids and dietary supplements that promise bigger muscles or more stamina for lifting.

One study suggests that an alarming trend in toy action figures' increasing muscularity is setting unrealistic ideals for boys much in the same way Barbie dolls have been accused of giving an unrealistic ideal of thinness for girls. "Our society's worship of muscularity may cause increasing numbers of men to develop pathological shame about their bodies…. Our observations of these little plastic toys have stimulated us to explore further links between cultural messages, body image disorders, and use of steroids and other drugs," says researcher Dr. Harrison Pope.

The majority of teenagers with eating disorders are girls (90 percent), but experts believe the number of boys affected is increasing and that many cases may not be reported, since males are reluctant to acknowledge any illness primarily associated with females. Studies have shown that boys, like girls, may turn to smoking to help them lose weight. Boys ages 9 to 14 who thought they were overweight were 65 percent more likely to think about or try smoking than their peers, and boys who worked out every day in order to lose weight were twice as likely to experiment with tobacco.

WEIGHTY MATTERS
William Underhill

Underhill adopts a tone that aims to entertain as well as inform the reader.

An important style tip for traveling fashionistas: If you plan to visit Britain this summer be sure to pack a hair shirt or two and maybe some sackcloth. The "skinny model" debate has leaped from the papers into the (appropriately plump) seat of government, and a little show of penitence might be wise. Yes, I am quite sure you have heard much of this before. How all those magazine pictures of pallid, panda-eyed models with coat-hanger shoulders are sapping the confidence of girls who can never hope to resemble Jodie Kidd or Kate Moss. How the struggle to shrink—and stay shrunk—is producing a generation of agonized and underweight underachievers.

But the level of hysteria [in Britain] has reached a new high—or low, depending on your orientation to the matter. The latest attack on extreme thinness comes from the British Medical Association (BMA), not some preachy pressure group. The BMA has announced that models and actresses in the late 1990s carried just 10 to 15 percent body fat, while the average for healthy women was 23 to 26 percent. And yes, constant exposure to "unachievable" images can trigger eating disorders. Conclusion: "More realistic body shapes need to be shown on TV and in fashion magazines."

A national issue

Tired as these breakthroughs might seem, they appear as fresh policy fodder to the government, which has decided to take a strong stand. Downing Street [the British prime minister's London residence] has summoned fashion industry leaders—teen mag editors, fashion model bookers, and the like, as well as experts on anorexia—to a Body Image Summit later this month. Heading the agenda will be the link between "inappropriate body images" and women's self-esteem. As many as 40 panelists are expected, including eating disorder expert and onetime Princess Di confidante Susie Orbach, as well as unnamed representatives of the (bring your cameras!) Storm model agency. Quite naturally, the government's minister for women, Tessa Jowell, isn't talking about anything so crude as blame; but we all know who'll be sitting on the sunny side of the table.

The British government's Body Image Summit took place on June 21, 2000, in London.

And this won't be just a chance to brainstorm. Oh no, no. The government is talking about "action." It has identified a real menace and it means business. Who knows, the next Labour election manifesto could contain a pledge—this is a government that loves targets—to raise women's self-esteem by 50 percent over the next five years. Quite possibly the summit will mark the start of a whole new era of good sense in which Barbie dolls have hips, men pull their weight in the kitchen, and world peace is restored.

Wit used well can help win you a debate, but it should be used with great care.

Motive and responsibility

Why the cynicism? As a father of preteen daughters, maybe I should be grateful. After all, something is badly wrong when 57 percent of the nation's 12- to 15-year-olds put "appearance" at the top of their worry list. Maybe I should support any serious attempt to correct the notion that only the truly svelte deserve happiness and success.

"We're very aware of the [thin] issue and I think we all try to use girls who look healthy."

—SAM BAKER, EDITOR,

COMPANY MAGAZINE (UK)

But a government-sponsored "summit"? First there's the question of motive. Any politician knows that fashion mavens [experts] make an easy target. We may buy the magazines but we distrust the folks behind them. These are the people who have grown rich by trading on our vanity and insecurity, who have persuaded my children to waste their (my) cash on tricolor sneakers. Now we learn that they are conspiring to ruin our health and well-being.

Voters will always support a government initiative that offers a chance for a little righteous indignation. (The truly skeptical might also like to note that an election looks likely next year and even that new baby might not prove enough to revive Prime Minister Tony Blair's sagging popularity with women voters.) But this is really none of the government's business. The aspirations and eating habits of young women are the business of parents or the young women themselves, not the

In 2001 Tony Blair, leader of the Labour Party, won a second term as prime minister.

British supermodel Jodie Kidd on the catwalk at a fashion show in New York in 1997. Some people believe that very thin models encourage girls and women to diet.

not the über-daddy state. The very idea of a national summit suggests that we can't be trusted to know best. (No surprise there. Under Blair, we're getting used to a hectoring, clean-your-teeth-twice-a-day tone from government as bad as anything we endured under Thatcher and the Conservatives.)

And the word "summit" is both chilling and laughable. Doubtless the PR team that drafted the press release wanted to convey the serious nature of the event. They attempted, in the choice of one word, to let us know that this gathering wouldn't be just another publicity blatherfest. Bad choice. That's just what "summit" means these days. A summit is a marathon of prepared speeches, empty declarations and photo ops; an occasion where the powerful gather to talk platitudes and then go home to continue degrading the environment, undermining each other's economies, and generally doing whatever best suits the national interest.

So maybe "summit" is all too apt. This certainly won't be the kind of confrontation that produces remedies. More likely, it will be a chance for all parties to flaunt their "concern." What "action" could the government take anyhow? Even this government couldn't seriously decree a minimum weight for models or ban 30-day bikini diets. The best we can expect is a voluntary code of conduct—just like [codes] for the press that have failed to curb the excesses of tabloid snoopery.

Let the public decide

One can expect the usual hand-wringing and excuses from the fashion-friendly who attend this affair. Nobody catches anorexia off the page, they will remind us. The magazines are only supplying what the readers want. Besides, diets are outré: detox cures and cleansing regimes are the order of the day. And "heroin chic" is out. Models really are getting a tad stouter. Just look at the latest Brazilian supermodel Gisele Bundchen (certainly no waif but most of the serious poundage is on the chest).

Sure that's all part of the truth. But the fashion industry isn't a powerless servant of public taste. The editors of women's magazines can—but don't—refuse to run ads or other shots showing models with jutting shoulder blades. Perhaps they know that it doesn't take government guidance to recognize jutting shoulder blades as freakish. My (well-rounded) 8-year-old certainly has such powers of discernment. If she's to be convinced that her worst enemies aren't pizza and ice cream, what's needed isn't a summit, it's more intemperate ranting to induce a sense of shame.

> The author is suggesting that the Blair government in Britain has adopted a "nannying" tone similar to that experienced under Prime Minister Margaret Thatcher.

See Topic 2 Do newsmakers have a right to privacy? pages 24-35.

> Do you agree with the author's conclusion that even consumers as young as eight are smart enough to pass their own judgment on "heroin chic"?

Summary

"Body Image and Advertising" states that consumers of all ages are bombarded with commercials that collectively project the ideal: "Thin is beautiful." This ideal, claims the report, gives many females and some males, too, a low self-image. However, statistics show that the beauty esthetic promoted by the use of waiflike models does not match real life: The vast majority of women are not, and can never become, waiflike in build. Their attempts to live up to the ideal lead many to dietary disorders and some to an early death. Moreover, the report implicates the media in perpetuating this impossible beauty ideal in order to sustain a culture of desire and thus sustain consumer spending.

In "Weighty Matters" William Underhill uses savage wit to pour scorn on what he describes as "hysteria" over the implications of a connection between media and body image. His article focuses on the Body Image Summit convened in London in 2000 by the British government in response to alarming medical association reports on dietary disorders. Underhill, for whom such a summit is yet another example of government meddling, is not convinced. Anorexia isn't catching, he says, and the magazines are only supplying the public with what they want. Even his eight-year-old daughter would know the difference.

FURTHER INFORMATION:

Books:

Fox, R. F., *Harvesting Minds: How TV Commercials Control Kids*. Westport, CT: Praeger Publishing, 1996.

Articles:

American Academy of Pediatrics, "Magazine Models Impact Girls' Desire to Lose Weight," American Academy of Pediatrics press release, 1999.

Goode, E., "Girls' Self Image Survives Effect of Glossy Ads," *New York Times*, August 24, 1999.

"How to Love the Way You Look," *Teen People*, October, 1999.

McLean Hopital, "Body Image Disorder Linked to Toy Action Figures' Growing Muscularity," McLean Hospital press release, 1999.

Marcus, A., "Body Image Tied to Smoking in Kids," Health Scout, Merck-Medco Managed Care, 1999.

Morris, L., "The Cigarette Diet," *Allure*, March 2000.

Wax. R. G., "Boys and Body Image," *San Diego Parent Magazine* 1998.

Useful websites:

www.womenswire.com/forums/image/D1022/ Article by M. Peacock, "Sex, Housework & Ads," 1998.

www.kidsnrg.simplenet.com/grit.dev/london/g2_jan12/green_ladies/media/ "Media Influence on Teens." Facts compiled by Allison LaVoie on the Green Ladies Website.

The following debates in the Pro/Con series may also be of interest:

In this volume:

Eating Disorders, pages 84–85

Topic 1 Should the media be subject to censorship?

Topic 7 Is advertising too powerful in American society?

DO THE MEDIA ENCOURAGE A DISTORTED BODY IMAGE?

YES: Statistics show that only a tiny fraction of consumers can achieve the waiflike look

YES: By using thin models to create a beauty myth, the media endlessly perpetuate demand for beauty products

IMPOSSIBLY THIN
Does the use of waiflike models mislead consumers?

MEDIA PRESSURE
Do the media have a secret agenda?

NO: Even today's preteens are sophisticated enough to distinguish fact from fantasy

NO: Television and the papers are merely reporting life; women's journals simply give consumers what they want

DO THE MEDIA ENCOURAGE A DISTORTED BODY IMAGE?
KEY POINTS

YES: The great amount of imagery to which people are subjected is bound to have an effect on body image, so the media should endorse responsible advertising

SLIM HOPE
Should the media adhere to an ethics code by which the body beautiful is represented in realistic terms?

NO: How can media watchdogs realistically place controls on imagery? Any enforceable measures would represent a loss of civil liberties

EATING DISORDERS

*"The experience of living in a severely anorexic body,
even if that body is housed in an affluent suburb, is the
experience of a body living in Bergen-Belsen."*
—NAOMI WOLF, AUTHOR OF *THE BEAUTY MYTH*

Eating disorders are a growing problem in modern society. Studies have shown that over half of adult Americans are overweight. About one-third of them are obese— that is, 20 percent over the normal and healthy weight for their size. "Drugs and Therapy Perspectives" reports that about 1 percent of women in the United States have a binge-eating disorder. Similarly, research also suggests that about four out of every 100 college-aged women have bulimia, and 1 percent of female adolescents have anorexia. So, why are eating disorders on the increase? Many sociologists, psychiatrists, counselors, and other critics lay the blame on the media and the pressure that they place on men and women to have the perfect body. Magazines, movies, and television are filled with images of very thin women and muscular men who, society is constantly shown, have ideal body shapes. But is this explanation too simplistic—should the media be blamed for this phenomenon?

Background

There are many descriptions of disorders similar to anorexia and bulimia (see table opposite) in ancient Egyptian, Persian, and Chinese scrolls. The Romans liked to overeat at banquets and then retreated to the vomitorium (a toilet chamber with vomiting facilities) so that they could be sick and then return to continue eating.

In 1689 Richard Morton first formally described anorexia nervosa in medical literature. He described his patient as being "a skeleton clad only with skin." In the beginning physicians thought that anorexia nervosa was linked to tuberculosis (T.B.) or was related to hormone or endocrine imbalances. It was only in the 1930s that researchers tried to identify the factors that influence the disease. Biological factors, such as temperament or chemical imbalances, can predispose anxious or compulsive behavior. There are psychological factors, too; people with eating disorders tend to be perfectionists with unrealistic expectations of themselves. Some sufferers develop disorders to avoid dealing with their sexuality or to exercise power over some aspect of their lives. Others feel that they are smothered by their families or are abandoned, ignored, or overly criticized.

Media and society

Every day through television and the cinema, and through newspapers and advertisements, people are told how they should look, what clothes to wear, what color their hair should be, how thin or fat they should be. The casts of *Ally McBeal*, *Buffy*, and *Friends* feature "lollipop" people—women and men with stick-thin bodies and disproportionately large heads. They are the role models for the young generation. Through the media people are told that to be happy and successful, they must have certain attributes: Women should be thin; men must be fit and muscular. So women diet and exercise, while men lift weights in an attempt to improve their physique. Media stereotyping helps explain why about 90 percent of people with eating disorders are women and 10 percent are men.

A study in Fiji showed that in 1995, before TV became widely accessible on the island, the ideal body shape was plump and soft. Fewer than 38 months later, after viewing of popular American shows like *Melrose Place* and *Beverly Hills 90210*, the incidence of eating disorders among teenage girls was on the rise. It is easy to forget that such media images are constructs. People should be more critical of the images they are fed on a daily basis. Society must encourage a more realistic and positive representation of people in the media or else live with the consequences.

THE MOST COMMON EATING DISORDERS

Anorexia nervosa—the pursuit of thinness
Literally means loss of appetite, but sufferers tend to be perpetually hungry, although they have an irrational fear of being fat. Characterized by depression, irritability, withdrawal, self-starvation, food preoccupation, ritual behavior, compulsive exercising, and absence of menstrual cycles. Untreated, it can be fatal.

Bulimia nervosa—diet–binge–purge
Characterized by recurring periods of binge eating during which large amounts of food are consumed in a short space of time. Sufferers know they are out of control, but worry about being fat. Behavior patterns include: bingeing, followed by purges through vomiting, laxative/diuretic abuse, and periods of fasting.

Compulsive overeating—binge eating
Sufferers compulsively overeat but don't purge themselves and are often overweight. Behavior patterns include: bingeing regularly, hoarding food and secret eating, feelings of guilt and shame, and a tendency to be depressed.

LESS KNOWN
Anorexia athletica—compulsive exercise
Sufferers compulsively exercise and may be fanatical about diet and weight. Behavior includes: skipping school, work, and homelife to exercise; constant dissatisfaction.

Body dysmorphic disorder (BDD)
Affects around 2 percent of the population in the United States. Behavior includes: excessive concern with appearance; constant belief that one is flawed.

Orthorexia nervosa
Sufferers have pathological fascination with eating "pure" foods. They obsess over what to eat. Eating is the primary focus of life.

Eating disorders affect people regardless of their age, race, or sex. Ninety percent of sufferers are women, but male cases are increasing. All of the above are treatable, but without treatment up to 20 percent of people with serious disorders die.

PART 2
ADVERTISING AND THE MEDIA

Advertising and the media are naturally intertwined. Media such as broadcasting, newspapers, and magazines typically rely on advertisers either for their entire income or for a significant part of their profits. Although advertising did exist before the development of mass media, and some media existed before the growth of a recognizable advertising industry, the arrival of the mass media—that is, the means to disseminate information and entertainment quickly to large numbers of people—coincided almost exactly with the development of the modern, vigorous advertising industry. With the arrival of mass circulation in the late 19th century newspapers became increasingly reliant on advertising. It was the desire to increase advertising that led to circulation battles in the last decades of that century and the rise of sensationalist "yellow" journalism.

Thereafter the development of mass media seemed inextricable from the development of advertising. Radio soon showed the power of electronic media supported by advertising, and few questioned that television would be an advertising-supported medium. The progression from newspapers to radio to television continues today with the Internet (see Part 3 of this volume).

Advertising raises questions not only about its impact on consumer behavior but also its effect on the media. Critics assume in one case that advertising works in a subtle and sophisticated way to exploit consumers, and in the other that the financial power wielded by advertisers gives them undue influence over the content of newspapers or broadcast shows. Supporters of advertising argue that it is less powerful and more transparent than it is accused of being.

The topics in this section consider various aspects of the power of advertising and whether it should be limited. Advertising is already controlled. Because it is classed as commercial speech—its purpose is to get consumers to buy something—it is subject to much more legal regulation than, say, political speech. The Federal Trade Commission (FTC) regulates advertisements to ensure fairness and that they do not make any false claims.

Protecting children

Advertising is an especially sensitive issue with regard to children, as discussed in *Topic 8 Is Advertising to Children Morally Wrong?* Some critics argue that children, especially the very young, do not understand the purpose of advertising and think that commercials are just another program. In the 1970s children were protected from "program-length commercials" that blurred the boundary between commercials and programs. When the regulations were lifted in the 1980s, children were again exposed to programs that were essentially advertisements for toys. These, and advertising for highly processed foods, motivate some to argue that children should be protected from advertising. Parents looking for relief from children who demand everything they see on TV favor such a move. Despite efforts by children's activists, no widespread acceptance for a total ban exists.

Another controversial question is whether it is morally wrong to use advertising to promote products that

Topic 10 Does Advertising Threaten Objective Journalism? addresses a different type of issue. How does advertising affect the industry it funds? For instance, would a media corporation such as ABC be willing to be critical of its parent corporation, Disney? The demands of advertising could potentially impinge on journalistic integrity. Although most mainstream journalistic organizations attempt to enforce separations between their editorial and business functions,

"Advertising is the greatest art form of the 20th century."

—MARSHALL McLUHAN, CANADIAN WRITER

harm the consumer. The prime example is tobacco, considered in *Topic 9 Should Tobacco Advertising Be Banned?* In numerous legal cases brought against tobacco producers by smokers in poor health a key claim is that advertising blinded consumers to the dangers of smoking.

The tobacco industry

In the 1970s cigarette advertising on television was banned. Big tobacco companies soon discovered other ways to advertise—in magazines and newspapers, in promotional campaigns, through cartoon characters allegedly aimed at children, and in the developing world. Public tolerance for restriction of tobacco advertising seems high, even if it involves restriction of freedom of speech. Other products may one day find themselves similarly regulated.

critics wonder whether journalists impose self-censorship over information and ideas that they sense would be difficult for their corporation.

Politics

Advertising is increasingly coming to serve as the primary process by which people learn about political parties and candidates (see *Topic 11 Is There Too Much Political Advertising?*). Negative advertising in particular is thought to pollute the political process and lead to public disaffection with politics. Declines in voter turnout since the advent of television might be related to the growing role in politics of image rather than substance. On the other hand, political advertising might well be one of the most efficient methods to educate citizens in a modern democracy today.

Topic 7
IS ADVERTISING TOO POWERFUL IN AMERICAN SOCIETY?

YES

"RISE OF THE IMAGE CULTURE: REIMAGINING THE AMERICAN DREAM"
MEDIA AND VALUES, ISSUE 57, WINTER 1992
ELIZABETH THOMAN

NO

"IN DEFENSE OF ADVERTISING: ARGUMENTS FROM REASON, ETHICAL EGOISM, AND
LAISSEZ-FAIRE CAPITALISM"
THE JOURNAL OF CONSUMER AFFAIRS, SUMMER 1995
GEOFFREY P. LANTOS

INTRODUCTION

The power of the media is a hotly debated subject. The ability of books, magazines, radio, TV, and movies to influence great masses of the population alarms some observers and excites others. One of the most controversial areas of media influence is advertising. Unlike the regular media, whose primary purpose might be to entertain or to inform, most advertisements have a purely commercial purpose: To influence consumer behavior.

People who are concerned that advertising is too powerful have two broad worries concerning its influence on individual consumers and on the behavior of broadcasters and publishers. Advertising is a huge business. The revenue from it provides funds for broadcasters, who often have no other source of revenue, and magazine publishers. Even when a magazine can pay for itself through its cover price, advertising often represents a valuable source of increased profit. It also fills pages, often with images that are as glamorous and attractive as anything in the magazine itself.

The financial power of advertisers is a cause of concern to some program-makers and editors. Few advertisers wish to advertise in a forum in which they are criticized. A cosmetics manufacturer—the makeup and fashion industries are traditionally large advertising spenders—might not wish to advertise in a magazine whose beauty editor has given its products a critical write-up. Other advertisers are reluctant to display their products in certain contexts—say, in the middle of a news broadcast about famine or war. Critics allege that advertisers will try to persuade editors what subjects to deal with, or that editors will subconsciously avoid some subjects. In this view advertisers' money effectively operates as a form of censorship. A counterview places its trust in the traditional refusal of reporters or editors to compromise their objectivity. It also emphasizes, for example, that TV advertising money, although it might be attracted mainly by popular, noncontroversial programs, can then be used to fund hard-hitting, less popular shows.

The power of advertising on the individual is a more complex debate. On one hand, businesses argue that they use advertising to educate the public about particular products. Once consumers have been told about a product's merits, they are free to make their choice in the marketplace.

Critics, on the other hand, see advertising as a form of pyschological persuasion that depends on subtle manipulation of consumers' aspirations and vulnerability. It might create unrealistic body images, leading to eating disorders, or it might encourage unhealthy or environmentally unsound behavior, such as cigarette smoking. This view suggests a division between, on the one hand, unscrupulous advertisers with advanced tricks to influence behavior and, on the other, consumers who are trusting and vulnerable.

Advertisers say that the two extremes do not exist. They argue that advertising does not put advertisers and consumers in opposition to one another, but creates a partnership between the two for the same end: more informed consumer behavior.

What seems like support for this scenario comes from classical economic theory, formulated in the early 18th century before advertising existed. One of the most important qualities of a free-market economy, according to classical theory, is that consumers are informed about the different products competing for their money. The world of advertising today remains at least in part a means of providing this information. That makes it necessary to maintain a healthy economy.

> *"Only for the phony is commercialism … a naughty word. To the truly creative, it is a bridge to the great audience, a means of sharing rather than debasing."*
> —ERNEST A. JONES, ADVERTISING EXECUTIVE

In a society without advertising producers might lack motivation to improve their goods, develop new ones, or innovate. In medicine, for example, pharmaceutical firms' new legal freedom to advertise has prompted consumers to demand drugs that they have seen advertised.

Two different views of the power and influence of advertising follow. Elizabeth Thoman, a media critic, argues that the emphasis on image in advertising lies behind many problems in American culture. A counterargument comes from Geoffrey Lantos, reviewing a book by Jerry Kirkpatrick, *In Defense of Advertising*. From this point of view advertising is a beneficial tonic for a society that can be pushed to new levels by competition and the free flow of information. To restrict advertising is antiindividualistic, anticompetitive, authoritarian, and elitist.

RISE OF THE IMAGE CULTURE: REIMAGINING THE AMERICAN DREAM
Elizabeth Thoman

Like most middle-class children of the 50s, I grew up looking for the American Dream. In those days there were no cartoons in my Saturday viewing, but I distinctly remember watching, with some awe, *Industry on Parade*. I felt both pride and eager anticipation as I watched tail-finned cars rolling off assembly lines, massive dams taming mighty rivers, and sleek chrome appliances making life more convenient for all.

Between his movie and political careers former president Ronald Reagan was a spokesman for General Electric (GE) and hosted its sponsored TV show from 1954 to 1962.

When I heard the mellifluous voice of Ronald Reagan announce on *GE Theater* that "Progress is our most important product," little did I realize that the big box in our living room was not just entertaining me. At a deeper level, it was stimulating an "image" in my head of how the world should work: that anything new was better than something old; that science and technology were the greatest of all human achievements, and that in the near future—and certainly by the time I grew up—the power of technology would make it possible for everyone to live and work in a world free of war, poverty, drudgery, and ignorance. I believed it because I could see it—right there on television.

The American Dream is a powerful idea in American life, but what do you think it actually means?

The American Dream, however, was around long before television. Some believe the idea of "progress" goes back to when humankind first conceived of time as linear rather than cyclical. Certainly the Judeo-Christian heritage of a Messiah leading us to a Promised Land inspired millions to strive for a better world for generations to come…. It is this search for "something-more-than-what-we've-got-now" that is at the heart of the consumer culture we struggle with today. But the consumer culture as we know it could never have emerged without the invention of the camera and the eventual mass-production of media images it made possible.

Selling an image

Holmes (1841–1935) was an eminent scientist, a noted poet, an essayist, and a humorist.

In 1859 Oliver Wendell Holmes described photography as the most remarkable achievement of his time because it allowed human beings to separate an experience or a texture or an emotion or a likeness from a particular time and place—and still remain real, visible, and permanent. He described it as a "conquest over matter" and predicted it would alter the physics of perception, changing forever the way people would see and understand the world around them. Holmes precisely observed that the emergence of this new technology marked the beginning of a time when the "image would become more important than the object itself and would in fact make the object disposable." Contemporary advertising critic Stuart Ewen describes the photographic process as "skinning" the world of its visible images, then marketing those images inexpensively to the public.

But successive waves of what might be called reality-freezing technology—first the photograph, followed by the phonograph and the motion picture camera—were only some of many 19th-century transformations that paved the way to our present image culture. As the wheels of industrialization began to mass produce more and more consumer goods, they also increased the leisure time available to use these products and the disposable income required to buy them.

> *Do you agree that an appearance on television can make something seem more "real" than it does off screen?*

"Our lifestyles in the First World are created to a large degree by a mass media system that is throwing 3,000 marketing messages a day into the average North American brain."
—KALLE LASN, EDITOR, *ADBUSTERS* MAGAZINE

Soon the well-being of the economy itself became dependent on an ever-expanding cornucopia of products, goods, and services. The Sears-Roebuck catalogue and the department store emerged to showcase America's new abundance, and by the turn of the century, as media critic Todd Gitlin notes, "production, packaging, marketing, advertising, and sales became functionally inseparable."

The flood of commercial images also served as a rough-and-ready consumer education course for the immigrants to America's shores and the thousands of rural folk lured to the city by visions of wealth. Advertising was seen as a way of educating the masses to the cycle of the marketplace and to the imperatives of factory work and mechanized labor— teaching them "how to behave like human beings in the

> *The merchandising company Sears, Roebuck & Co. was founded in 1893. In the postwar era it was the largest retailer in the United States.*

machine age," according to the Boston department store magnate Edward A. Filene. In a work world where skill meant less and less, obedience and appearance took on greater importance. In a city full of strangers, advertising offered instructions on how to dress, how to behave, how to appear to others in order to gain approval and avoid rejection.

Granted, the American "standard of living" brought an end to drudgery for some, but it demanded a price for all: consumerism. Divorced from craft standards, work became merely the means to acquire the money to buy the goods and lifestyle that supposedly signified social acceptance, respect, even prestige. "Ads spoke less and less about the quality of the products being sold," notes Stuart Ewen, "and more about the lives of the people being addressed."

What goods do you own, or would you like to own, that in your opinion raise your status among other students?

In 1934, when the Federal Communications Commission approved advertising as the economic basis of the country's fledgling radio broadcasting system, the die was cast. Even though early broadcasters pledged to provide free time for educational programs, for coverage of religion, and for news … it wasn't long before the industry realized that time was money—and every minute counted. Since free enterprise dictates that it's better to make money than to lose it, the American commercial broadcasting system was born. But it was not until the 1950s that the image culture came into full flower. The reason? Television.

What price progress?

Kalle Lasn, a cofounder of the Canadian media criticism and environmentalist magazine *Adbusters*, explains how dependence on TV first occurred and continues today each time we turn on our sets:

It can be effective to quote a long passage when that passage makes a point forcefully.

> *In the privacy of our living rooms we made a devil's bargain with the advertising industry: Give us an endless flow of free programs and we'll let you spend 12 minutes of every hour promoting consumption. For a long time, it seemed to work. The ads grated on our nerves but it was a small price to pay for 'free' television….What we didn't realize when we made our pact with the advertisers was that their agenda would eventually become the heart and soul of television. We have allowed the most powerful communications tool ever invented to become the command center of a consumer society defining our lives and culture the way family, community, and spiritual values once did.*

This does not mean that when we see a new toilet paper commercial we're destined to rush down to the store to buy its new or improved brand. Most single commercials do not have such a direct impact. What happens instead is a cumulative effect. Each commercial plays its part in selling an overall consumer lifestyle. As advertising executive Stephen Garey noted in a recent issue of *Media and Values*, when an ad for toilet paper reaches us in combination with other television commercials, magazine ads, radio spots, and billboards for detergents and designer jeans, new cars and cigarettes, and ... cereals and computers, the collective effect is that they all teach us to buy. And to feel ... dissatisfied and inadequate unless we have the newest, the latest, the best.

How important is it to you that you own the newest or best product? Is it as important for bedroom furniture, say, as it is for sneakers or cell phones? If not, why not?

Just like our relatives at the turn of the [20th] century, we learned to take our identities from what we own and purchase rather than from who we are or how we interact with others. Through consuming things, we continue the quest for meaning which earlier generations sought in other ways—conquering the oceans, settling the land, building the modern society, even searching for transcendence through religious belief. With few places on earth left to conquer, the one expanse of exploration open to us is the shopping mall.

Escaping consumerism

We'll never stop living in a world of images. But we can recognize and deal with the image culture's actual state, which might be characterized as a kind of midlife crisis— a crisis of identity. Three responses are typical:

Thoman lists ways in which people typically address the image culture problem, but expresses pessimism about all three.

1) Denial. Hoping that a problem will go away if we ignore it is a natural response, but business as usual is no solution.

2) Rejection. Some critics believe they can use their television dials to make the image culture go away, and urge others to turn it off, too. But it's impossible to turn off an entire culture. Others check out emotionally by using drugs, alcohol, addictions of all kinds to vainly mask the hunger for meaning that comes when reality and images don't converge.

3) Resistance. A surprisingly active counterculture exists and is working hard to point out the dangers of overreliance on the image culture. But such criticism is negative by nature, and critics tend to remain voices crying in the wilderness.

By convincing us that happiness lies at the other end of the cash register, our society has sold us a bill of goods. To move beyond the illusions of the image culture we must begin to grapple with some deeper questions: Where is the fine line between what I want and what all in society should have? What is the common good for all?

IN DEFENSE OF ADVERTISING
Geoffrey P. Lantos

NO

X This excellent, thought-provoking book [*In Defense of Advertising* by Jerry Kirkpatrick] thoroughly debunks popular, hostile misconceptions about consumer advertising, all of which boil down to the notion that advertising is a coercive, offensive, monopolistic force which must be heavily regulated by the government. Jerry Kirkpatrick, Professor of Marketing at California State University, Pomona, demonstrates that, in fact, advertising is a rational, morally good, productive, and even benevolent instrument of laissez-faire capitalistic production and the division of labor.

The reviewer starts by summarizing the book's central argument, which he then goes on to explain in detail.

This he accomplishes by describing and refuting the false philosophic and economic worldview underlying the "social" and economic criticisms of advertising, using unique theoretical applications of philosophy, economics, and psychology. He shows the fallacies underlying this "antireason, antiman, antilife, authoritarian worldview that permeates our culture." His aim is to get practitioners, academics, and thoughtful laypersons alike to check their assumptions and consider instead novelist-philosopher Ayn Rand's proreason philosophy of objectivism as well as Austrian economist Ludwig von Mises' proindividualist laissez-faire economics as the foundations of advertising's defense.

Russian-American writer Ayn Rand (1905–1982) is known for The Fountainhead *(1943) and* Atlas Shrugged *(1957), novels that served as vehicles for her philosophical views. Von Mises was a staunch supporter of consumerism.*

Beacon of a free society

This alternative world view, he logically demonstrates, leads to a positive moral evaluation of advertising's role: capitalism is the social system resulting in greatest economic progress, and advertising is the "beacon" of a free society guiding individuals to the fruits of that progress, rather than the evil serpent that tempts consumers with original sin to pursue selfish gain and disrupts the Garden of Eden of pure and perfect competition in which advertising is nonexistent.

The author wishes to provide readers "intellectual ammunition" with which they can confidently defend … advertising against three major criticisms: it is (1) coercive, (2) offensive, and (3) monopolistic. The first two constitute the so-called social criticisms and view advertising as being superfluous, inherently dishonest, immoral, and fraudulent. The third objection, the economic criticism, alleges that advertising increases prices and wastes society's scarce resources. All three criticisms assert that advertising adds no value to products. A major premise underlying the author's analysis is that these objections assault consumers' reason.... It is advertising's appeal to buyers' rational self-interest for the rationally selfish profit motive of capitalists that Kirkpatrick defends. Thus, he argues that the proper theoretical foundations for advertising are reason, ethical egoism, and laissez-faire capitalism.

If advertisers "selfishly" want to sell us goods, and we "selfishly" want to buy them, then isn't everyone happy?

Determinism and dichotomy

The authoritarian worldview of the critics pictures people as blind, helpless pawns who need guidance from an authoritative elite.... The first of two philosophic doctrines forming [this] worldview is determinism, which says that people lack a rational volitional nature, that is, free will; rather, the external environment and individual's inner instincts are deterministic factors for behavior. The logical conclusion is that advertising is harmful to consumers, either directly as a powerful force in the environment or indirectly as a devious means of tapping their inner instincts. The second philosophic doctrine shaping the critics' worldview is the mind/body dichotomy, which assumes that our minds (consciousness and reason) are at constant war with our bodies and the material world. Thus, people face a choice between the sacred, moral world of the mind or the profane, practical world of matter. This dichotomy stacks the deck against advertising, which lives in the material world.

If determinism is basically the law of fate, then, argue the critics of advertising, consumers are helpless to resist their destiny.

The alternative worldview, which is "liberal" in the classic sense, provides the rational basis for egoism, capitalism, and advertising. First, it sees each individual's life as the purpose of ethics and people as self-determined, self-responsible individuals who require political freedom so as to pursue their own values and happiness. This worldview provides a more cogent defense than the typical one, which is based on a standard of social welfare, such as the "common good," derived from the morality of altruism. According to Ayn Rand capitalism is morally justified because it is the only economic system which allows us to rationally exercise free will in evaluating communications and making choices in the marketplace. This negates determinism, and it follows that advertising cannot force people to buy.

Lantos does not suggest that the egoist worldview is better than the altruistic, but that it offers a better defense against critics who argue that advertising forces people helplessly to buy.

In praise of egoism

Second, contrary to intrinsicism, Rand's theory of objectivism holds that peoples' minds are active and contribute to

What the author is saying in simpler terms is that ideas and objects do not have an intrinsic worth; each person evaluates them as he or she sees fit and can do so without the help of an expert.

Here egoism refers to the philosophical doctrine in which self-interest is a motive and goal for all conscious action. It is not the same as egotism, which is excessive self-interest to the detriment of others.

process formation, that is, knowledge and rational values are objective not subjective. Thus, things and ideas have no intrinsic value and should not be judged by the "revelations" of an authoritative elite, but rather by the value significance they acquire through the beneficial or harmful effects they have on people's goals (while not violating others' rights), as human life is the standard of moral value and each individual's life has its own moral purpose. This rational egoism calls for the end of altruistic sacrifice as no one has the right to sacrifice either others or one's self to other people. Thus, Rand defends advertising as morally good, not because it contributes to society's well-being, but because it appeals to the self-interest of individual consumers for the selfish gain of individual producers. In other words, says Kirkpatrick, advertising is morally justified because "it represents the implementation of an ethics of egoism—the communication of one rational being to another rational being for the egoistic benefit of both."

Kirkpatrick [concludes] that, rather than advertising, it is the Federal Trade Commission which has coercive power because in a free-market economy the only legitimate, objective protection for producers and consumers offered by the law should be in enforcement of the common law against fraud, several of the conditions of which the FTC has dispensed with. The result is that now ads must not be misinterpreted by the "ignorant, unthinking, credulous, and gullible consumer." The unintended consequence has been that ads today contain fewer facts and more puffery and sophistry, both of which are forms of irrational persuasion.

Taste is a personal option

Chapter 4 annihilates the second "social" objection to advertising, that advertising is offensive. It affronts the consumer's sense of good taste by insulting and degrading his/her intelligence, promoting low- and poor-quality products as well as morally offensive products, and encouraging harmful and immoral behavior.

The major problem with these arguments, says Kirkpatrick, is that they deny that values are objective, that is, they are a product of the relationship between material objects and the volitional consciousness that evaluates them. For Kirkpatrick, tastes are "morally optional values" according to a rational standard of ethics, that is, they are discretionary, not universal and obligatory, as are moral values. Thus, no one's (e.g., the elitists') moral values can be said to be superior to others'.

This obliterates the intrinsicist idea that advertising is offensive because it promotes immoral (tasteless) products and encourages immoral or harmful (tasteless) behavior. Furthermore, critics disagree about which ads are immoral because they each have their own set of intrinsic values about what are moral ads and products.

Intrinsicness implies that an object or idea has an inbuilt and therefore universal value; Kirkpatrick argues that value is established by individuals: that is, taste is personal.

"Advertising is shrill, noisy, coarse puffing, because the public does not react to dignified allusions. It is the bad taste of the public that forces the advertisers to display bad taste."
—LUDWIG VON MISES, ECONOMIST

Advertising and the law

A discussion of advertising and the law concludes the fourth chapter. The author agrees with Rand that an act should be considered illegal only when it violates individual rights, that is, when physical force against others is used. Advertising critics use physical force through laws against consumers by restricting products they may buy and conditions under which they may buy them and against producers by telling them which products they may advertise and under which conditions they may do so. The resulting restriction of the free flow of information is censorship, contrary to the intent and meaning of the U.S. Constitution's First Amendment guarantee of freedom of speech, and it is based on the ideas that consumers lack free will and certain products are inherently evil.

In the final chapter, Kirkpatrick reminds us that "advertising is just salesmanship, the product and expression of laissez-faire capitalism. Unfortunately, this is precisely why the critics hate advertising; namely, that it is the means by which millions of self-interested individuals become aware of the self-interested achievements of millions of other individuals. Advertising is the means by which millions of men learn how to enhance their tastes and increase their standard of living above the ordinary, humdrum existence of their forbears." The reader is supposed to recognize that the practice of advertising is a moral profession and it is the practitioners, not the critics, who occupy the moral high ground.

Would your life be poorer without advertising? If so, in what ways?

Summary

For Elizabeth Thoman her fond memories of television in the 1950s serve as a starting point for her message: The "reimagination" of the American Dream. She suggests that this dream has become little more than a hunger for goods or a metaphor for consumption. Since the advent of photography the world has been increasingly crammed with images, many of them created expressly to feed society's growing desire to have the latest and best of everything. The insidious ubiquity of advertising and its powers of persuasion have multiplied with the postwar proliferation of the television and its capacity to bombard the viewer with images. The net result, says Thoman, is that material possessions have replaced personality as the criteria by which identity is assessed. The shopping mall has replaced the church as the meeting hall. People can resist this image-led culture of consumerism, but to do so they must first address the fine line between needs and wants.

Geoffrey Lantos and Jerry Kirkpatrick praise advertising, but do so largely through the arguments of philosopher Ayn Rand and economist Ludwig von Mises that frame the latter's book. Advertising, say Lantos and Kirkpatrick, is not sinful, but is instead the guiding light of a free-market society. They raise arguments used by critics of advertising and counter each one. For example, to the claim that advertising exploits only the weak-minded, they reply that the capitalist system is the only one in which people are at liberty to exercise their free will in making their own judgments about objects advertised to them. Such objects do not have an intrinsic value fixed by a well-meaning elite; ordinary people can judge value for themselves. Advertising cannot be thrown out on grounds of bad taste or immorality, for taste is the perogative of the individual. Control of advertising is arguably unconstitutional in that it limits free speech. Advertising is good because it caters to the self-interests of the supplier and the self-interests of the consumer.

FURTHER INFORMATION:

Books:

Beniger, J., *The Control Revolution*. Cambridge, MA: Harvard University Press, 1987.

Chewning, Richard C., John W. Eby, and Shirley Roels, *Business through the Eyes of Faith*. San Francisco: Harper & Row, 1990.

Klein, Naomi, *No Logo: Taking Aim at the Brand Bullies*. New York: Picador, 2000.

Lasn, Kalle, *Culture Jam: The Uncooling of America™*. New York: Eagle Brook/William Morrow, 1999.

McLuhan, H. Marshall, *Understanding Media: The Extensions of Man*. New York: McGraw-Hill Book Company, 1964.

Useful websites:

www.adbusters.org/home/
Homepage of *Adbusters* magazine.

The following debates in the Pro/Con series may also be of interest:

In this volume:

 Topic 8 Is advertising to children morally wrong?

IS ADVERTISING TOO POWERFUL IN AMERICAN SOCIETY?

YES: Advertising is everywhere, from TV, billboards, and magazines to the Internet

YES: Advertising has enslaved people to consumerism, persuading them that they need better, newer, and more products

SATURATION
Is there too much advertising?

PERSONAL FREEDOM
Are people victims of consumerism?

NO: Advertising is the oil of the capitalist system, offering people freedom of choice, so the more, the better

NO: People can think for themselves; ads may be crude and tasteless, but they give people what they want

IS ADVERTISING TOO POWERFUL IN AMERICAN SOCIETY?

KEY POINTS

YES: The decline of "junk culture" would benefit society by restoring power to the consumer

YES: Advertising is purely profit-motivated and doesn't care if it encourages people to buy products that might be harmful to them, like cigarettes

BIG BROTHER
Should advertising be controlled?

EFFECT ON SOCIETY
Is advertising detrimental to people?

NO: Control would be authoritarian and unconstitutional in limiting personal freedom

NO: Advertising provides a service to society by supplying people with information that they would not have access to as easily

Topic 8
IS ADVERTISING TO CHILDREN MORALLY WRONG?

YES
"CHILDREN AND ADVERTISING IN
U.S. SOCIETY"
A.VASUDEVAN

NO
"PESTER POWER: A REPORT ON ATTITUDES
IN SPAIN AND SWEDEN"
DECEMBER 1999
THE ADVERTISING ASSOCIATION

INTRODUCTION

In the United States in the late 1970s the Federal Trade Commission considered banning advertising aimed at children. The reasoning behind this was that children could not adequately understand the purpose of advertising, so they should not be exposed unfairly to persuasive techniques. Any number of concerns were at issue. Children's diets, influenced by advertising for fatty and sugary foods, seemed to be becoming more unhealthy. Children, seeing many different toys and other goods on TV, might pester their parents for these things. Also, advertising for alcohol, cigarettes, and other unhealthy products might reach children. All in all, there was significant concern that television advertising, and advertising in general, was not good for children.

The ban was never passed. After the Reagan Administration nixed the idea of an advertising ban, the question has never really risen again in the United States. Advertising to children is a staple of television and is even moving into other media. The United States has passed only very minor legislation on children's television (the Children's Television Act of 1990), requiring broadcasters to include a certain amount of programming for children, but the legislation does not touch the issue of advertising itself.

In the United States concerns have focused more on programs than on advertisements. Few recent initiatives aim to strongly limit children's advertising, except in the case of alleged tobacco marketing to children. In general, media have been deregulated since the 1980s, and the trend is no different for children's advertising.

The question remains, though, should advertising to children be allowed? In general, U.S. audiences might be willing to tolerate a little more regulation of advertising. However, would they be willing to go as far as they have in Sweden and Norway, where there is a total ban on children's advertising? In Italy cartoons cannot be interrupted by advertising. Greece allows no TV advertisements for toys, Belgium does not allow advertising breaks in children's programs, and other European Union (EU) states have a variety of restrictions. In fact, the general movement of the EU toward more restrictions is worrisome to some advertisers in Europe, who could stand to lose a sizable market.

"Advertising [is] the science of arresting human intelligence long enough to get money from it."
—STEPHEN LEACOCK, HUMORIST

Some people believe that childhood should be a haven from commercialism, which will be a major part of children's lives soon enough. Already, they say, advertising tends to creep into every aspect of children's lives, even school. A study by the American Association of Pediatrics showed that children of 12 years of age and under view around 20,000 ads per year through different media. Whittle Communications' *Channel One* program was one such controversial example, broadcasting free news programs into schoolrooms, but with commercials. Whittle offered video equipment to schools that might not otherwise have been able to afford it, but critics worried that introducing advertising in schools was a bad precedent. The precedent has had followers, however,

with companies such as Coca-Cola establishing agreements with schools to supply a given product, such as soda. However, not surprisingly, advertisers feel that a ban on advertising to children is not warranted.

The following two articles examine the main arguments in the debate. The first article—"Children and Advertising in U.S. Society" by A. Vasudevan—examines the morality and effects of advertising on children. Vasudevan uses various studies to show that advertising affects every aspect of U.S. life. She argues that advertising can influence everything from the food children eat to whether they drink alcohol or smoke cigarettes. She concludes that there should be more stringent monitoring and regulation of the advertising industry in the United States.

The second article—"Pester Power: A Report on Attitudes in Spain and Sweden"—is a study commissioned by the U.K. Advertising Association. It asserts that children pestering their parents for products is not a major public concern. The study compares Sweden, which has a ban on children's TV advertising, to Spain, which does not. It finds similarly low rates of concern about advertising to children. The study does not deal with other issues, such as whether children's health improves in a no-advertising environment, and it does not look at the First Amendment issues that could be raised. Although commercial speech is subject to different kinds of restrictions in the United States than explicitly political speech, it would be difficult to sustain a total ban on a class of advertising, even when there might be significant public interest in doing so.

CHILDREN AND ADVERTISING IN U.S. SOCIETY
A. Vasudevan

Advertising is one of the most powerful and pervasive forces in U.S. society. Its effect on adults and children has been a matter of concern for many decades since sociologists and educationalists began to acknowledge that people could be influenced by successful selling techniques, which in turn could substantially increase sales for specific products, such as alcohol and cigarettes.

In the past the most effective way of selling products to children was to target the parent audience; however, today most advertisers recognize the importance of children in buying decisions. Many U.S. advertisers therefore target children in three main ways:

- As buyers.
- As influences on their parents' buying habits.
- As future adult consumers.

Techniques

Since the 1980s advertisers have adopted a range of techniques and invested in a multitude of sophisticated products aimed at encouraging and manipulating how and where children spend their money. Consequently, there has been an increase in advertising vehicles geared specifically toward children such as: the use of promotional toys based on characters from cartoons, TV shows, and movies to promote brand loyalty; advertising in schools; children's magazines; radio or TV networks, such as Channel One, which children watch at school; and free promotional merchandise. Today increased access to new technology, such as the Internet, means that parents are finding it more and more difficult to monitor what their children hear and see and subsequently how much influence the advertising world has on their purchasing decisions. This has served to enforce the belief that advertising to children is wrong and that there should be greater regulation of advertising practices. The following article looks at the influence and effects of advertising on children and adolescents and argues that, for the most part, advertising is both manipulative and harmful.

According to The Industry Standard online advertising will earn almost $28 million by 2005. Look at www.the standard.com/article 10,1902, 16284,00.html

How influential is advertising

Society has become increasingly concerned with the impact that the media has on children—especially the effect of advertising on children's perceptions of themselves and the world in which they live.

In 1999, for example, the American Academy of Pediatrics estimated that the average American child viewed around 20,000 TV ads per year: 2000 of those were for beer and wine. The children's market was viewed as so important that between 1993 and 1996 advertising expenditure for that market increased by around 50 percent to $1.5 billion and *USA Today*, in December 1997, estimated that children aged 12 and under would spend or influence the spending of around $500 billion in the U.S. economy.

George Comstock argues in *Television and the American Child* (1991) that young children cannot distinguish between television programs and commercials and that they do not recognize that commercials are trying to sell something. Similarly James McNeal in *Kids As Customers* (1992) asserts that brand loyalty can begin in children as young as two. The two most advertised products to children in the United States are foodstuffs and toys.

Advertising in schools

Children spend around 20 percent of their time at school and advertisers have always been keen to pursue school-marketing strategies. Although there have always been links between business and education— through sponsorship of sport, for example—the use of commercialism in U.S. schools has rocketed in recent years.

Today direct advertising in schools can be found in a number of ways:

Book covers—in 1998 around 25 million students (over half of U.S. students at the time) received free book covers, advertising products like Frosted Flakes.

Reward coupons—companies like Pizza Hut and McDonald's supply food and drink coupons as prizes in U.S. reading programs.

Soft drink machines—Coke and Pepsi, for example negotiate with schools to supply them with their products.

"Educational posters" advertise candy in school hallways.

Channel One—the TV channel, viewed in around 12,000 schools in the United States every day by about 8 million adolescents. It features a 12-minute news show plus two minutes of "age-appropriate" ads, promoting products like jeans and soft drinks.

In 1993 Colorado Springs, CO, became one of the first U.S. public school districts to supplement revenue by offering space to corporate advertisers. It raised $69,000 for the 54 schools in the district in two years.

- Athletic fields, gyms, libraries, and so on—sponsored by big corporations who place their names and logos in prominent positions around the school.

All of these advertising vehicles have helped to build up brand loyalty among students and ultimately have increased product sales. However, advertising in schools often occurs irrespective of whether the product promoted is appropriate for the school market and appears often without parental approval.

Advertising and perceptions of self

The media influences every aspect of life and commercials broadcast during children's programming have affected everything from the clothes children wear to the food and drink they consume.

The 1990 Children's Television Act limits commercial time during children's programming to 12 minutes per hour during the week and 10.5 minutes at weekends but advertisers have become very adept at manipulating the existing rules and regulations. For example, advertising during children's programming quite often promotes unhealthy or highly calorific foods and some critics argue that has led to a rise in obesity among U.S. children. Similarly, the way children are portrayed in adverts has influenced the way in which they see themselves and behave toward others.

According to "Advertising Images of Girls and Women," a report by the organization Children Now, the power of the media lies in supplying appealing role models to children who usually combine both beauty and success. Similarly, advertising also helps to determine male-female/ boy-girl relationships and behavior.

The report found that the majority of ads focusing only on one gender usually featured boy actors and ads featuring girls were in most cases for appearance-related products. It also found that while ads featuring boys took place in a wide variety of settings, those featuring girls were usually set inside the home, often against a pink or soft background. The authors concluded that, "From childhood to adolescence, stereotyped images of females and males in advertising are reinforced in the children's television and prime-time programs kids avidly watch. The result is a continuum of limiting messages that often tell girls and boys alike that female appearance is central, that boys can do and achieve things girls can't, and that boys have more value than girls."

Go to www. childrennow. org/medial medianow/mnfall 1997.html at the Children Now site to view the full text of "Advertising Images of Girls and Women," Fall 1997.

Can you think of any recent TV or movie ads that do not use stereotypical images to sell or market products? Do the ads work?.

The adolescent audience

A joint study by Children Now and the Kaiser Family Foundation, which looked at messages sent to girls across six media, including TV commercials and advertisements in teen-focused magazines, found that:
- men outnumbered women 58 percent to 42 percent in TV commercials in the United States.
- 70 percent of ads for women were still for appearance-related products compared to 9 percent for men.
- 26 percent of women in TV commercials received comments on their looks compared to 7 percent of men.
- 32 percent of women were thin compared to 6 percent of men.
- 81 percent of ads in teen magazines promoted cosmetics, clothing, and toiletries and were directed at women.

Apart from beauty products, many of the goods advertised to adolescents are harmful. For example, alcohol producers spend over $2 billion per year in advertising and promotion and recent U.S. ads have focused on promoting the "fun" aspects of drinking—such as attending raucous parties, and having greater sex appeal if you drink. Recent studies have shown that nearly 90 percent of high school seniors have tried alcohol at least once. Similarly, cigarette manufacturers spend over $3 billion per year on advertising. Despite a U.S. ban on TV advertising of cigarettes, tobacco-sponsored sporting events and advertising at stadiums has as much, if not more impact on younger audiences. A recent report has shown that the Camel logo is as recognizable to six-year-old children as Mickey Mouse. According to the American Association of Pediatrics in 1988 adolescents spent around $1.26 billion on cigarettes and smokeless cigarettes, and around two million teenagers begin smoking each year. In the United States, tobacco-caused illnesses are responsible for one in six deaths per year.

In the United States cigarette advertising was banned from TV and radio in 1969. For a discussion of tobacco advertising see Topic 9 Should tobacco advertising be banned? on pages 112–123.

Conclusion

The advertising industry in the United States spends billions of dollars each year promoting products to children, many of which are harmful to their health and wellbeing. The result is that more and more children feel under pressure to conform to certain stereotypical behavior promoted by the media—whether it be wearing the latest Nike trainer or wearing a size 0 dress. Stronger laws are needed to monitor and regulate advertising to children and prevent the advertising industry from committing further abuses in their bid to increase sales.

PESTER POWER
The Advertising Association

NO

Assessing the importance of what has come to be known as "pester power" is difficult. Assessing the extent to which such behavior is a result of commercial television or children's advertising generally, or other factors, is clearly even more difficult given the numerous factors that influence children's desire for toys, candy, and various forms of food and drink.

This exercise is a first attempt at assessing the general importance of pestering behavior as assessed by adults, and then looking at differences between countries with few controls (in this exercise Spain) and a country with a ban on television advertising to children (Sweden).

Given the emotive nature of the subject matter, it was believed to be essential to put "pester" questions in a general framework of other questions relating to shopping. If pestering is of a real importance then it should emerge during shopping trips to a greater extent than on other occasions.

Two questions were asked. The first was a general question relating to shopping:

The questions were asked of representative samples of adults in Spain and Sweden using local "omnibus" surveys (national surveys of 1,000 people over 18 in each country).

Question 1

"Which of the following do you think are the two worst things about shopping?" Seven possible responses were allowed:

In-store promotion over the sound system

Children pestering parents

Not enough staff

Changing display positions

Poor quality staff

Queues at checkout

Parking problems

A second question was asked of all respondents who mentioned "children pestering parents" as one of the worst things about shopping in the first question.

Question 2

"Which two of the following do you think should be done to make shopping more agreeable?"

Don't display toys and candy where children can reach them

Ban advertising displays intended to attract children

Ban children's advertising

Ban in-store commercials

Ban children in busy stores

Have in-store activity areas for children

Results

The results are shown in tables I, II, III, and IV (below). It can be seen from Table I that of all the various aspects of

Table I

"Which of the following do you think are the two worst things about shopping?"

	SPAIN	SWEDEN
In-store promotion	9%	11%
Children pestering	7%	9%
Not enough staff	34%	34%
Changing displays	32%	37%
Poor quality staff	30%	29%
Queues at checkout	51%	62%
Parking	15%	14%

(Results shown as percentage of people mentioning pestering as either one of the two worst things.)

shopping that people disliked, children pestering parents was the lowest of all the factors listed. Only 7 percent of adults in Spain and 9 percent in Sweden found this a problem.

Table II
"Which of the following do you think are the two worst things about shopping?"

	SPAIN	SWEDEN
In-store promotion	5.3%	5.5%
Pestering	3.4%	4.4%
Not enough staff	18.9%	17.2%
Changing displays	17.9%	18.9%
Poor quality staff	16.5%	15.0%
Queues at checkout	28.4%	31.7%
Parking	8.6%	7.2%

(Results shown as percentage of all reasons given by respondents for disliking shopping.)

Table II
When the answers are rebased to allow for the fact that all respondents were allowed two reasons for disliking shopping, only approximately 4 percent of adults found "pestering" to be a problem—the lowest level of answers for any of the questions. Again, Sweden scored higher than Spain.

Table III
The results shown in Table III indicate that even those people who felt pestering to be a problem did not ... feel children's advertising should be banned. Only 9 percent in Spain and 19 percent in Sweden wanted a ban on children's advertising.

Table IV
When viewed as a proportion of the whole sample, the small proportion who felt that pestering by children was a problem, who also wanted a ban on advertising to children, was very small indeed. Less than 1 percent of people in Spain wanted this and only 1.7 percent in Sweden.

Table III

"Which two of the following do you think should be done to make shopping more agreeable?

	SPAIN	SWEDEN
Don't display toys and candy where kids can reach	34%	71%
Ban advertising display for children in shops	22%	17%
Ban children's advertising	9%	19%
Ban in-store advertising	8%	4%
Ban children in busy stores	16%	4%
Have in-store activity areas for children	60%	64%

(Results shown are answers given by people who mentioned "pestering" as a problem—not the whole sample.)

Conclusion

In summary, it is clear that only a small proportion of people in either Spain or Sweden believe that children pestering parents is of any major significance, and only an extremely small proportion of these people felt that an advertising ban would be an appropriate solution.

Table IV

"Which of the following things should be done to make shopping more agreeable?"

	SPAIN	SWEDEN
Don't display toys and candy where kids can reach	2.3%	6.4%
Ban advertising displays for children in shops	1.5%	1.5%
Ban children's advertising	1%	1.7%
Ban in-store advertising	1%	1%
Ban children in busy stores	11.1%	1%
Have in-store activity areas for children	4.2%	5.8%

(Results shown as percentages of whole sample.)

Summary

There is no question that advertisers look very closely at children and teenagers as target groups. In the United States youth spending, or youth-directed spending, is an enormously large component of the overall total advertising market ($12 billion a year is spent on advertising to children, who spend more than $500 billion every year).

In the first article, "Children and Advertising in U.S. Society," A. Vasudevan argues that advertising is one of the most pervasive and powerful forces in U.S. society. She asserts that advertisers have targeted children, investing billions of dollars in sophisticated marketing vehicles that encourage children and adolescents to eat unhealthily, diet, smoke cigarettes, and drink alcohol. Thus advertising has a negative effect on children and adolescents by encouraging them to value and judge themselves and the world around them by the standards set by big business and advertising firms.

The authors of "Pester Power," a study of advertising in Spain and Sweden commissioned by the U.K. Advertising Association, found that advertising does not influence children and their parents' buying choices enough to warrant a ban. The difference between the two countries' advertising policies—Spain has few controls, Sweden has a ban on television advertising to children—did not seem affect the results of the survey.

FURTHER INFORMATION:

Books:

Fox, Roy F., *Harvesting Minds: How TV Commercials Control Kids*. Westport, CT: Praeger, 1999.

Macklin, Carole M. and Les Carlson (editors), *Advertising to Children Concepts and Controversies*. Thousand Oaks, CA: Corwin Press, 1999.

Unnikrishnan, Namita and Shailaja Bajpal, *The Impact of Television Advertising on Children*. Thousand Oaks, CA: Sage Publications, 1996.

Articles:

Oldenburg, D. "Ads Aimed at Kids." *The Washington Post*, May 3, 2001.

Useful websites:

www.aap.org
American Academy of Pediatrics site.
www.carv.org
Children's Advertising Review Unit.
www.mediaandthefamily.org
National Institute on Media and the Family site.

The following debates in the Pro/Con series may also be of interest:

In this volume:

Part 1: Media and Society, pages 8–9

Topic 3 Do people watch too much television?

Topic 7 Is advertising too powerful in American society?

Topic 9 Should tobacco advertising be banned?

Topic 10 Does advertising threaten objective journalism?

IS ADVERTISING TO CHILDREN MORALLY WRONG?

YES: The current limits are too high, particularly since many programs are actually program-length commercials

LIMITS
Should there be stricter limits on children's advertising?

YES: Brand loyalty can begin to be established as early as age two

BRAND LOYALTY
Do advertisements promote brand loyalty among children?

NO: Children in countries that have banned children's advertising do not pester their parents to buy any more than those in countries that have no bans in place

NO: There is little evidence that advertisements have this effect on children

IS ADVERTISING TO CHILDREN MORALLY WRONG?

KEY POINTS

YES: Many of the products advertised, such as alcohol, tobacco, and high-fat foods, are harmful to health

YES: Approximately two million teenagers start smoking each year, and there are at least nine million underage drinkers

HEALTH
Are advertisements harmful to children's health?

NO: There is little evidence that advertisements cause children to influence their parents to buy certain products

NO: There are legal restrictions on children buying harmful products

111

Topic 9
SHOULD TOBACCO ADVERTISING BE BANNED?

YES
"TOBACCO ADVERTISING"
DUTCH FOUNDATION ON SMOKING AND HEALTH/NETHERLANDS HEART FOUNDATION
MARC C. WILLEMSEN AND BOUDEWIJN DE BLIJ

NO
"MORE TAXES AND LESS FREE SPEECH"
INDEPENDENCE INSTITUTE: ISSUE BACKGROUNDER 99-K, FEBRUARY 11, 1999
LINDA GORMAN

INTRODUCTION

Tobacco advertising on TV was banned in the United States in the 1970s, although it remains legal in other forms. The same is true in numerous other countries. Why should tobacco advertising be singled out in this way? Partly it is controversial because smoking itself is controversial. This form of advertising specifically promotes behavior that is now known to damage health. Critics of tobacco advertising claim that if it did not exist, fewer people would smoke. They argue, for example, that children would be less likely to smoke if they were not exposed to positive images of smoking. Even supporters of this view, however, admit that tobacco advertising plays only a small part in getting people to smoke—and is more effective at influencing brand choice among people who already smoke. Peer pressure, parental behavior, and so on are also important in people's original decision to take up smoking.

Tobacco advertising also raises a moral issue. Should people be protected from persuasion even if they willingly accept the risks attendant on smoking? There is also the question of whether advertisers who promote smoking should be charged something toward the health costs associated with smoking? If so, should this tendency end with tobacco or extend to manufacturers of other potentially dangerous products, such as guns?

In the early days of television cigarette advertising was a staple, and many people smoked. The dangers of smoking were not as well understood. Some ads plugged cigarettes that doctors recommended and that were claimed to improve the smoker's health. Edward Bernays, called the "father of public relations," took credit for spurring a boom in cigarette smoking when previously people had smoked cigars or pipes, by making cigarettes seem more acceptable.

Cigarette smoking was ubiquitous in the 1950s and into the 1960s. The habit's social acceptability fell with the release of negative health studies and the declaration of the Surgeon General in the mid-1960s that smoking was harmful to health. Other products that cause health problems are not subjected to the same stigma as smoking, however. Other factors should be considered as well, and the ban on advertising might have played a significant role. When ads on TV were banned, smoking rates were at or above 40 percent. Within only 13 years only 25 percent of people were smoking.

The TV ban meant that exposure to brand images was being lost. Cigarette advertisers sought alternate outlets, one being print media. More creative campaigns were devised; some had cartoon characters that critics thought were aimed at children. "Joe Camel," a campaign that emphasized the cool aspects of smoking by using a James Bond-like camel, was singled out as evidence that cigarette firms were marketing their product to children. Though the accusation was never proven, tobacco companies have now agreed not to engage in this practice.

Few people would support tobacco advertising today, but it continues to raise real questions. Do people have a right to smoke? If they do, how can advertising be held responsible for individuals choosing to exercise such a right? As long as tobacco is legal, should its producers be denied the right to market the product legally? Don't smokers have the right to receive information about brands of cigarettes? More, should the state interfere with the free flow of communication? Especially with tobacco advertising, where regulation has already mandated specific and easily understood health warnings, what more should be done?

"Advertising is essential to the growth and promotion of tobacco, and advertising is inextricably linked with consumption."

—INTERNATIONAL UNION AGAINST CANCER

The first of the following articles reviews research that argues that there is a relationship between tobacco advertising and smoking rates. This puts the research on virtually the same level as research on media and violence; there is a broad consensus that the media have some effect. The second article deals with a recent proposition in Congress that would impose additional tax burdens on tobacco companies. The article outlines an argument against such measures.

TOBACCO ADVERTISING
Marc C. Willemsen and Boudewijn de Blij

To say that tobacco advertising stimulates tobacco sales may seem a simple and moderate statement. In reality, tobacco control activists often meet serious opposition in defending this fact. Achieving the restriction or banning of tobacco advertising is one of the fiercest battles to face. Tobacco lobbyists usually assert that advertising does not increase the overall quantity of tobacco sold. Rather, the tobacco industry maintains that advertising merely enhances the market share of a particular brand, without recruiting new smokers.

The authors provide reliable data with which a lobbyist can construct his or her own argument.

These arguments are not always easy to counter. This fact sheet gives health advocates the arguments and research data needed to face well-prepared tobacco lobbyists in public debate. The data cited are all presented in reputable scientific journals or congresses. They demonstrate that tobacco advertising entices young people to begin smoking and that restricting or banning advertising has a measurable effect on smoking behavior.

Research on tobacco advertising and consumption

It is not possible to conduct a randomized, controlled trial to study the effect of an advertising ban. Such a trial would require long-term exposure of one group of people to cigarette advertising, while ensuring that a control group would be completely unexposed. This is neither feasible nor ethical.

One of the problems associated with collecting data on dangerous materials or practices is that conducting tests exposes people to unacceptable risks.

Scientists funded by the tobacco industry have argued that in the absence of data from such a trial, it can never be proven that banning tobacco advertising will reduce tobacco consumption. However, most researchers agree that reliable conclusions can be drawn from other types of studies. Three main types of studies have examined the relationship between tobacco advertising and consumption:

1. Econometric research on the link between expenditure on advertising and tobacco consumption;
2. Research comparing tobacco consumption within a country before and after an ad ban;
3. International comparison of trends in tobacco consumption and antitobacco measures.

1) Econometric research

Numerous studies have investigated the relationship between expenditure on tobacco advertising and consumption of tobacco. Adjustment must be made for important factors such as product price, available income, etc., to avoid drawing wrong conclusions. As econometric studies look at total expenditure and total consumption, no specific conclusions regarding effects on young people can be drawn.

Most econometric studies have found that increased expenditure on tobacco advertising increases demand for cigarettes, while banning advertising leads to a reduction in tobacco consumption.

A recent meta-analysis of 48 econometric studies found that tobacco advertising significantly increased tobacco sales. Recent reviews by the United States Institute of Medicine, the United States Department of Health and Human Services, and the World Health Organization reached the same conclusion.

Quoting reputable scientific bodies is always effective.

2) Research before and after an ad ban

These studies, conducted independently within several different countries, such as Finland and New Zealand compare tobacco consumption before and after a complete ban on advertising, controlling for other factors. [In spite of] inadequacy of data collection or poor implementation of the ban, they have yielded convincing data that a complete ban on advertising makes an important contribution toward reducing smoking prevalence.

3) International comparisons of trends

This type of study—known as a cross-sectional time-series analysis—compares trends in tobacco advertising and consumption. An important study commissioned by the New Zealand government examined trends in consumption and advertising in 33 countries during 1970-1986. It demonstrated that the higher the degree of governmental control on tobacco advertising and sponsorship, the larger the annual reduction of tobacco consumption. Corrections were made to account for differences in income, tobacco prices, and public information.

A cross-sectional time series analysis in 22 OECD countries for the period 1960-1986 concluded that increasingly strict regulation of advertising causes corresponding reductions in tobacco consumption. The degree of restriction on tobacco marketing was scored in each country: for example, Iceland, Finland and Norway, countries with a comprehensive ad ban and strong warnings on tobacco products, scored 10, while

The Organization for Economic Cooperation and Development (OECD) was founded in 1961 to stimulate world trade and economic progress. It includes the United States among more than 25 other nations.

others with less strict measures, such as a ban only on TV, radio, or cinema advertising, had a lower score. On a scale of one to ten, an increase of 1 point was found to translate into a 1.5 percent reduction in tobacco consumption. One drawback was that other types of antitobacco measures, such as public information campaigns, were not corrected for.

Another study of 22 OECD countries during 1964–1990 came to a different conclusion. This study suggested that advertising bans have no effect on tobacco consumption. No attempt is made to explain why this conclusion differs so radically with those of other researchers. The tobacco industry often quotes this study when attacking restrictions on advertising.

The effect of tobacco advertising on young people

A recent review of the available literature concludes that isolated actions have little effect in reducing youth smoking, arguing that only in combination with measures like increased health education can an advertising ban be expected to affect adolescent smoking. Any advertising ban must be comprehensive and cover other promotional activities (see next paragraphs). The tobacco industry targets young people in their advertising campaigns, and research has shown that young people are aware of, remember, understand, and are receptive to tobacco advertising. Bans on advertising have an impact on youth norms and attitudes regarding smoking. A combination of increases in tobacco prices and a complete advertising ban proved to be more effective than either measure on its own.

Why do you think the tobacco industry might target the young?

Outdoor advertising and indirect promotion

Outdoor advertising—for example, billboards or posters—has always been used heavily by the tobacco industry. Voluntary restrictions on outdoor advertising, such as agreements not to place ads on billboards within a certain distance of schools, have been less than effective. One study showed that, despite such an agreement, during a six-month period in 1994, tobacco advertising was posted on two-thirds of billboards near schools. In 1995, tobacco advertising was posted near 40 percent of the schools.

Not all tobacco promotion takes traditional forms, such as billboard, print or TV advertising. A large proportion takes more subtle forms. Indeed, the tobacco industry undertakes much more "indirect" advertising than other industries. Indirect advertising includes: sponsorship of sports or cultural events; displays at points of sale; "brand stretching", where tobacco brand names are used as part of other product names (e.g., Marlboro Classics clothing); product placement in television and film shows; direct mailings; special sales promotions, etc. Indirect advertising is being used increasingly where direct advertising is not permitted. Studies show that young people are easily attracted by this kind of advertising.

"Today's teenager is tomorrow's potential regular customer, and the overwhelming majority of smokers first begin to smoke while still in their teens.... The smoking patterns of teenagers are particularly important to Philip Morris."

—1981 PHILIP MORRIS, INC. REPORT

[There is] evidence … that tobacco advertising plays an important part in encouraging nonsmokers to begin smoking. [It] is a particularly important factor among young people. Comprehensive bans on tobacco advertising and promotion can result in a considerable reduction of tobacco consumption on a national level. Laugesen and Meads conclude that where a complete ad ban is coupled with an intensive public information campaign on smoking, a reduction in tobacco consumption of 6 percent can be achieved. A recent report by the World Bank supports this conclusion.

According to the American Medical Association, 90 percent of new smokers are children and teenagers.

COMMENTARY: Promotion and sponsorship

Big tobacco companies spend around $14 million each day on advertising and promotion. As direct advertisements face increasing restriction, the lion's share of this budget has been allocated to indirect promotion, such as sport sponsorship. In the United States a major sport that prominently enjoys tobacco sponsorship is motor racing (Marlboro, Rothmans, Benson & Hedges). Children in particular have come to associate cigarettes and tobacco with the excitement of fast cars and the glamor and high social status enjoyed by sporting stars.

Marlboro's penetration of the burgeoning eastern European and Asian markets has been eased by sponsorship of rock concerts in Hungary and of radio shows in Beijing, China. R.J. Reynolds (makers of the Camel and Salem brands) has sponsored pop programs on Hong Kong TV and live discos in China. At such events representatives typically hand out free cigarettes, as well as branded merchandise such as sunglasses, key rings, and tee-shirts.

Another avenue for tobacco companies is the movie industry. Philip Morris reportedly paid $350,000 to have its cigarettes featured in the James Bond movie *License to Kill*. The antismoking lobby says that this constitutes hidden advertising. But is giving government the power to restrict speech by controlling advertising worthwhile even if it does reduce smoking? Should individuals be responsible for their decision to smoke?

would be in danger of being turned over the District Attorney by local health puritans, for "indirectly" encouraging teenagers to smoke?

A license for government control

The author shows effectively how well-intended laws can do more harm than good.

Censorship of Advertising: Prohibiting "advertising, promotion, or marketing" targeting people under 18 is equally naïve. Eighteen is a legal boundary, not an advertising one. Promotions that appeal to people in their early 20s often appeal to those in their late teens as well. Some automobile advertisements appeal both to teenage boys and middle-aged men. In effect, the "indirect" advertising ban gives state government control over the public activities of tobacco companies because there is no practical way to "prove" that a particular activity does not appeal to minors.

Setting aside the damage such a precedent would do to free speech, there is no evidence to suggest that handing state government this kind of control over private activity would really reduce smoking. Contrary to popular belief, authorities as diverse as the United States Surgeon General's office, the government of the United Kingdom, and the Belgian health minister agree that tobacco advertising does not appear to affect tobacco consumption. The opposite impression has arisen out of confusion over the fact that increasing a person's awareness of a particular brand does not necessarily mean that that person has an increased propensity to smoke.

Although there is evidence that the Joe Camel advertising campaign induced smokers to switch to Camels, there is little evidence that it increased the overall proportion of youth smokers.

For example, the much-hyped studies showing that preschoolers were as familiar with Joe Camel as Mickey Mouse say nothing about smoking behavior. Studies showing that 85 percent of six-year-olds associated Joe Camel with cigarettes also showed that less than 4 percent thought cigarettes were good. Most six-year-olds probably associate Bugs Bunny with carrots. This does not imply that they love eating them for dinner. Smoking levels increased in European countries with outright tobacco advertising bans, and the percentage of youth smokers, defined as the percent of high school seniors who use any cigarettes, has fallen from 27 to 20 percent since 1975. In spite of tobacco advertising.

Cartoons under fire

Censorship of Cartoons: This bill also gives the state legislature the power to define cartoons so that it can ban them in marketing tobacco products. Cartoons are any depiction of anything ("object, person, animal, creature, or any similar caricature") that has comically exaggerated features, gives human characteristics to anything not a human, or endows humans with "extrahuman abilities." Some antitobacco extremists consider smoking such an evil, abhorrent, and immoral activity that any ad merely showing smokers merely having a good time would endow them with "extrahuman" abilities. They reason that human smokers, drug addicts by definition, cannot possibly have a good time when pursuing their filthy habit.

Moves to ban cartoons

Should cartoon makers have a moral duty not to portray antisocial behavior?

Since the ban applies not just to direct advertising but also to promotion, there is a risk that a zealous prosecutor could bring a case against noncommercial cartoons which portray smoking. For example, *The Simpsons* cartoon series has literally hundreds of instances of characters smoking.

Wile E. Coyote cartoons make fun of explosives, violence, and hunting. Some argue that such cartoons harm children by encouraging violence. Look for Mr. Coyote to join Joe Camel on the Colorado banned cartoons list in the next bill that plans to save the children by savaging the First Amendment.

Summary

In "Tobacco Advertising" Willemsen and de Blij frame their argument by providing statistics that support the view that tobacco advertising should be banned. They quote three major strands of research. The first looks at advertising expenditure and smoking rates, concluding that the majority of studies find that increased spending on advertising leads to a rise in smoking, and reduced spending has the opposite effect. The second strand of studies examines the efficacy of total bans on tobacco advertising (i.e., within one country), concluding that such bans can, in ideal circumstances, produce a measurable drop in smoking. The third strand of research looks at comparative smoking rates and advertising control across different countries. It finds that comprehensive bans on advertising are the most effective means of reducing tobacco consumption. The article also exposes the way in which tobacco companies try to recruit young smokers.

Linda Gorman's article "More Taxes and Less Free Speech" focuses on a bill intended to outlaw the marketing of cigarettes to minors—through, for example, the use of cartoons. She argues that the bill is founded on false logic. Smoking, she says, already brings in money for the government; tobacco advertising does not cause smoking rates to rise; and it is impossible anyway to tailor ads that do not appeal in some way to minors. Above all, she claims, government control over tobacco ads is unconstitutional and an infringement on the freedom of speech.

FURTHER INFORMATION:

Books:

Lynch, B.S. and R. J. Bonnie (editors), *Growing Up Tobacco Free: Preventing Nicotine Addiction in Children and Youths*. Washington, D.C.: Institute of Medicine, National Academy Press, 1994.

Petrone, Gerard S., *Tobacco Advertising: The Great Seduction*. Atglen, PA: Schiffer Publishing, 1996.

White, Larry C., *Merchants of Death: The American Tobacco Industry*. New York: Beech Tree Books, 1988.

Articles:

Evans, N., A. Farkas et al, "Influence of Tobacco Marketing and Exposure to Smokers on Adult Susceptibility to Smoking." *Journal of the National Cancer Institute*, 87, 1995.

Nelson, E, D. White, "Children's Awareness of Cigarette Ads on Television." *Health Education Journal*, 1992: 51.

WHO, "It Can be Done: A Smokefree Europe." World Health Organization, 1990.

Useful websites:

www.ama-assn.org/special/aos/tobacco/fact.htm
AMA factsheet on minors and tobacco advertising.

www.ymn.org/newstats/advertising.shtml
Youth Media Network (California) factsheet on tobacco and advertising.

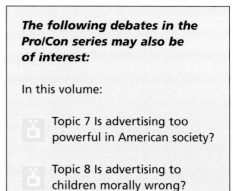

The following debates in the Pro/Con series may also be of interest:

In this volume:

Topic 7 Is advertising too powerful in American society?

Topic 8 Is advertising to children morally wrong?

SHOULD TOBACCO ADVERTISING BE BANNED?

YES: The Department of Health and Human Services and the World Health Organization, among others, believe so

YES: The government is obliged to act in the interests of public health

CAUSE AND EFFECT
Do tobacco advertising and promotion lead to an increase in smoking?

FREE SPEECH
Does government have a duty to control tobacco advertising?

NO: Not even the Surgeon General's office is convinced that a rise in tobacco advertising causes more people to smoke; ads merely reinforce brand loyalty among existing smokers

NO: Government control is unconstitutional, infringing the Fourteenth Amendment and the right to free speech

SHOULD TOBACCO ADVERTISING BE BANNED?
KEY POINTS

YES: Cartoon characters such as Joe Camel and pop culture promotions are aimed directly at young people

YES: 5,000 U.S. smokers die each day, so tobacco giants have to recruit new smokers from the youth sector

YOUNG SMOKERS
Does tobacco advertising target young people?

NO: The advertising is directed at adults; minors are inevitably attracted to tobacco ads, just as they are attracted to auto ads

NO: The tobacco industry has always denied that it targets the youth sector

THE TOBACCO INDUSTRY

Tobacco use is the leading preventable cause of death in the United States, causing more than 400,000 deaths each year and costing more than $50 billion in medical bills. Of particular concern is the number of young people who take up smoking every year, and there are calls for tobacco advertising to be banned. Whether this would have a direct effect on young people smoking is not clear, particularly while smoking is still presented as glamorous in some aspects of popular culture.

1952 British researchers publish first evidence of a "real" link between smoking and lung cancer.

1954 The tobacco industry faces its first liability lawsuit by a lung cancer victim, but the suit is dropped 13 years later.

1964–1970 Surgeon General Luther Terry concludes that smoking causes lung cancer. The Federal Cigarette Labeling and Advertising Act orders a health warning on all cigarette packs.

1971–1980 Broadcast advertising for cigarettes is banned. All airlines must now provide nonsmoking sections. The warnings on cigarette packs and advertising are strengthened. Nicotine gum is accepted as an aid to help quit smoking. The government bans smoking on short domestic flights.

1992 Nicotine patches are introduced as an aid to quit smoking.

1994 The executives of the seven largest American tobacco companies swear in congressional testimony that they believe nicotine to be nonaddictive. They deny that they have manipulated nicotine levels.

May 1994 Mississippi files suit against tobacco companies to win back Medicaid costs—the first of many states to do so.

November 21, 1995 Jeffrey Wigand, former employee of Brown & Williamson Tobacco, is sued for breach of contract. He blows the whistle on the company's practices in an interview with CBS's *60 Minutes* news show.

March 15, 1996 The Liggett Group, a cigarette manufacturer, agrees to pay more than $10 million in Medicaid bills after settling court action with five states. On the 18th a former Philip Morris scientist reveals that nicotine levels in cigarettes have been controlled to encourage smoking and sales.

April 18, 1996 The first nonprescription nicotine gum is released.

August 1996 New regulations restricting tobacco advertising aimed at teenagers are proposed by the U.S. Food and Drug Administration. On the 21st President Clinton approves the FDA regulations. On the 23rd the president declares nicotine addictive.

October 1996 The tobacco companies file a motion in a North Carolina court asking for the FDA regulations to be overturned.

November 5, 1996 Florida files criminal charges against the tobacco industry.

December 1996 The Justice Department files a 149-page brief that outlines the FDA's case for the regulation of tobacco.

1997 A federal judge rules that the government can regulate tobacco as a drug but also states that the industry should be allowed to continue advertising.

March 1997 On March 20 the Liggett Group settles its lawsuits with a further 22 states and agrees to pay out $750 million. It becomes the first tobacco company to admit that cigarettes are addictive and can cause cancer. On March 26 the Federal Trade Commission begins to investigate whether R. J. Reynolds Tobacco's "Joe Camel" advertisements are aimed at children.

Late 1997 There is a landmark settlement. The tobacco industry has to spend $386 billion over 25 years, mainly on antismoking advertising, increase the size of warnings on its product, decrease prosmoking advertising, and face fines if young smokers increase. Mississippi agrees to a $3.6 billion deal. Florida reaches a similar settlement of $11.3 billion.

1998 Texas settles its claim against the industry for $15.3 billion. The tobacco executives testify before Congress, stating now that nicotine is addictive and that smoking may cause cancer. Minnesota settles its action for $6.6 billion. The Senate rejects a proposal backed by President Clinton to increase tax on cigarettes by $1.50 per pack. The Senate goes on to disable a settlement bill that would have cost the tobacco companies $516 billion dollars over 25 years.

November 1998 Forty-six states agree to a settlement of $206 billion over health costs for treating smokers. Cigarette prices are expected to rise as a result.

1999 Patricia Henley is awarded $51.5 million in damages against Philip Morris. This is later reduced to $26.5 million. Philip Morris is currently appealing the award. A jury in Portland, Oregon, awards the family of Jesse Williams $79.5 million against Philip Morris in punitive damages plus $821,485 in compensatory damages for medical costs and pain and suffering caused by smoking. The punitive damages are later reduced to $32 million. Philip Morris is currently appealing against this. Elsewhere a Florida jury says that five tobacco companies have been engaged in "extreme and outrageous conduct; in making a defective product that causes emphysema, lung cancer, and other illnesses."

September 1999 The Justice Department begins to sue the tobacco industry to recover billions of government dollars spent on smoking-related health care.

November 5, 1999 Michael Mann's movie *The Insider* is released. It dramatizes the relationship between tobacco industry whistleblower Jeffrey Wigand and *60 Minutes* investigator Lowell Bergman.

March 2000 A San Francisco jury orders Philip Morris and R. J. Reynolds, the two largest tobacco companies in America, to pay $20 million in punitive damages. This follows a $1.7 million compensatory damage award to one Leslie Whiteley for medical costs and pain and suffering. Her husband, Leonard, is awarded $250,000 for loss of companionship. Both companies are appealing the decisions.

July 2000 A jury orders the tobacco industry to pay $145 billion in punitive damages to Florida smokers—the highest sum so far.

The tobacco industry has at last admitted that its product is addictive and that it causes fatal diseases. While some people would like to see a total ban on all tobacco advertising, others argue that tobacco is legal, and so the industry should be allowed to advertise. See *Topic 9 Should Tobacco Advertising Be Banned?* for a discussion on this issue.

Topic 10

DOES ADVERTISING THREATEN OBJECTIVE JOURNALISM?

YES

"THE POWER OF THE PRESS HAS A PRICE"
EXTRA!, JULY/AUGUST 1997
LAWRENCE SOLEY

NO

"THE WALL"
LOS ANGELES TIMES, DECEMBER 20, 1999
DAVID SHAW

INTRODUCTION

There are few media systems throughout the world that do not depend on advertising for at least a portion of their revenue. In the case of many broadcasting stations or online broadcasters advertising is the sole source of revenue. Because TV networks and other media are commercial concerns, this puts them under an inevitable pressure: They have to create output that attracts not just viewers but also advertisers (the two are often the same, however—the more viewers, the more advertisers are usually attracted).

This reliance on advertising creates some concerns about feature magazines or comedy and drama shows on television. It raises particular issues, however, when it comes to journalism and current affairs. How can journalists and newspapers be critical of the very corporations, institutions, or industries that fund them? Does a firm that advertises in a certain publication thus avoid legitimate criticism from it?

The issue has been thrown into sharp relief by specific cases. ABC News withdrew an interview on cigarettes when threatened by lawsuits from tobacco giant Philip Morris Inc. Threat of legal action also led a Fox station in Florida to withdraw a news item that was critical of a product manufactured by Monsanto, the pioneers of genetically modified foods.

If big companies can exert influence through threat of legal action, how much more influence is wielded behind the scenes? People who are suspicious of advertisers' influence, including many journalists themselves, argue that one of the most powerful ways in which that influence operates is not overtly, through legal action or direct protest, but through journalists' own self-censorship. According to this argument, journalists are aware—at least unconsciously—of the value of advertising to their newspaper and, therefore, to their own job security.

They therefore automatically shape their stories to satisfy, or at least not to anger, those advertisers. This is a particular fear in smaller communities, where there are only a limited number of advertisers, who can thus exert undue influence and are more likely to find editors who will bow to it. Newspapers in larger towns and cities, where there is a greater variety and number of potential advertisers, can usually afford to be more objective.

Advertising is not new in broadcasting or in print journalism. The latter, in particular, has developed various ways to attempt to preserve objectivity. Most newspapers carefully separate the editorial from the business function. Advertising salespeople should not be in frequent contact with reporters or editors, so that the people who create the content can feel free to report on what they see fit, regardless of the advertising in their paper.

The ethics of individual journalists should also guard them from advertising pressure. Journalists must be mindful of both the rights and duties associated with the overall right of freedom of the press. They have a duty to protect that freedom from censorship, not only from outside forces but also from their own instincts to self-censorship.

The demand for rigorously "objective" journalism to counter the influence of advertising was one of the impulses behind the creation of journalism schools in the early 20th century. They were a reaction to the so-called "yellow journalism" of the late 19th century, when competition for circulation often overcame ethical standards. The new schools promoted a professional approach that adhered scrupulously to ethical standards.

Yet objectivity is not without critics. Some people argue that objectivity cannot exist and is an unrealistic goal. Newspapers and reporters are often associated, more or less explicitly, with a particular political stance—left, right, or center—for example. Certain papers and news organizations are thought to be "of record," however, meaning that they distribute the news in its most unadulterated, truthful form.

Another criticism is that objectivity, like the need to attract readers and advertisers, leads papers into the "center" of opinion, where the sympathies of most readers lie. This affects the ways in which certain stories can be treated. Expressions of views that are unpopular or simply novel might diminish that audience.

> *"The most stupid boast in … journalism is that of the writer who says, 'I have never been given orders; I am free to do as I like.'"*
> —GEORGE SELDES, JOURNALIST

The articles in this section deal with the issue of how news media face advertisers. The first argues that violations of journalistic ethics in television news occur more commonly than one might think. The second article describes the "wall" within newspapers that separates the editorial from the business side. Though it is sometimes breached, the article argues that the wall works well overall.

THE POWER OF THE PRESS HAS A PRICE
Lawrence Soley

Sixty years ago, reporter and press critic George Seldes wrote in *Freedom of the Press* that advertisers, not government, are the principal news censors in the United States. Not only do advertisers pressure newspapers to kill or alter stories, he concluded, but newspapers censor stories out of deference "toward the sources of their money" without being told.

Seldes (1890–1995) was one of the foremost American journalists of his age. What does Soley gain by quoting him?

Sixty years later, advertisers are still muscling newspapers. A survey of 55 members of the Society of American Business Editors and Writers at the society's 1992 conference revealed that advertiser pressure was common. Eighty percent said that the pressure was a growing problem, and 45 percent knew of instances where news coverage was compromised by advertisers. "Business journalists have always struggled against advertiser pressures, but our members are telling us it's getting worse," said Sandra Deurr, the business editor of the *Louisville Courier-Journal* and former society president.

A survey of local news editors … found that auto dealers were the most frequent sources of pressure. "They want all stories involving auto sales to have a rosy outlook," one editor observed, "and they whine about negative economic stories, even if they're on a national level from AP."

AP (Associated Press) is the oldest and largest wire service (news agency) in the United States. It is a highly reliable source, feeding the latest stories to the nation's press.

Advertisers appear to be muscling broadcasters as well. In Los Angeles, veteran KCBS-TV consumer reporter David Horowitz was let go in 1996 after automobile advertisers repeatedly complained to management about his stories on car safety. According to Horowitz, management had first tried to stop his investigations with comments such as, "I'm concerned about the story not because it's right or wrong, but because it may cost us advertising." According to *Chicago Sun-Times* columnist Robert Feder (2/12/96), Chicago's WLS-TV killed a story on fire hazards in Ford vehicles because it "didn't want to risk offending auto dealers who advertise heavily on the station."

Pressures are common

To determine whether these actions are typical, I sent a questionnaire about advertiser pressures to 241 members of Investigative Reporters and Editors employed at commercial television stations. The questionnaires asked reporters about advertiser muscling of their news operations and their stations' responses to these pressures.

Nearly three-quarters of the respondents reported that advertisers had "tried to influence the content" of news at their stations. The majority of respondents also reported that advertisers had attempted to kill stories.

Moreover, the responses show that advertisers tried to use monetary leverage as part of their pressure. More than two-thirds reported that advertisers threatened to withdraw their advertising because of the content of news stories. Forty-four percent of the respondents reported that advertisers had "actually withdrawn advertising because of the content of a news report." The responses of reporters at large and small market stations did not differ.

> *Soley does not specify how many respondents he had. Why might that be?*

> *Small news stations are usually thought to succumb more to advertiser pressure, but these uniform results suggest otherwise.*

"Money is always the first thing we talk about. The readers are always the last thing we talk about"

—LEO WOLINSKY, MANAGING EDITOR,

LOS ANGELES TIMES

Citing another censorious industry [in addition to auto dealers], one reporter noted that "we are currently battling with the local restaurant association and the members who advertise on our station whether we should air the city's weekly restaurant inspection ratings." The reporter added, "In this instance, my bosses are backing me." Grocery stores and "lawyers who advertise on television" were also mentioned as sources of pressure.

The more important question is not whether advertisers have directly pressured television stations, but whether the stations have yielded to the pressure. Questioned whether advertisers "succeeded in influencing a news report at your station," nearly as many said their stations had capitulated (40 percent) as had withstood the pressure (43 percent).

> *Soley seems to concede that it is natural for advertisers to try to influence broadcasters. Do you agree?*

Self-censorship

Two questions addressed the issue of self-censorship. Asked whether there had been "pressure from within your stations to not produce news stories that advertisers might find objectionable," 59 percent of respondents said there had been. One respondent wrote, "I have experienced direct pressure from my general manager (with no defense from my news director) to not only 'tread lightly' on advertisers, but also to be careful about 'our corporate neighbors in the community.' Disgusting!"

Do you think journalists have a duty toward their local community? What might it be?

A reporter in California, who claimed to have been sacked for offending advertisers, sent a copy of a memo he received from his news director, reading, "If you're involved in a story which you know might reflect badly on an advertiser, please let me know, so I can give sales a 'heads up.'"

"We believe we can be subsidized by the advertiser by giving him value for value received and without compromising more than a small fraction of our journalistic soul. That small fraction we are frankly willing to sell for a price."

—HENRY LUCE, FOUNDER, TIME INC.

Several respondents provided in-depth descriptions of the internal pressures at their stations. One wrote, "I've found that many general managers at TV stations (including my own) are former TV sales people and therefore know the advertisers very well. It is common for advertisers to call a station and express their 'concerns' about a story. While I have never been asked to lie or mislead viewers, I have been asked to soften a story an advertiser might find objectionable."

Another commented that "I'm not sure if 'pressure' is the right word. It's probably better described as 'story steering.' For example, if a story is suggested on car dealers, something might be said like, 'there's a lot better things for us to look into, don't you think?'" Similarly, one reporter wrote that direct pressure wasn't applied at the station, but there was "just a general understanding to avoid a specific area."

As for whether there had "been pressure from within your station to produce news stories to please advertisers," 56 percent of respondents reported that there was. Several reporters wrote comments about this pressure. The most frequent comment suggested that "sales people come in and request stories be done on their clients" or that sales people set up "interviews and tell us about them after they're promised." Another wrote there was pressure "to interview advertisers on positive stories and not on negative stories with the guidance of management."

Another reporter provided a directive [from] the news director: "From time to time, we do stories where we need an expert of sorts … no one company or person in particular, just someone who knows about a certain subject. Sales has asked me to check with them in those situations, feeling that … we might as well call on one who does business with the station. So, whenever it's one of those situations (like we need a realtor, we need a bail bondsman, we need a coffee shop owner), please give sales a call and see if they have someone who's available and media friendly."

In such instances what pressures might bear on the "expert" to give impartial advice?

A little help from their friends

While other groups try to influence or suppress coverage, advertisers wield a unique economic club over television stations by withdrawing or threatening to withdraw advertising. However, advertisers do not exert the pressure by themselves. As one respondent wrote: "The pressure comes from outside the station and within the station and often the two sides are working together to either kill stories or alter them. I know of an instance where a sales executive actually met with the focus of an investigative report over lunch and told him what the story would be about. How did the sales executive know the content of an investigative report before it aired? A news executive told him."

Soley gives an example of a branch of the "wall," as described in the next article.

Keeping advertisers sweet

Not all news executives have sold out. But with pressures for greater profits, the incentive to produce news stories that will either please or not offend advertisers is great. The problem was summarized by an investigative reporter, who wrote: "The pressure from outside influences doesn't bother me; it's always been there and I suspect it always will be. However, there seems to be a frightening trend for the powers that be at corporate [headquarters] to give in to that pressure and pretend everything [is] business as usual."

Unfortunately, in many cases, that's all it is, Business. A gold-card advertiser can keep the dirty secrets secret and in some cases keep their victims in the dark. Those victims are our viewers who expect more and many times rely too much on the so-called power of the press. What they don't know is—power has a price, and it's for sale.

Soley concludes that members of the public are the ultimate losers when their news sources can longer be trusted.

THE WALL
David Shaw

As Terence Monmaney, a medical writer for the *Los Angeles Times*, wrote in a memorandum to top executives at the paper last month, newspaper stories "serve many millions of people locally and nationally who may not even realize that the information behind improvements in their schools, cops, hospitals and government (among other things) got into the public domain as a result of ... a newspaper's determined efforts. Few businesses strive to market a product that helps people who do not buy it, yet journalists aim to do just that—by pumping into society the oxygen of news."

Many newspapers have suffered financially for telling readers what they didn't want to hear—most notably during the civil rights movement of the 1950s and early '60s, when several Southern papers covered (and editorially supported) efforts to win equal rights for blacks. The *Lexington Advertiser* in the delta country of Mississippi was firebombed by angry readers, boycotted by advertisers, and finally forced into bankruptcy. Later in the 1960s, and into the early '70s, newspapers throughout the country gave broad, ongoing coverage—and, sometimes, editorial support—to protests by campus activists, antiwar demonstrators, feminists, and environmentalists at a time when many, if not most, readers opposed the protesters and the coverage they received.

Loyalty to journalism's tenets

Shaw points out that papers gain credibility through telling the truth, rather than merely appease the public or their advertisers.

This behavior runs contrary to both common sense and common business practice, but newspapers realize that if they do not tell the truth, to the best of their ability to determine it, they will not only fail to fulfill their professional obligation, they will ultimately fail as businesses because readers won't trust them. "Every newspaper I've worked for has done things that were not in their own best interest but were in the best interest of their readers and their communities," says Dennis Britton, former editor of the *Denver Post* and *Chicago Sun-Times* and former deputy managing editor of the *Los Angeles Times*.

Newspapers have often risked government reprisals in order to report news they deemed important to society—

most famously in the Pentagon Papers and Watergate cases in the 1970s. In the former, the *New York Times* and then the *Washington Post* published a secret history of the Vietnam War in the face of threats by the administration of President Richard Nixon to seek criminal indictments against the papers and their executives. Three years later, the *Post* vigorously pursued the Watergate break-in story, despite fears—later confirmed by transcripts of Nixon's conversations with top aides—that his administration might retaliate by causing "damnable, damnable problems" when the *Post* tried to renew the federal licenses required to operate the company's lucrative television stations.

The Watergate scandal cost Nixon his presidency; the Washington Post is still running.

The wall—a conflict of interests?

The wall itself is a metaphor for another fundamental difference between journalism and other businesses. In a typical business, everyone is expected to work together toward the common goal of improving the company's financial performance—i.e., making more money; while newspapers certainly must be profitable to survive, making money has traditionally been the sole province of the business side of the paper—the people who sell ads and subscriptions and promote and market the paper.

The "wall" refers to the barrier within newspapers which separates the editorial from the business side.

The editorial side—the reporters and editors—feel they owe their primary loyalty not to the bottom line nor even to the company—the newspaper—but to the basic tenets of journalism. As a result, they have not only been free to ignore the issue of profitability but have often done things guaranteed to offend, even damage—and perhaps cost the paper—the advertisers who provide that profitability.

Indeed, this may be the single characteristic that most distinguishes the newspaper business from any other—its willingness (and often its obligation) to bite the hand that feeds it. Advertisers provide 80 percent of the revenue for most newspapers, and yet newspapers routinely publish stories critical of or contrary to the best interests of their biggest advertisers or whole groups of advertisers.

This figure has risen from less than 50 percent in 1880 to more than 60 percent in 1920.

Negative stories about advertisers don't appear every day, of course, and there are numerous embarrassing examples of newspapers, especially in smaller towns, bowing to pressure from advertisers. Several newspapers, for example, have caved in to automobile dealers after suffering costly advertising boycotts triggered by stories that disclosed some of the dealers' shady practices. To the astonishment and dismay of many in the media, a nationwide survey of 105 newspaper editors and 60 publishers published this month in *Editor &*

COMMENTARY: The *LA Times* sells its integrity

A flagrant breach of the wall between editorial and advertising was made in October 1999 by the publishers of the *Los Angeles Times* when they secretly implicated their editorial department in a revenue-sharing deal with the city's new stadium, the Staples Center.

The Times Mirror Company, the paper's parent, was one of the 12 leading financial partners in the $400-million stadium. The chief executive officers of both parent and paper helped broker the deal by which Times Mirror, to fulfill part of its financial commitment to the stadium, would devote the editorial content of a 168-page Sunday supplement to the stadium and then give the stadium half of the edition's $2 million advertising revenue. To this procedure the publishers added an extraordinary twist. They chose not to inform the editorial department of the deal.

When other publications leaked news of the shared-revenue deal, the editorial staff expressed fury at the fact that their journalistic integrity had been compromised. To the outside world it appeared that they had had an undisclosed financial connection with their editorial subject. Several writers and editors quit in disgust, heads rolled in the boardroom, and the paper began the slow process of regaining the credibility it lost.

It is understandable that a publisher might care chiefly about money, but why might an editor compromise integrity to protect an advertiser?

Publisher magazine showed that 19 percent of the publishers and 11 percent of the editors thought it was acceptable for newspapers to consider "killing or holding a story that might negatively portray an advertiser." About 9 percent of the sample said they had "already killed or altered such a story."

But more than half those respondents were from papers with less than 100,000 circulation. Such acts are the exception, not the rule, in the recent history of the country's better newspapers, especially the major metropolitan dailies. In the same *Editor & Publisher* survey, more than 80 percent of the respondents said a newspaper should never kill, delay, or alter a story that might negatively portray an advertiser, and 76 percent said they had never done so; 86 percent said reporters should never be asked to include an advertiser in a story. Four out of five editors and almost every one of the publishers said advertisers had pulled their ads to protest unfavorable coverage, and virtually every respectable newspaper has had advertisers do likewise—sometimes for months at a time.

The better newspapers, regardless of size, do not soften their coverage to woo back advertising dollars. "Early this year, we ran a number of stories, one in particular, that was

critical of how home-builders in the Chicago area stretched the truth in brochures they put out," says Howard Tyner, editor of the *Chicago Tribune*. The home-builders pulled "a million dollars' worth or more" of advertising, according to Dennis Grant, vice president for advertising at the *Tribune*.

---

*"There is no such thing as
Objective Journalism. The phrase
itself is a pompous contradiction in terms."*
—HUNTER S. THOMPSON,
JOURNALIST AND AUTHOR

David Scribner, editor of the *Berkshire Eagle*, a 32,000-circulation newspaper in Pittsfield, Mass., says a local health care network canceled all its advertising for "a whole year" because of the paper's critical coverage of the network. "They wouldn't even let patients in their hospital get our paper delivered to their rooms," he says. But like the *Tribune*, the *Eagle* continued its critical coverage. "Frankly," Scribner says, "when you have an advertiser pissed off at you, you know you're doing something right."

Scribner's comment touches on a core issue: An advertiser who objects to editorial criticism may well deserve it.

Keeping the flame of impartiality

"Because we're funded by advertisers … there's a natural suspicion on the part of readers that's inherent in the relationship between newspapers and their advertisers," says Jeffrey S. Klein, a former senior vice president at the *Los Angeles Times* and now president of 101communications, an Internet magazine publisher based in the San Fernando Valley.

Jack Fuller, president of Tribune Publishing Co. in Chicago, makes a similar argument. "We're attempting to persuade the public that we're doing our best to tell them the truth, regardless of the consequences to us," he says. "That's counterintuitive. It's not easy for people to believe that." Because of that, Fuller says, newspapers must "go out of their way to do things that will give people the confidence that we really do behave that way." Newspapers must also do everything they can to avoid even the appearance of a conflict of interest or any kind of impropriety involving their advertisers or the people and institutions they cover.

People, says Fuller, are suspicious of any business that appears to shoot itself in the foot— in essence, of the tension between journalism and advertising.

Summary

In his title Lawrence Soley says that the power of the press to inform the public has a price; he goes on to explain in the article that through bribes or intimidation unscrupulous advertisers can exploit that power to their advantage. He bases his argument on the results of two surveys, one of which he conducted personally. The findings appear to prove that advertisers frequently "muscle" in on TV stations and newspapers, and that the networks and papers themselves are also self-censoring—that is, they voluntarily alter or pull news stories rather than offend valuable advertisers. Respondents to his survey describe the full range of muscling, from monetary threats and punitive action by outside advertisers to subtle "story steering" and cronyism. Ultimately, warns Soley, it is the public that suffers, because the news sources they trust have sold their integrity in the name of business.

David Shaw gives a guarded vote of confidence in the so-called wall, the purposefully maintained barrier between the journalists and the advertising or business staff at any TV station or newspaper office. He uses much of his essay to describe the paradox at the heart of every good paper. A journalist's first loyalty is to the truth and to telling it regardless of what readers might or might not want to read. But this duty is often at complete odds with the business ethic, and there is an honorable tradition, continued today, of papers publishing stories that provoke readers to cancel their subscription or advertisers to pull out in anger. Of course, Shaw admits, the truth sometimes suffers, particularly at smaller papers where advertisers hold greater relative power, but this is the exception rather than the rule. It is incumbent on a news source to go out of its way to win the trust of the public, whose natural inclination is to mistrust a commercial enterprise as paradoxical as the press.

FURTHER INFORMATION:

Articles:

Miraldi, Robert, "Muckraking and Objectivity: Journalism's Colliding Traditions," in *Contributions to the Study of Mass Media and Communications*, No. 18. Westport, CT: Greenwood Press, 1990.

Useful websites:

www.journalism.indiana.edu/Ethics/
Ethics Cases Online, provided by the Bloomington School of Journalism at the University of Indiana.
www.scottlondon.com/articles/journalism.html
London, Scott, "Just What Ails Journalism?" Published in the *Santa Barbara News-Press*, April 22, 1995.
www.cjr.org/year/00/1/lacron.asp
Risser, James, "Chronology of a Crisis."

www.washingtonpost.com
Site of the *Washington Post*.

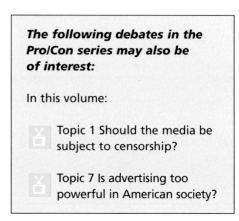

The following debates in the Pro/Con series may also be of interest:

In this volume:

Topic 1 Should the media be subject to censorship?

Topic 7 Is advertising too powerful in American society?

DOES ADVERTISING THREATEN OBJECTIVE JOURNALISM?

YES: Isolated from commercial pressure, a journalist should, and can, approximate the truth to the best of his or her knowledge

YES: The pressure within a paper to keep advertisers happy is often as pervasive as the pressure from the advertisers themselves

OBJECTIVITY
Is it impossible for a journalist to be completely objective?

SELF-CENSORSHIP
Do publishers alter stories to please advertisers?

NO: Even without pressure from advertisers, journalists are always subject to their own subjective interpretation of the truth

NO: The ethics of journalism are usually respected by publishers, even when large ad budgets are at stake; self-censorship is the exception, not the rule

DOES ADVERTISING THREATEN OBJECTIVE JOURNALISM?
KEY POINTS

YES: Companies that advertise in the press have a right to prevent journalists from criticizing their business

YES: The journalist's duty is to report the truth; the publisher is primarily concerned with sustaining circulation. Their goals are mutually exclusive.

INFERNAL PACT
Does the press's dependence on advertising inevitably raise a conflict of interests?

NO: If a truthful news report directs criticism on a business, that criticism is justified

NO: Advertising staff and journalists accept the need for a "wall." Problems only arise when the wall is willfully breached.

Topic 11

IS THERE TOO MUCH POLITICAL ADVERTISING?

YES

"GOUGING DEMOCRACY: HOW THE TELEVISION INDUSTRY PROFITEERED ON ELECTION 2000"
WWW.BETTERCAMPAIGNS.ORG
ALLIANCE FOR BETTER CAMPAIGNS

NO

"POLITICAL ADVERTISING REGULATION: AN UNCONSTITUTIONAL MENACE?"
POLICY ANALYSIS NO. 112, SEPTEMBER 22, 1988
STEPHEN BATES

INTRODUCTION

Advertising is an integral part of almost any election campaign in the United States. Presidential candidates and their supporters are the biggest spenders, but any election for national-level office is accompanied by a degree of television advertising. While advertising in general has numerous critics because of the power it wields in U.S. society, political advertising raises specific concerns because it is seen as being directly connected with the health of democracy in the United States.

Political advertising is almost as old as formal politics. It can be as simple as a printed slogan—"Vote for X"—or a paid-for announcement of an individual's policies. What particularly worries its critics, however, are highly sophisticated TV ads that rely on advertising techniques that use imagery and complex pyschology to make their points, rather than political procedure.

The main criticisms of political advertising are twofold. One arises from the fact that it makes political campaigning more expensive. In the 2000 elections a New Jersey multimillionaire was elected to the U.S. Senate despite his lack of political experience at least in part because he was backed by an effective—and expensive—advertising campaign.

The second debate concerns the effect of advertising on the nature of political debate. TV ads in particular, argue critics, need to be brief and hard-hitting. They therefore tend to simplify complex issues to easily memorable images or slogans. This in turn has the effect of making politics seem like a contest between black-and-white views, which it rarely is. In addition, advertisements allow candidates to say what they want without giving their opponents a chance to question or contradict them—unless they decide to answer with an ad of their own. To that extent political advertising allows politicians to sidestep debate with their opponents or the questions of an audience of voters.

Negative advertising, in which politicians set out to criticize or weaken their opponents, is also a cause for concern. All sorts of psychological tools are dragged in: Beyond attacking specific policy proposals, these ads may challenge candidates' integrity, honesty, and personal life. Some observers believe that George Bush's victory in the 1988 presidential campaign was at least partly due to commercials that attacked his opponent, Michael Dukakis. One notorious example concerned murderer Willie Horton and suggested that Dukakis, as governor of Massachusetts, had willingly let killers out of jail to commit more crimes.

The campaigners who use negative advertising argue that the character and record of an opponent are fair game, and that they are alerting voters to weaknesses in a candidate. Critics allege that Americans' disillusion with politics in general may partly be the result of the way that political advertising has stifled any discussion of real political issues. In fact, research is not clear about the effectiveness of negative advertising. It may not work particularly well. Voters continually tell surveys that they do not like it.

Many people do not agree that political advertising is damaging the U.S. political system. They see it as a vital way for politicians to connect with the public and also as an important expression of free speech, as enshrined in the First Amendment. Voters are perfectly capable of distinguishing slick but empty images from real information on a candidate's attitudes and policies.

Even if it is accepted that there is too much political advertising, could anything be done about it? At the moment it is something of a vicious cycle: If candidate A turns to negative ads, it will be difficult for candidate B to turn the other cheek; after candidate B has responded, candidate A will respond in turn, and so on.

It is also notoriously difficult to enforce restrictions on political advertising. Because it is political speech, it enjoys the highest form of First Amendment protection. Political ads are not subject to content restriction, and the law guarantees candidates' access to airtime. It would take major legislation to even be able to consider restrictions on campaign spots, and such legislation might not get through the courts.

Proposals for campaign finance reform—limiting the amount candidates can spend during an election, say, or funding all candidates from public money—may be the best avenue for those who wish to change how political advertising works. Such proposals have been discussed recently, but they are also difficult to pass.

This section deals with two aspects of political advertising. The first article looks at how television stations are profiteering from political advertising. Though rules guarantee candidates access to television advertising at the lowest possible rate, TV stations often threaten to bump candidates' spots unless they pay the higher rates. The technique effectively blackmails candidates into paying the higher rates.

The second article argues that political advertising is, at base, free speech. Ads should not be curtailed and even may offer the best way of reaching voters. The article argues that most proposals for regulating political advertising would not work and would be unconstitutional.

GOUGING DEMOCRACY
Alliance for Better Campaigns

Long before the election that refused to end finally did, a clear winner had already emerged from Campaign 2000—the nation's local television stations. The industry took in at least $771 million from the sale of 1.2 million political ads in 2000, according to a report by the Campaign Media Analysis Group (CMAG)....This was a five-fold increase over the amount of political ad spending in 1980.

Several factors have fueled this rapid growth. For candidates, broadcast TV has long been the most important and widely watched medium for communicating with voters. However, a reduction in political coverage by broadcasters and the desire by candidates to control their message has led candidates more than ever to rely on paid ads to communicate with voters via television. The continuing fragmentation of audiences has also played a role. Even as broadcast channels lose viewers to cable and the Internet, they alone are able to offer candidates the ability to reach a broad audience (albeit not as broad as it once was). In a universe made up of niches, any medium that reaches across niches has added value. Finally, the surge in issue advocacy advertising, party advertising, and ballot initiative advertising—much of it financed by unlimited contributions from special interests—has added to the all-ads, all-the-time culture of politics on television.

The collapse of the LUC system

In 1971 Congress enacted the "Lowest Unit Charge" system to insulate candidates from price gouging by local television stations. The law requires that, as a condition of receiving their free licenses to use the public's airwaves, television stations must offer reduced rates to candidates in the closing weeks of all elections. Specifically, broadcasters must offer qualified candidates an LUC rate, the one given to the station's most favored product advertiser.

In order to comply with the law, local stations publish a candidate or LUC rate card in the weeks and months preceding all elections. But these rates come with a catch: Ads sold at the LUC rate can be preempted by the station, often without any notice, if another advertiser wants that

The four televised debates between presidential candidates John F. Kennedy and Richard M. Nixon in 1960 were a milestone in political broadcasts. As many as 120 million Americans watched at least one debate.

particular time slot and is willing to pay more for it. When this happens, candidates are entitled to have their money refunded or have their ad run at a later date. This is cold comfort for the candidate. Unlike many product advertisers, whose chief objective is to build brand loyalty over the long haul and who can therefore afford to be flexible about when their ads run, candidate advertisers need assurance their ads will run exactly when and where they place them.

> *"The stations know it's their way or the highway.... They've just become vacuum cleaners for political money."*
> —PETER FENN, DEMOCRAT MEDIA CONSULTANT

At these local stations, candidate ad prices rose from week to week as the fall campaign season unfolded. For example, in Philadelphia, a battleground for the presidential race and Senate campaigns in Pennsylvania, New Jersey, and Delaware. the LUC rate on CBS affiliate KYW for a preemptible, 30-second spot on the 6 p.m. local news climbed from $575 the week of Labor Day to $859 in the final week of the campaign—almost equaling the $900 nonpreemptible rate charged in early September. Even so, just a tiny fraction of candidate ads that aired during the fall campaign were sold at this ever-rising LUC rate; candidates were too concerned about getting bumped, so they purchased ads at the nonpreemptible rate, which itself was also rising. By the week before the election, a nonpreemptible spot on KYW's 6 p.m. news cost $1,065.

Clutter on the air

Issue advertising also contributed indirectly to an increase in advertising by candidates, who frequently felt compelled to respond to attacks launched against them by issue groups. Moreover, the sheer clutter of all political ads made each spot less effective—which, perversely, often induced candidates to buy even more spots. In Detroit, for example, 21 different political groups were on the air during the closing weeks of the fall campaign, forcing candidates to buy more ads than in previous years to get their message out. "There's so much

Issue groups lobby politicians on specific issues (such as abortion rights, religious tolerance, etc.). They have a constitutional right to buy airtime, though they lack the privileges, such as LUC rates, enjoyed by strictly political candidates.

Lazio lost the New York senatorial seat to Hillary Clinton in August 2000.

clutter on the air, you have to buy at levels that were unheard of a decade ago," [Rick Lazio's 2000 media buyer Brad] Mont said. "A month out from Election Day last year, I was buying 2000 gross rating points per week for Lazio in upstate markets. Ten years ago, for a big-ticket Senate race, I'd be buying maybe 800 GRPs per week at that stage. But it's just so hard to get a message out that you have to hammer, hammer, hammer."

Up through the early 1990s, the Federal Communications Commission (FCC) encouraged political candidates to lodge formal complaints against stations if they thought they were not getting the full advantage of the LUC system; some of these complaints resulted in broadcasters making substantial compensatory payments to candidates. Since 1995, however, the FCC has encouraged stations and candidates to work out their differences. As a result of this policy shift, there have been no formal complaints since 1995.... But while the LUC law remains on the books, its original intent—to peg candidate ad rates to discount prices paid by volume product advertisers—is no longer served. In practice, the system has come to mean that candidates' rates will be driven up sharply by the demand spike created by the election itself, but not quite to stratospheric levels paid by other advertisers during the campaign season.

The public interest obligations of broadcasters

Unlike newspapers, magazines, and other communications media, commercial broadcasters have always been public trustees. The Communications Act of 1934 ... granted broadcasters free and exclusive licenses to use the public airwaves ... on the condition that they agreed to serve "the public interest, convenience, and necessity." Regulations regarding political discourse always have been a part of this public interest standard, even though the most well-known of them—the Fairness Doctrine, which required stations to air competing views on controversial public issues—was repealed by the FCC during the Reagan administration. The political discourse rules that remain in effect are:

- Lowest Unit Charge—Guarantees federal, state, and local candidates the ad rates given to a station's most favored commercial advertiser;
- Reasonable Access—Requires stations to offer airtime to federal candidates who can afford to pay for it;
- Equal Time—Requires stations that have sold spots to one candidate to give his or her opponent the opportunity to buy comparable airtime at a comparable price.

In 1997 the federal government doubled the amount of spectrum space it licensed to television broadcasters in order to facilitate the industry's transition to digital technology. Estimates of the value of this additional spectrum space ranged up to $70 billion. Congress gave it to the broadcasters for free—provoking cries of protest about "corporate welfare" from liberals as well as free-market conservatives.

Against this backdrop, President Clinton appointed an advisory panel to assess how to update the public interest obligations of television broadcasters in the wake of this valuable gift of the public's assets. In the area of political discourse, the panel, which was made up of broadcasters, scholars, and public interest advocates, recommended that television broadcasters voluntarily air five minutes a night of candidate-centered discourse in the 30 days before all elections. However, during the 2000 campaign—the first national election conducted after the panel's recommendation—the typical local television station in a major market aired just 45 seconds of candidate-centered discourse per night in the month before November 7.... The major broadcast networks [aired] just 64 seconds a night of candidate-centered discourse per network.

The author points out an abuse of privilege by the television industry. Do you think government should force networks to donate airtime to political coverage?

Conclusion

In the Information Age, the most precious natural resource the public owns is the airwaves. For seven decades, the government has granted free and exclusive use of the most valuable portions of these airwaves to the broadcast industry, in return for its commitment to serve the public interest. During election campaigns, however, the industry has placed its own bottom line ahead of the public interest. It routinely gouges candidates on their ad rates, violating the spirit if not the letter of a 30-year-old law designed to protect candidates from such practices.

That law has never worked well. The FCC tried to close some of its loopholes in the early 1990s, but the gouging has grown ... in recent years, largely the result of the flood of soft money into the political process. Moreover, these dynamics are self-perpetuating. Just as more money creates the chance for more gouging, more gouging generates the need for more money. Given the dismal track record of price controls in market economies, it is hard to see how the LUC system can be fixed. The wiser course is to scrap it altogether and replace it with a ... system of mandatory free airtime for parties and candidates who meet qualifying thresholds and agree to an overall voluntary limit on campaign spending.

Soft money refers to funds donated to the nonfederal accounts of political parties. Such funds can be of unlimited size; many are used to subsidize the enormous media costs of electoral campaigns.

POLITICAL ADVERTISING REGULATION: AN UNCONSTITUTIONAL MENACE?
Stephen Bates

NO

Opening with a list of points can be an effective debating tool.

Last spring, you could have confidently made four predictions about the fall campaigns:

First, many candidates will rely heavily on negative television commercials. For guidance here, forget professional codes of ethics, party leaders' admonitions, and candidates' precampaign promises; look instead at recent history. In 1986 attack ads became so prevalent that the *Washington Post* labeled it the "Year of the Negative." In early 1988 several presidential candidates aired attack ads, and some hit home. In fact the demise of one candidate, Paul Simon, was widely attributed to his refusal (until it was too late) to air negative ads. In the fall, televised rhetoric in the presidential election is likely to be at least as harsh, and many races for lower offices will be much rougher. Inevitably a few campaigns … will air undeniably cheap shots.

The author lines up many of his opponents' claims so that he can go on to debunk them.

Second, more than one political columnist will point to those cheap shots and shake his head over the republic's future. Recall 1982, when David Broder fretted that negative campaigning could "cripple a healthy democracy." Recall 1984, when Jack Germond and Jules Witcover wrote that "voters are brainwashed, misled, and deceived." Third, opinion surveys will show that the vast majority of voters side with the columnists. In a 1983 Harris poll, 82 percent of the people polled said political ads are too negative. In an election year that percentage is likely to go even higher.

The fourth prediction follows from the first three: voters and policymakers will talk about regulating or banning political ads, especially negative ones. They will say that such ads divert money from people-oriented political activities, weaken the political parties, give unchecked power to sleazy political consultants, mislead and alienate viewers, reduce voter turnout, and debase political rhetoric.

Mark Shields is a political columnist and commentator who has worked with CNN and the Washington Post.

Such criticisms are off-base. In a modern political campaign, commercials constitute a candidate's "best opportunity," as Mark Shields has written, "to explain why the race is being made, how he differs from his opponent and what he wants to do in office." Proposals to clean up commercials would undercut that opportunity, perhaps eliminate it entirely. Voters would end up knowing less about candidates. But even if such commercial spots did harm the political system in clear-cut, demonstrable ways, the proposed regulations would almost certainly be ruled unconstitutional. Campaign speech, including political ads, enjoys maximal First Amendment protection. In short, practical considerations and the Constitution both argue against regulating political commercials.

Proposals for curbing political ads

In recent years ... proposals to regulate political candidates' TV commercials have been advanced. These proposals are likely to reappear this year. Some proposals would ban all ads. Other would ban only short (30- and 60-second) political ads. The proposals that are likely to get the most attention would ban production material in some or all ads. The ads could show only the speaker addressing the camera. They could no longer include "voice-overs; anonymous faces; actors playing the part of politicians; demagogic scene settings; devices such as graphs, charts and the like; talking cows; nuclear weapons and any other paraphernalia that would [add] emotive content to a political message."

This refers to a 1960s TV ad attacking Barry Goldwater. In it a child picked daisies against the backdrop of a nuclear explosion.

Political spots in the modern campaign

All of the criticisms of political television advertising fail under close scrutiny. The Inouye-Rudman bill states that campaign costs have increased to the point that they "threaten both access to and equity within the political process" and that television commercials are the principal reason for this state of affairs. True, the cost of political campaigns has risen steeply, and television advertisements seem to be the main culprit. In the general elections of 1952 (the first year in which TV ads played a significant role), television and radio costs accounted for 4.3 percent of total political spending. By 1986 the figure had increased more than fivefold, to 24.3 percent, and in some races well over half of expenditures went to TV. The amounts involved have become enormous: the 1984 presidential nominees spent about $50 million on TV time, and the 1986 House and Senate candidates spent about $86 million. Although those figures are huge, they are dwarfed by the airtime expenditures of commercial advertisers. In 1986 [U.S. manufacturer] Proctor & Gamble spent more than five times what the House and Senate candidates were spending on TV airtime: $456 million. If, as campaign finance scholar Herbert

The 2000 election campaign, which was eventually won by Republican George W. Bush, saw a dramatic increase in the amount of money spent on political advertising. According to one report, five times more was spent on TV ads in 2000 than in 1980.

Alexander has said, political advertising costs are the "tuition we pay for our education on the issues," then the question may be whether candidates are underspending, not overspending.

More important than absolute cost is cost-effectiveness, and in this regard television spots stand out. According to one estimate, a 1983 campaign spent about 0.5 cents to reach a voter by television. The cost for a newspaper ad was 1.5 cents; for direct mail, 25 cents. Out-of-home alternatives, such as political rallies, are even less efficient.

In 1996 the total of $400 million spent on TV airtime by U.S. candidates and political parties represented about 1 percent of that year's total broadcast TV ad revenues.

> *"The public always says that they hate negative ads, but the truth is, they are what seem to get the public's attention."*
> —CHERON BRYLSKI, PR SPECIALIST

In some campaigns, of course, media markets do not match electoral boundaries, thus making TV advertising inefficient. For this reason more than half of the candidates for the House use little or no television. For most large-area races, however, the situation is much as Mark Shields has described it: "Political television spots are the contemporary political campaign." The proposals to restrict political commercials would hamper the candidate's most efficient way of communicating with voters.

It is their access to a broad spectrum of viewers that makes TV ads effective in large-area races.

No magic bullets

There is nothing magical about political advertising, positive or negative, with or without production material. It does not overwhelm the viewer's natural skepticism or subvert his rational faculties. It provides information that some voters accept, some reject, some ignore, and some misunderstand. In most races … voters obtain information from other sources as well, particularly the news media. Of more than a hundred statewide races he has worked on, Robert Goodman believes his work has made the decisive difference in "only three or four." "The very best people in this business," Democratic consultant Robert Squier has said, "probably understand only about 5 to 7 percent of what it is that they do that works. The rest is all out there in the unknown."

Many critics say that TV ads can mislead people; here the author transfers blame to people who misunderstand the ads.

Summary

These two articles both agree on one point: Money matters. Amendments to election rules for many years have tried to eliminate the influence of cash from the electoral process, but it is difficult to eradicate entirely.

The article by Alliance for Better Campaigns (ABC) presents reasons why broadcast TV is now the medium of choice for political campaigning: It reaches large numbers of voters and gives candidates control over their ad content. But, says ABC, the system is widely abused, not least by the TV industry. The networks are leading political clients in a dance through the guidelines laid down by the Federal Communications Commission, specifically with regard to the Lowest Unit Charge system. Far from guaranteeing a political client its budget rate, a TV network charges what it likes, knowing that at critical points in a campaign a political client will pay whatever it takes. As a result, TV advertising is becoming the costly preserve of wealthier candidates and betraying the ideals of democracy, especially where soft-money funds are used. ABC concludes that the broadcasting industry is failing in its duty.

Stephen Bates argues against the regulation of political advertising on both practical and constitutional grounds. Not only would it deprive candidates of an effective medium through which to address their electorate, it would also be an infringement of First Amendment freedom of speech. To the charge that spending on political ads has risen through the roof, Bates replies that the sums involved nevertheless pale into insignificance against the TV budgets of, for example, pharmaceutical giants. If anything, more should be spent on airing political ideals, given the effectiveness of TV advertising. Bates diverts some responsibility toward viewers, some of whom misunderstand or misinterpret the ads; he also downplays the overall effect of TV advertising.

FURTHER INFORMATION:

Books:

Patterson, Thomas E. and Robert D. McClure, *The Unseeing Eye*. New York: G. P. Putnam's, 1976.

Articles:

Phillips, Leslie, "Voters Getting the Campaign They Want." *USA Today*, October 30, 1992.

Rabin, Phil, and Carolyn Myles, "TV Political Ads to Start Showing Viewers Who's Paying." *Washington Times*, March 18, 1992.

Useful websites:

www.uiowa.edu/~commstud/resources/pol_as.html
A useful page of media sources on the subject.

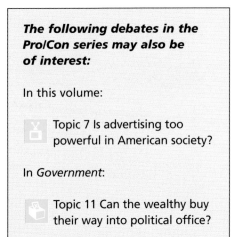

The following debates in the Pro/Con series may also be of interest:

In this volume:

Topic 7 Is advertising too powerful in American society?

In *Government*:

Topic 11 Can the wealthy buy their way into political office?

IS THERE TOO MUCH POLITICAL ADVERTISING?

YES: The gloss on political ads tends to mask a candidate's real political concerns

YES: There should be federal control to clamp down on widespread malpractice and misrepresentation

GET THE MESSAGE
Do political ads mislead the public about the real issues?

FREE SPEECH
Should the government regulate political advertising?

NO: The public is smart enough to discern good from bad; TV ads are an invaluable vehicle for political dissemination

NO: Political advertising is protected by the First Amendment; to control it would be unconstitutional

IS THERE TOO MUCH POLITICAL ADVERTISING?

KEY POINTS

YES: Advertising is so costly that only the wealthiest candidates can afford TV ad campaigns; democracy suffers as a result

YES: The only people to make money out of the ads are the advertisers themselves, who flaunt FCC guidelines

PRICE OF SUCCESS
Do political ads cost too much and benefit wealthy candidates?

NO: In some countries parties pool resources for central campaigns; this strategy could work in the United States

NO: On a cost-per-voter basis TV campaigns can be cheaper than press, direct mail, and rallies

PRESENTATION SKILLS

The Roman orator Cicero laid down three duties for a speaker: to be clear, to be interesting, and to be convincing. He argued that if an orator followed these rules, he or she would keep the audience's attention and convince it of anything. A speaker's delivery and body language are also very important.

GOOD PRESENTATION

The following is a list of key factors in making a good presentation:

1. Determining the purpose
2. Picking a topic for debate
3. Researching the topic
4. Identifying the audience
5. Substantiating ideas
6. Defining ideas
7. Using relevant visual aids
8. Delivery and body language

We will look at each aspect in a little more detail.

1. Determining the purpose

Consider the purpose of the speech you are giving. Is it for an end-of-year report, a debate, or a celebration of some kind? Verifying the location, time of the speech, and the type of audience will help you achieve that end.
There are three main types of speech:
• Informative—usually reports or briefings that inform the audience about a new topic in a concise, instructive way.
• Persuasive—the type of speech used during a debate. Its aim is to convince the audience of a proposition of fact (where the audience has to choose the truth), policy (recommending a specific course of action), or value (usually examining the worth of something or someone).
• Entertaining—usually aims to amuse or entertain, such as a wedding speech.

2. Picking a topic for debate

The topic you pick can be something that you are interested in, a debate subject that has been set, or something you have an in-depth knowledge of. You could also pick the topic from the audience's interests—the more it appeals to the audience, the better the speech will be received.

3. Researching the topic

You can research the subject by referring to books, newspapers, reference works, periodicals, and the Internet. Another method of research might be to conduct interviews with people. See *Government, Research Skills*, pages 58–59.

4. Identifying the audience

The aim of any speaker is to be perceived as credible and knowledgeable about the topic he or she is discussing. This depends partly on the speaker's ability to identify and adapt to any type of audience. The makeup of the audience depends on variables such as age, occupation, religion, ethnic background, socioeconomic status, gender, education, and political views. The speaker must consider the audience's wants, reactions, and behavior and be able to identify with them. He or she must also be able to adapt and communicate the knowledge to his or her audience.

5. Substantiating ideas
Using facts, statistics, quotations, anecdotes, and testimonials will give your argument credence. Substantiating points in this way confirms that you have thoroughly researched your topic. Telling a story connected with the subject is another way of conveying ideas and is also a useful tool for keeping an audience's attention. Humor can also be a good way of relaying information and entertaining the audience but should be used judiciously.

6. Defining ideas
It is essential that you keep to a cohesive, structured plan in your speech. The introduction and conclusion are very important and should grab the audience's attention, introduce/summarize the topic, and present/summarize the main ideas. In the case of a debate or a persuasive speech use the problem/solution strategy in the main body of your speech. Use the first part of your speech to define the problem and the latter half to provide solutions. Similarly, the cause/effect strategy is useful. Outline the cause of the problem first—for example, the causes of social violence in the United States—and then state the effects of the problem.

7. Visual aids
Aids can include maps, diagrams, sketches, actual people, photos, films, and posters. They help enhance the audience's understanding, provide speaker credibility, and help the speech have a lasting effect.

8. Delivery and body language
- Be aware of delivery—always be cool, rational, and reasoned when speaking.
- Body language—try to appear relaxed, avoid excessive hand movements, punching the air or pointing.
- Language—keep your language simple, clear, and avoid expletives.
- Speak truthfully—that is, don't lie.
- Use audacious but not slanderous statements to attract your audience.
- Be humorous but not cruel.
- Avoid excessive emotion, or be emotive with restraint.
- Use credible sources (see visual aids, above).
- Be concise, clear, and factual.

Presentation skills will help you in every area of your life. They are particularly relevant in the debating arena.

Topic 12
SHOULD THE INTERNET BE POLICED?

YES

"AGAINST RACIAL DISCRIMINATION ON THE INTERNET"
WWW.HUD.GOV/LIBRARY/BOOKSHELF18/PRESSREL/PR00-165.HTML
DEPARTMENT OF HOUSING AND URBAN DEVELOPMENT

NO

"CENSORSHIP IN A BOX:
WHY BLOCKING SOFTWARE IS WRONG FOR PUBLIC LIBRARIES"
AMERICAN CIVIL LIBERTIES UNION REPORT, 1998

INTRODUCTION

The right to freedom of speech is protected by the First Amendment in the United States, but the media are subject to many types of censorship. Generally speaking, electronic media that are licensed by the government, such as radio and television stations, can be restricted more broadly than newspapers, magazines, and cable television. Licensed broadcasting stations use the "people's airwaves." Since those signals come into the house freely, children could be exposed to material that their parents might not want them to see or hear. We pay for newspapers, magazines, and cable, so these media have more freedom from censorship than broadcasting stations.

Should the Internet be regulated like broadcasting, or should it be completely unrestricted? Naturally, people are divided on this issue, but the Supreme Court made a determination in the case of *Reno v. American Civil Liberties Union* when it said, "Unlike communications received by radio or television, the receipt of information on the Internet requires a series of affirmative steps more deliberate and directed than merely turning a dial. A child requires some sophistication and the ability to read in order to retrieve material and thereby to use the Internet unattended."

The court decided that the Internet was not really like broadcasting because surfing the Web required many conscious steps for a person to receive information and that fewer restrictions should be placed on Internet communication. Some groups contest this assertion, and in fall 2000 members of Congress responded by sponsoring a new bill called the Children's Internet Protection Act. This act, which went into effect in April 2001, stops federal funding to schools and libraries if the library does not provide some kind of blocking software on its general access computers. Currently the federal government provides funds so that "qualified" libraries can pay the costs of accessing the Internet. Libraries that choose not to install blocking software would therefore not be eligible for federal telecommunication funds.

> *"I'm afraid of a world where somebody exceedingly clever could wipe all the information off everybody's computers."*
>
> —A. S. BYATT, WRITER

Both the American Library Association and the American Civil Liberties Union (ACLU) oppose the act for a variety of reasons. Some First Amendment supporters say that the software is not advanced enough to be usable, even though those who want controls say that the newest generation of software is a huge improvement over early blocking programs. Those opposing censorship believe that the First Amendment wording is absolutely clear: "Congress shall make no law … abridging the freedom of speech, or of the press." Supreme Court Justice Oliver Wendel Holmes said that the best test of truth is the power of a thought to get accepted in the competition of the market. The debate is not yet over.

The United States has many laws that restrict speech, and as a society we have come to accept them. For example, as a prank you cannot yell "Fire!" in a crowded theater, nor can you advocate violent overthrow of the government or taking lives. These restrictions are meant to preserve order and protect the common good. There is another classification of restricted speech—pornography—which is classified as "obscene," and which receives no First Amendment protection. Child pornography is illegal either in print or on the Internet because it is considered obscene. Thus the debate about what can and cannot be regulated continues as each new technology provides us with new challenges.

The Internet has thousands of sex- and violence-related sites, and it is clear that parents have legitimate concerns about protecting children from viewing such sites. While the issue of Net censorship generally seems to center around the question of whether there ought to be blocking programs to protect children from viewing certain sites, perhaps the focus of the debate should actually be broader.

The following two articles provide opposing views on the question of internet policing. In the first the case against a neo-Nazi group that made death threats against a fair housing advocate on its Website is outlined, and a full account of the justice system's response is given. There is also an overview of the Children's Internet Protection Act that restricts access to material harmful to minors.

In the second article the American Civil Liberties Union argues that censoring the Net by using blocking software is a direct violation of the First Amendment. It concedes that blocking software may be suitable for parents to use, but argues that it is unconstitutional for the government to be judging what is offensive and controversial by requiring libraries and schools to use the software.

AGAINST RACIAL DISCRIMINATION ON THE INTERNET
Department of Housing and Urban Development

YES

A neo-Nazi group is a modern-day political organization that is inspired by the racist beliefs of the German Nazi Party led by Adolf Hitler from the 1920s until 1945. The prefix "neo" means "new" or "revived."

Housing and Urban Development Secretary Andrew Cuomo said today that an administrative law judge's decision to award more than $1.1 million in damages to a fair housing advocate who received death threats by a hate group leader on his web site "sends a clear message that racial discrimination on the Internet will not be tolerated."

The decision stems from threats made by Ryan Wilson and his Philadelphia neo-Nazi group ALPHA HQ against Bonnie Jouhari and her teenage daughter. Jouhari's job was to promote fair housing, including helping housing discrimination victims file complaints under the Fair Housing Act. HUD brought the suit against Wilson and his group for violating the Act. "The Clinton Administration will not permit the Internet to be used as an open sore for hate, prejudice and bigotry," Cuomo said. "And HUD means business when it comes to enforcing the nation's fair housing laws. If you violate them, even in cyber-space, you will pay the price."

What problems can you see in policing the Internet? Since cyber-space crosses all national and international frontiers, in what ways can an individual nation-state offer protection to its citizens?

Damages paid for emotional stress

Cuomo said that the award—which totaled $1,166,863—includes the largest emotional distress award by a court to a single victim in a fair housing case—$750,000 was awarded to Jouhari's daughter. It is also one of only a few published decisions involving emotional distress damages from Internet hate. In his decision Chief Administrative Law Judge Alan W. Heifetz wrote: "If dedicated and talented fair housing advocates and their families may be targeted, intimidated, and harassed with impunity, then the enforcement mechanism of that Act will be rendered impotent."

Jouhari, who is white, was a fair housing specialist at the Reading-Berks Human Relations Council in Reading, PA. She was also the founder and chairperson of the Hate Crimes Task Force for Berks County, PA, and served on the Governor's Interagency Task Force on civil tension.

Jouhari and her daughter, Danielle, fled their home near Reading, PA, after the threats and moved to Washington State.

The two have since moved several times and now reside in an undisclosed location.

In January, Cuomo announced that HUD had charged Wilson and ALPHA HQ with violating the Fair Housing Act. The charge was a result of threats posted on Wilson's Internet web site and statements made by him in a TV interview against Jouhari in the summer of 1998.

Wilson's web site carried Jouhari's picture, labeled her a "race traitor" and threatened to lynch traitors "from the nearest tree or lamp post." The site also carried an animated picture of Jouhari's office being blown up by explosives. Wilson also stated on his web site that Jouhari had a "mongrel" daughter, a reference to the fact that her daughter's father is black. The web site has since been removed from the Internet as the result of a Pennsylvania state court order.

To "lynch" someone means to put them to death without legal authority. In the past lynching usually involved a mob that took it upon themselves to hang a person they felt to be guilty of a crime without allowing that person any recourse to the justice system.

On February 29, Judge Heifetz issued a default decision against Wilson and ALPHA HQ because Wilson failed to respond to the housing discrimination charge within 30 days, as required under law. Following that ruling, a hearing was held in April in Philadelphia to determine if Wilson must pay damages to Jouhari and her daughter, and penalties to the federal government.

In the decision announced today, Judge Heifetz noted that Jouhari and her daughter suffered not only a loss of employment income, but emotional distress "through a relentless campaign of domestic terrorism" over a two-year period. A forensic psychologist testified the daughter was suffering from severe Post-Traumatic Stress Disorder with Delayed Onset, triggered by her exposure to the threats on the ALPHA HQ web site and the events that followed.

In addition to the monetary relief, the judge has prohibited Ryan Wilson and ALPHA HQ from posting, publishing, or distributing in any public forum (including the Internet) any pictures or references of Jouhari or her daughter. Wilson is also prohibited from discriminating against Jouhari and her daughter or anyone associated with them, and from retaliating against them or anyone else because of their case.

Equal protection for all Americans

According to Rev. Jesse Jackson, "The scales of justice must provide equal protection under the law for all Americans. When leaders like Secretary Cuomo take their oath of office seriously and enforce the law to its full extent, it serves as a deterrent to those who challenge the system."

"Secretary Cuomo is certainly a hero to me," Ms. Jouhari said. "He stuck his neck out to help us. I hope that today's

Rev. Jesse Jackson is the most politically influential black leader in the United States today. Having formed the National Rainbow Coalition, a liberal political group, in 1984 Jackson became the first black politician to run a major national campaign for the office of president.

COMMENTARY: The Children's Internet Protection Act

The Children's Internet Protection Act (CIPA) came into effect in the United States in April 2001. Under the terms of the act any school or library that receives government funding for Internet access must restrict access to visual material on the Net that is deemed to be obscene, child pornography, or harmful to minors. In March 2001 the American Library Association (ALA) and the American Civil Liberties Union (ACLU) filed a lawsuit against the CIPA, saying that it violated the First Amendment. Conservative groups such as Concerned Women for America (CWA) have spoken out against the lawsuit. One CWA member wrote: "The ALA and the ACLU are accomplices with the worst kind of criminals by trying to undo the CIPA."

Many children have easy access to computers and the Internet, and this makes them particularly vulnerable to offensive material located on the Net.

decision serves as a deterrent to anyone else who thinks they can get away with such torture. That's been my objective." Elizabeth Kleinberg, legal representative for Jouhari added, "It was critically important that HUD act decisively in this case. Unless those who champion the rights of others, like Ms. Jouhari, are themselves protected, the enforcement of civil rights laws will be greatly compromised." Wilson has 15 days from today's decision to file an appeal to the Secretary of HUD, who routinely designates a HUD official to act on ALJ decisions. Parties may appeal a final HUD decision to the Third Circuit Court of Appeals.

Civil rights laws are intended to prevent racial discrimination in U.S. society. The struggle to pass such laws was a long and turbulent one. The Fair Housing Act was part of the Civil Rights Act of 1968, which outlawed racial discrimination in the sale or rental of housing.

Discrimination outlawed by Fair Housing Act

The Fair Housing Act bars housing discrimination on the basis of race, color, religion, sex, disability, family status and national origin. It covers the sale, rental, financing and advertising of almost all housing in the nation. After a charge is filed, it is heard by an ALJ, unless a party asks that it be heard in federal court. HUD, like many other federal agencies, has [judges] who make independent decisions in administrative law matters before the Department, such as fair housing cases.

The Ku Klux Klan is a secret organization committed to white supremacy over all other groups.

This is the second victory HUD has won for Jouhari and her daughter. In May, the United Klans of America and Roy Frankhauser, a self-described chaplain of the Ku Klux Klan, settled a complaint in which he was charged with threatening Jouhari in 1998. Frankhauser agreed to pay damages, to publicly apologize to Jouhari and her daughter, and to perform 1,000 hours of community service. He also agreed to display a HUD Fair Housing poster at his house and broadcast HUD fair housing public service announcements as part of his "White Forum" public access television show..

The crime of racial discrimination can be punished in a variety of different ways. Which ones do you think might prove most effective in helping a person change his or her racist views? Can you think of any other useful measures?

Damages and penalties in the decision

- $750,000 in emotional distress damages to Jouhari's daughter
- $250,000 in emotional distress damages to Jouhari
- $77,793.75 for future therapeutic expenses and lost wages to the daughter
- $33,683.64 in tangible damages, including relocation expenses, salary loss, and future
- Therapeutic expenses for Jouhari
- $33,000 in civil penalties to be paid by Wilson
- $22,000 in civil penalties to be paid by Wilson, doing business as ALPHA HQ
- $385 in sanctions to be paid by Wilson for failing to appear at scheduled depositions

CENSORSHIP IN A BOX
American Civil Liberties Union (ACLU)

NO

In libraries and schools across the nation, the Internet is rapidly becoming an essential tool for learning and communication. According to the American Library Association, of the nearly 9,000 public libraries in America, 60.4 percent offer Internet access to the public, up from 27.8 percent in 1996. And a recent survey of 1,400 teachers revealed that almost half use the Internet as a teaching tool. But today, unfettered access to the Internet is being threatened by the proliferation of blocking software in libraries.

For more information on blocking software take a look at www.cityscope.net/blocking/html.

In 1995, the National Telecommunications and Information Administration of the U.S. Department of Commerce concluded that:

> *Public libraries can play a vital role in assuring that advanced information services are universally available to all segments of the American population on an equitable basis. Just as libraries traditionally made available the marvels and imagination of the human mind to all, libraries of the future are planning to allow everyone to participate in the electronic renaissance.*

Today, the dream of universal access will remain only a dream if politicians force libraries and other institutions to use blocking software whenever patrons access the Internet. Blocking software prevents users from accessing a wide range of valuable information, including such topics as art, literature, women's health, politics, religion, and free speech. Without free and unfettered access to the Internet, this exciting new medium could become, for many Americans, little more than a souped-up, G-rated television network.

Censorship in a box

Like any technology, blocking software can be used for constructive or destructive purposes. In the hands of parents and others who voluntarily use it, it is a tool that can be somewhat useful in blocking access to some inappropriate material online. But in the hands of government, blocking software is nothing more than censorship in a box. The ACLU believes that government has a necessary role to play in promoting universal Internet access. But that role should focus on expanding, not restricting, access to online speech.

Reno v. ACLU: A momentous decision

Our vision of an uncensored Internet was clearly shared by the U.S. Supreme Court when it struck down the 1996 Communications Decency Act (CDA), a federal law that outlawed "indecent" communications online.

The ACLU and 19 other organizations initiated a constitutional challenge to the CDA in February 1996.

Ruling unanimously in *Reno v. ACLU*, the Court declared the Internet to be a free speech zone, deserving of at least as much First Amendment protection as that afforded to books, newspapers, and magazines. The government, the Court said, can no more restrict a person's access to words or images on the Internet than it could be allowed to snatch a book out of a reader's hands in the library, or cover over a statue of a nude in a museum.

The nine Justices were clearly persuaded by the unique nature of the medium itself, citing with approval the lower federal court's conclusion that the Internet is "the most participatory form of mass speech yet developed," entitled to "the highest protection from governmental intrusion." The Internet, the Court concluded, is like "a vast library including millions of readily available and indexed publications," the content of which "is as diverse as human thought."

Blocking software: For parents, not the government

In striking down the CDA on constitutional grounds, the Supreme Court emphasized that if a statute burdens adult speech—as any censorship law must—it "is unacceptable if less restrictive alternatives were available."

Commenting on the availability of user-based blocking software as a possible alternative, the Court concluded that the use of such software was appropriate for parents. Blocking software, the Court wrote, is a "reasonably effective method by which parents can prevent their children from accessing material which the parents believe is inappropriate."

The rest of the Court's decision firmly holds that government censorship of the Internet violates the First Amendment, and that holding applies to government use of blocking software just as it applied when the Court struck down the CDA's criminal ban.

In the months since that ruling, the blocking software market has experienced explosive growth, as parents exercise their prerogative to guide their children's Internet experience. According to analysts at International Data Corporation, a technology consulting firm, software makers sold an estimated $14 million in blocking software last year, and over the next three years, sales of blocking products are expected to grow to more than $75 million.

An increasing number of city and county library boards have recently forced libraries to install blocking programs, over the objections of the American Library Association and library patrons, and the use of blocking software in libraries is fast becoming the biggest free speech controversy since the legal challenge to the CDA.

What kind of speech is being blocked?

Most blocking software prevents access to sites based on criteria provided by the vendor. To conduct site-based blocking, a vendor establishes criteria to identify specified categories of speech on the Internet and configures the blocking software to block sites containing those categories of speech. Some Internet blocking software blocks as few as six categories of information, while others block many more.

In a study conducted by the Electronic Privacy Information Center (EPIC) a "family-friendly" search engine prevented access to almost 90 percent of relevant material on the Net.

Blocked categories may include hate speech, criminal activity, sexually explicit speech, "adult" speech, violent speech, religious speech, and even sports and entertainment.

Using its list of criteria, the software vendor compiles and maintains lists of "unacceptable" sites. Some software vendors employ individuals who browse the Internet for sites to block. Others use automated searching tools to identify which sites to block. These methods may be used in combination ....

Examples of the inaccuracy of blocking software are highlighted. How does this help support the point being made?

Typical examples of blocked words and letters include "xxx," which blocks out Superbowl XXX sites; "breast," which blocks website and discussion groups about breast cancer; and the consecutive letters "s," "e," and "x," which block sites containing the words "sexton" and "Mars exploration," among many others. Some software blocks categories of expression along blatantly ideological lines, such as information about feminism or gay and lesbian issues. Yet most websites offering opposing views on these issues are not blocked. For example, the same software does not block sites expressing opposition to homosexuality and women working outside the home.

Clearly, the answer to blocking based on ideological viewpoint is not more blocking, any more than the answer to unpopular speech is to prevent everyone from speaking, because then no viewpoint of any kind will be heard. The American Family Association (AFA), a conservative religious organization, recently learned this lesson when it found that

CyberPatrol, a popular brand of blocking software, had placed AFA on its "Cybernot" list because of the group's opposition to homosexuality.

Blocked for intolerance

The AFA's site was blocked under the category "intolerance," defined as "pictures or text advocating prejudice or discrimination against any race, color, national origin, religion, disability or handicap, gender or sexual orientation. Any picture or text that elevates one group over another. Also includes intolerance jokes or slurs." Other "Cybernot" categories include "violence/profanity," "nudity," "sexual acts," "satanic/cult," and "drugs/drug culture."

In a May 28 news release excoriating CyberPatrol, AFA said, "CyberPatrol has elected to block the AFA website with their filter because we have simply taken an opposing viewpoint to the political and cultural agenda of the homosexual rights movement." As one AFA spokesman told reporters, "Basically we're being blocked for free speech."

The AFA said they are planning to appeal the blocking decision at a June 9 meeting of CyberPatrol's Cybernot Oversight Committee, but expressed doubt that the decision would be overturned. The conservative Family Research Council (FRC) also joined in the fight, saying they had "learned that the Gay Lesbian Alliance Against Defamation (GLAAD) is a charter member of CyberPatrol's oversight committee," and that "it was pressure by GLAAD that turned CyberPatrol around." Until now, AFA, FRC, and similar groups had been strong advocates for filtering software, and AFA has even assisted in the marketing of another product, X-Stop. AFA has said that they still support blocking but believe their group was unfairly singled out.

Indeed, as the AFA and others have learned, there is no avoiding the fact that somebody out there is making judgments about what is offensive and controversial, judgments that may not coincide with their own. The First Amendment exists precisely to protect the most offensive and controversial speech from government suppression. If blocking software is made mandatory in schools and libraries, that "somebody" making the judgments becomes the government.

The AFA is an organization that is in favor of blocking software, yet it has been blocked itself by a blocking software company. Can you think of other organizations that might find themselves in a similar position?

The AFA has its own filtering software that it sells on its site (www.afa.net). The program does not even have an adult override.

Summary

Both essays provide an insight into the troubling nature of censorship. The Founders did not want government to determine what information should be available to Americans, and the First Amendment was added to the Constitution to prevent this happening. Pornography, hateful speech, acts of school-related violence, and the existence of the Internet create a far different America than anything the Founders could have ever imagined. Would the framers of the Constitution advocate an open Internet, or would they consider filtering or ratings to be acceptable curtailments?

In the first article the Department of Housing and Urban Development adopt a factual approach in outlining the issues raised by cyber-crime. It details the response of the U.S. justice system and the government to a case of racial hatred and discrimination perpetrated by a neo-Nazi group against a fair housing advocate and her child. The judge in the case, Alan W. Heifetz, rules that users of the Internet for the purposes of intimidation and harassment are to be treated in the same way, under law, as would any other criminal. The article also highlights the Children's Internet Protection Act that restricts access to material harmful to minors. The American Civil Liberties Union (ACLU) takes the opposing viewpoint that any moves to restrict access to the Net is a violation of the First Amendment. The government's role should be to expand access to online speech, it says. The authors point out that blocking software is unsophisticated in that it will sometimes block inoffensive sites, and that there is an ideological bias that favors conservative, "family values" sites—but, as the article points out, this bias can sometimes backfire on such groups, as it did with the American Family Association.

FURTHER INFORMATION:

Books:

Friedman, Samuel Joshua, *Children and the World Wide Web*. Lanham, MD: University Press of America, 2000.

Kolbert, Kathryn and Zak Mettger (editors), *Justice Talking: Censoring the Web*. New York: New Press, 2001.

Peck, Robert S., *Libraries, the First Amendment and Cyberspace: What You Need to Know*. Chicago: ALA Editions, 1999.

Wallace, J. and M. Mangan, *Sex, Laws and Cyberspace*. New York: Henry Holt & Co., 1997.

Useful websites:

www.ala.org
American Library Association website
www.epic.org/filters&freedom/

"Filters and Freedom: Free Speech Perspectives on Internet Content Controls," edited by David L. Sobel.

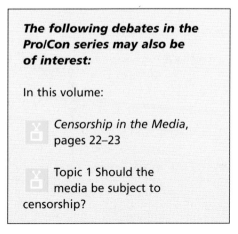

The following debates in the Pro/Con series may also be of interest:

In this volume:

Censorship in the Media, pages 22–23

Topic 1 Should the media be subject to censorship?

SHOULD THE INTERNET
BE POLICED?

YES: Some material on the Net is offensive, and restricting access, particularly to children, is appropriate

YES: Civil libertarians put children at risk by placing freedom of expression first

PROTECTING USERS
Should users be protected from certain material?

FREEDOM OF EXPRESSION
Is restricting access more important than freedom of expression?

NO: Restricting access to the Internet is an infringement of the First Amendment

NO: Blocking software is appropriate for parents but not for government

SHOULD THE INTERNET BE POLICED?
KEY POINTS

YES: Crimes are committed on the Net every day, and by not policing it, we condone those crimes

YES: The government has a responsibility to protect its citizens from harm. The same laws that apply in the everyday world should also apply in cyber-space.

THE GOVERNMENT
Should the government take an active role in policing the Net?

NO: The First Amendment exists to protect offensive and controversial speech from government suppression

NO: By enforcing blocking software in public libraries the Net will turn into nothing more than G-rated TV

Topic 13
WILL THE INTERNET CREATE A GLOBAL CULTURE?

YES
"GLOBALIZING THE INTERNET"
WWW.GUARDIANUNLIMITED.CO.UK
SUNDER KATWALA

NO
"ELECTRONIC EMPIRE"
COMMUNICATIONS OF THE ACM, MARCH 2001
ANTHONY M. TOWNSEND AND JAMES T. BENNETT

INTRODUCTION

At the start of the 21st century one of the most hotly debated cultural and economic phenomena was globalization. The word refers to the spread of multinational companies, products, music, TV shows, and similar items throughout the world, regardless of national boundaries. For some people this is a nightmare vision: In economic terms western multinationals will exploit the developing world for cheap labor and materials; in cultural terms western entertainment—particularly American movies, music, or TV shows—will swamp and eventually destroy more regional or experimental cultural traditions. Other people, however, are excited by the prospect of overcoming national barriers, especially with regard to culture and knowledge. They imagine a world in which all scholars or artists are part of a single community, and access to knowledge is open to all.

The idea of such a cultural unity is not new. Many people point out that in previous ages—such as the Renaissance in Europe—scholars throughout the Christian world were linked in a vast network reinforced by the use of Latin as a common language and the recent introduction of printing. More recently media scholar Marshall McLuhan coined a famous phrase of the 1960s, the "global village." McLuhan saw that national mass media, particularly television, had a tendency to erase some of the differences in regional culture that existed in the United States. Communication satellites had started to become a reality, and McLuhan concluded that it would soon be possible to receive and transmit TV signals around the world. The effect would be to make the world smaller and more uniform, a global village.

McLuhan's vision of a worldwide television network never emerged, for a number of reasons. First, media systems tend to be nationally based. There are different models of media control in different countries. American media, for example, are privately owned and sponsored by advertising, but the same does not hold around the world. Most developing countries, for instance, have small government-owned, nationalized media with limited choices; a number of other countries still try to control their media. China, for example, limits its citizens' access to foreign media. National boundaries can still act as barriers to the free flow of information.

Could it be possible, however, that the Internet will become a vehicle for the growth of global culture? The Internet has advantages over other media. It is not owned by any one country or organization. Censorship is more difficult because the Internet was designed to allow many different computer systems to distribute information broadly. If a server's message is blocked at one point, information packets can be rerouted via alternative networks.

"[The Internet is] the most participatory form of mass speech yet developed … a never-ending worldwide conversation."

—FEDERAL COURT JUDGES, PENNSYLVANIA, 1996

In the United States many First Amendment supporters believe that there ought to be completely free access to information on the Internet. In 1996 judges in the federal court in Pennsylvania ruled that the Communications Decency Act, which aimed to regulate the Internet, represented an unconstitutional infringement on free speech. Free access to information on the Internet could make cyberspace a place of great diversity, bridging political, geographic, and cultural barriers.

But even if a "global village" is attainable, is it desirable? Some people are concerned about the influence that major media enterprises, such as AOL–Time/Warner, could have on developing cultures. Critics such as media scholar Nicholas Garnham are concerned that a few media companies will exert too much control over the flow of information around the world. Likewise, would familiarity with the American consumer lifestyle, gained via Internet access, fundamentally harm the cultures of developing nations?

The articles in this section reflect two divergent points of view regarding the globalization of culture. First, Sunder Katwala argues that the free flow of information allowed by access to the Internet has transformed the global economy, putting oppressive political regimes under greater pressure to liberalize in order to take part in the market-based global economy. Productivity is often technologically driven, Katwala argues, which means that education will become the most important economic policy. The authors of the second piece take a different point of view, arguing that, technology aside, there will be other factors at play. Businesses and people need nations to protect and project their interests, they say. The authors' gloomy prediction is that control of Internet content to manipulate consumption and ideology will transform the Internet into another mechanism of coercion and control.

GLOBALIZING THE INTERNET
Sunder Katwala

YES

Like all technologies, the impact of the Internet will depend on the uses to which our societies put it. It will be used for repression and liberation, for commerce and community. But not all technologies are neutral. The Internet has a profoundly globalizing, flattening, and democratizing bias, bringing societies closer together, in anything from commerce to cultural exchange.

What is the nature of the Internet? Its primary impact is to speed up the flow of information, making the cost of creating barriers to these information flows much higher, and ultimately impossible to police; levelling playing fields by making more and more information previously available to an elite few accessible to all. It completes a long process of technological advance from the telegraph to the fax to email, whereby global communication could become possible, faster and then instantaneous. It offers everybody online a range of information that previously required the resources of a research department of a large multinational. And, following a century in which states have poured resources into mighty instruments of coercion and control, we enter an age in which the mightiest of regimes seems powerless in the face of a click of a mouse.

Do you think the Internet will make information accessible to all? Look at the Internet usage figures in the box on page 175, and calculate the percentage of people using the Internet compared to total population for each region. What do the results tell you?

The powerful are under greater scrutiny
Information is power, it has been said, and with some justice, although this is not the whole story. A wider dispersal of information, within societies and between them, does not mean the end of political tyranny or, indeed, the ability of the powerful to seek to manipulate market processes to their own ends. But those who seek to maintain concentrations of economic or political control will have to do so under much greater scrutiny. Alternative accounts—both sides of the story—will be much more widely available.

The broad social and economic impact of this could be immense. There is a tendency to understate these because, in the late 1990s, the narrow economic impact of the Internet was overstated. The dot.com phenomenon was another example of the "stock market" bubble, repeated periodically over centuries, and which once saw Dutch "tulipmania," with tulip bulbs valued higher than gold. The Internet was never going to turn the rules of economics on their head, making the aim of the game to secure the largest losses possible. But the more profound change will come not because the Internet rewrites the economic rule book or puts our societies onto an entirely new path. In fact, the Internet's impact will be greater because it does not entirely cause the transformations it looks set to facilitate—these are more powerful because they reinforce, speed up, and entrench the most important aspects of social and economic change.

In the global political economy, the fall of the Berlin Wall in 1989 was the symbol for the failure of collectivist, state-planned economic management. There are different models of the market economy, but all successful economies will be market-based. More subtly, large developing countries like India and China that had sought to develop more self-sufficiently outside the global economy now sought to liberalize and integrate within it.

Transforming the global economy

The Internet has an important effect because of the nature of this new global economy. The technological transformation of both economies and the financial markets created capital flows across borders on an unprecedented scale, dramatically transforming ideas about the global economy. The barriers to entry to global markets is lowered (a well-chosen URL and the search engine can decrease the cost of numerous different national marketing campaigns), and the ability of consumers to compare prices, even across borders, grows.

While we traditionally think of international economic activity as trading produce or manufactured goods, the Internet has facilitated a much more rapid growth in the global trade in services, worth over $40 billion of United States exports—from software and entertainment to financial and professional services. This has also changed the outlook of corporations. The largest—from General Motors in the U.S. to BMW in Germany—saw themselves primarily as national champions. Now, across economic sectors, major cross-border mergers are commonplace for some of the world's largest firms like Daimler-Chrysler. This has become possible because faster communication enables much larger companies to share information internally more widely. They are also much "flatter" organizations—a "knowledge economy" requires those with the knowhow to make more decisions; the old hierarchical corporation has too many of the defects of the state-planned economy.

Find out what other cross-border mergers have taken place recently, either in the United States or elsewhere.

COMMENTARY: McLuhan's global village

The Canadian media scholar Marshall McLuhan, who theorized the development of the "global village."

The Canadian media scholar Marshall McLuhan (1911–1980) was born in Edmonton, Alberta, and studied at Manitoba and Cambridge universities. His first book, *The Mechanical Bride* (1951), analyzed advertising and propaganda methods. In 1953 he founded the journal *Explorations* to publish work on language and media.

In his book *Understanding Media* (1964) McLuhan came up with his famous observation "The medium is the message." By this he meant that the form of a medium can be more important than its content: *What* is being said is influenced by *how* it is said.

In 1967 McLuhan formulated another influential concept: "Time has ceased; 'space' has vanished. We now live in a global village … a simultaneous happening." The vital role in creating this global village, McLuhan predicted, would be played by the mass media. In some ways the growth of the Internet has made the global village even more of a reality. Webcams allow us to watch live events as they happen; websites give us news that is only minutes old; e-mail enables us to write to someone on the other side of the world and get a reply within seconds.

Some people argue, however, that the dominance of western, particularly U.S., media does not create the shared meanings that a global village or culture implies. The United States, for example, exports more television programs than any other country in the world. More people in North America use the Internet than in any other region, and the majority of websites are of American provenance.

Critics see this dominance as leading to a kind of cultural imperialism rather than a global village. The Internet excludes many people from developing countries who have no access to computers and also people in countries such as Afghanistan, where the Internet has been banned. The power and influence of the media lie mainly with a limited number of western corporate interests. Although the media do have the ability to transform political and cultural values throughout the world, some people argue that it does not necessarily follow that we are all living in a homogenized "global village."

This shift in the focus of economic activity—with productivity often technologically driven—will not be a happy and brave new world for all. It implies a growing division between the skilled and the unskilled. Policy-makers will need to equip their citizens to participate—education will become the most important economic policy.

Political repression becomes more difficult

But in global terms, this will have an important liberalising impact. Many governments would ideally choose to combine the market economy with political repression. The nature of a technologically driven market economy makes that more and more difficult. Simply rejecting these technologies is easy—but few wish to emulate North Korea or the Afghan Taliban. But countries like China will find it difficult to participate on their own terms. There will be an economic imperative to spread skills, technological knowhow, and information technology much more widely—to loosen control. Attempts at surveillance will be ineffectual and largely symbolic.

A report by Reporters Sans Frontiere, in August 1999, stated that people living in the North Korea capital, Pyongyang, were prohibited from accessing the Internet and from viewing anything other than the "propaganda" generated by the government.

This does not mean that the Internet will end repression—many regimes, as they give up on censoring English-speaking elites, crack down on the local language press ever more strongly. But more and more information filters through: Controlling what a society can know—largely possible 20 years ago—is now almost impossible. Again, this reinforces a preexisting trend toward increasing global democratization and global political norms from human rights to war crimes: The Internet has enabled the growth of a global civil society able to pursue these goals more rapidly and effectively.

The Internet cannot replace national economies and national identities, but it may transform them. Economies and identities will overlap and become more plural. These changes are open to democratic debate and choice but are likely to persist because they go with the grain of the way our domestic and global societies are evolving.

ELECTRONIC EMPIRE
Anthony M. Townsend
and James T. Bennett

NO

As we continue into the *terra nova* of the electronic frontier, there is no set destiny that determines how the electronic society evolves. For all of the promise of true democracy, free markets, unrestrained speech, and the creation of a global village, there remains the distinct possibility that the tools empowering this utopia will just as likely be used to enslave, repress, and balkanize the planet. In addition, if history is any teacher, the latter is a much more likely scenario. Two forces array themselves against the realization of a global village: First, human nature requires borders to distinguish the we from the them; second, nations will continue to serve the purpose of power elites, and these power interests will preserve sovereignty and distort the information infrastructure to serve this end.

"Balkanize" means to break up into small, mutually hostile political regions, as the Balkans were after World War I (1914–1918).

The social curse

Regardless of our technological prowess, we remain the same crude species that lurched out of the cave a few thousand years ago. Although we have achieved remarkable feats of civilization, we remain essentially bound by our evolution and instinct. It is critical to understand that humankind has evolved as social creatures, with as powerful a social instinct as bees, wolves, or ants. This social imperative drives a significant portion of our lives as we struggle to mate and prosper in the complex social hierarchies we inhabit. We define ourselves by the groups we belong to, and just as importantly, we define ourselves in juxtaposition to the others.

With the Internet, we are inundated with others, with information about ideas and customs well beyond our parochial experience. Many believe this expanding familiarity with humanity's rich diversity will yield a pan-human empathy that will render nations, borders, and traditional antipathies into obsolete artifacts of a less-informed age.

Unfortunately, there is little in human history that supports this expectation; nations represent the largest salient aggregation with which humans identify, and because they need to identify as a member of us, and in contrast to them, there must always be nations and national culture. The Internet, particularly when combined with other mass media, begins to blur cultural and national distinctions as it overloads us with information. In many respects, it creates a pressure to assimilate into a larger, heterogeneous global culture. However, as a species, we are not comfortable with too high a level of heterogeneity, and so we rebel by reestablishing our identity as a member of the largest group with which we are comfortable. It is important to note that some of the most powerful nationalist movements begin as rebellions against assimilation: fascists and national socialists fighting the assimilation of European communism, the communist Chinese and fundamentalist Moslems fighting the cultural assimilation of the West; and more recently, the rise of a variety of nationalist parties in Europe fighting the assimilation of the European union. Thus, it is almost inevitable that as globalization continues to blur national distinctiveness, the nationalist impulse will assert itself and people will seek to reassert the sovereignty of their nation and preserve its integrity.

Find out what the dominant characteristics of nationalist movements have been and are today.

The Internet and the power elite

In capitalist economies in general, and in information economies specifically, there is a pressing need for stable national governments, because ultimately, the government is the guarantor of the basis of wealth (for instance, through control of the banking system) and of the social and physical infrastructure of trade. Even the most profoundly multinational of firms has little interest in losing the predictability and stability of the countries in which they operate. Hence, while they may work to influence the regulatory environment in their favor, they will tolerate little that would broadly destabilize nations in which they have a significant interest.

Thus, because of its economic and strategic importance, the control of the Internet will be absolute. We are already seeing well-intentioned legislators in a number of countries working to restrict what can and cannot be published on the Internet. Whether it's hate speech banned in Australia, political communication in China, indecency in the U.S., or tobacco advertising just about anywhere, it is all part of a pattern of reducing the freedom of the medium. Contrary to the popular myth, the content of the Internet can be controlled. People live in real space, and in real space the laws of sovereign nations continue to apply. Thus, while you can access any information you wish, you can also be locked up for doing so if you violate local laws prohibiting your access.

For a discussion about tobacco advertising see Topic 9 Should tobacco advertising be banned? on pages 112–123.

Thus, freedom on the Internet is already illusory; as governments develop more sophisticated monitoring tools, they will continue to effectively restrict the demand side of Internet content.

We do not own the Internet

One of the great myths of our era is the Internet is everyman's medium; we see it popularly as a happy anarchy of participants and a free market of ideas. What we forget is we do not own the Internet and only use it according to the rules of those who do. At its most basic level, the Internet relies on an infrastructure of wires owned by a handful of corporate entities, and ultimately, whoever owns the wires really controls the Internet.

"I think there is a world market for maybe five computers."

—THOMAS WATSON, CHAIRMAN OF IBM, 1943

This is certainly not a popular view; most people believe the Internet represents the greatest open market of ideas and communication in human history. While true at this particular moment in its evolution, it is an unlikely description of the Internet's future. Like all frontiers, once civilization discovered the Internet, it began to fence it in and create law and order. We are already seeing smaller ISPs [Internet service providers] being squeezed out of the market by bigger players with a better deal on high-speed data lines; the mom-and-pop ISP is soon a thing of the past.

Manipulating content

Do you agree with the authors that mass media such as radio, movies, and TV have acted like a sleeping pill on people so that they accept the status quo? What arguments can you think of to refute this point?

Business will also control the supply side of the Internet; the mega-mergers between access service providers and content providers will continue unabashed until the Internet has all of the rich diversity of ideas of broadcast television. The combination of superiorly crafted content and economies of scale in delivery will soon obviate the small, dissident voices that characterize the contemporary Internet. However, unlike radio, cinema, and television, which have narcotized generations into obeisance to the status quo, the Internet has the capability of returning information about the user to the content provider. This enables a bold new era of

---

COMMENTARY: How many people are online?

It is difficult to estimate accurately how many people are online in the world, but surveys suggest that in November 2000 something in the region of 407.1 million people were accessing the Internet. Nua.com (www.nua.com.ie) is a site dedicated to providing an online source of information on Internet demographics and trends. Based on nua.com's observation of published surveys over two years, this worldwide figure can be broken down into regions as follows:

Africa	3.11 million
Asia/Pacific	104.88 million
Europe	113.14 million
Middle East	2.4 million
Canada and the U.S.	167.12 million
Latin America	16.45 million
Total	**407.1 million**

---

manipulation of content to create consumer demand; the bidirectional flow of the Internet will empower a level of consumer manipulation of unimagined proportions.

Once the corporate community realized the importance of the Internet to productive activity, it became inevitable that the Internet would become a closely held, regulated, and controlled commercial commodity. Business organizations may regularly rail against the regulators, but they actually thrive on the predictability of regulation and rely on their ability to appeal to regulators to control the excesses of their competitors. Organizations look to strong national government to provide a consistency in regulatory control that can't be duplicated by trade organizations or extra-national entities.

No second Troy

Therefore, contrary to the utopian wisdom of most observers of the evolving information economy, we do not see a global village in the near future. Both businesses and people need nations, to both protect and project their interests in a world too diverse to apprehend. While global trade will continue to expand, it will do so between nations and between populations that clearly identify with their own nation state. As for the Internet, the increasing control of content to manipulate both consumption and ideology will soon transform the most promising communicative medium in human history into yet another mechanism of coercion and control.

What evidence can you find to counter the authors' assertion that Internet content will be increasingly controlled?

Summary

There is no easy answer to the question of whether or not the Internet will create a global culture, but these articles provide some ideas to ponder. In the first, "Globalizing the Internet," Sunder Katwala puts forward the view that the Internet has a globalizing, flattening, and democratizing bias, which will bring societies together. The mightiest of regimes, he says, could become powerless with the click of a mouse. A technology-driven market economy makes political repression more difficult, and controlling what a country can know becomes almost impossible. Katwala sees the Internet transforming national economies and identities.

Townsend and Bennett, the authors of "Electronic Empire," take a different point of view. They contend that regardless of the technology, the stumbling blocks to becoming more global are cultural. Are we tribal by nature? Will there always be the tendency to shun heterogeneous culture and fight assimilation? This viewpoint suggests that technology cannot be the sole mechanism to promote diversity and understanding. Townsend and Bennett say that it is a myth to think of the Internet as everyone's medium. The Internet runs over an infrastructure that is owned by a few large corporations, and eventually those owners will assert ownership over the technology and the content. They present a gloomy conclusion that the Internet will become a mechanism for coercion and control. Are we doomed to act in our own self-interest and behave tribally? Or could the Internet, with its incredible potential for diversity of viewpoints, promote tolerance and provide a better mechanism for sharing our common interests and understanding our differences?

FURTHER INFORMATION:

Books:

Herman, Andrew, and Thomas Swiss (editors), *The World Wide Web and Contemporary Cultural Theory: Magic, Metaphor, Power*. New York: Routledge, 2000.
Morris, Nancy, et al. (editors), *Media and Globalization*. Lanham, MD: Rowman & Littlefield Publishing, 2001.
Pavlik, John V., *New Media Technology*. Boston: Allyn & Bacon, 1996.
Gauntlett, David (editor), *Web Studies*. London: Edward Arnold, 2000.

Useful websites:

www.cis.washington.edu
Center for Internet Studies, University of Washington.
www.accenture.com
Panel discussion on globalization and the Internet.

www.internetindicators.com/globalinternet.html
Statistics on the Internet and the global economy.

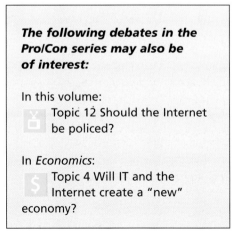

The following debates in the Pro/Con series may also be of interest:

In this volume:
Topic 12 Should the Internet be policed?

In *Economics*:
Topic 4 Will IT and the Internet create a "new" economy?

WILL THE INTERNET CREATE A GLOBAL CULTURE?

YES: There will be a trend toward global democratization, bringing societies together

YES: The barriers to entry to global markets are lowered; already major cross-border mergers are commonplace

DEMOCRATIZATION
Will the Internet promote democratization?

ECONOMY
Will the Internet promote a global market economy?

NO: As national distinctiveness becomes blurred, the nationalist impluse emphasizing difference from others will assert itself

NO: Power elites will distort the information infrastructure to preserve the sovereignty of nations and to promote national economic interests

WILL THE INTERNET CREATE A GLOBAL CULTURE?

KEY POINTS

YES: There will be much greater scrutiny of those who seek to control power and what a society can know

YES: The technology-driven market economy makes political repression more difficult

FREEDOM OF IDEAS
Will the Internet be an open market of ideas?

NO: The Internet will become a closely controlled and regulated commercial commodity

NO: Control of Internet content will turn it into another mechanism of coercion and control

Topic 14
DOES NAPSTER ENCOURAGE COPYRIGHT INFRINGEMENT?

YES

"FACING THE MUSIC"
CURRENT EVENTS,
VOL. 100, ISSUE 21, MARCH 16, 2001

NO

"RANTS ABOUT FREE DOWNLOADS"
TWICE, VOL.16, ISSUE 6,
MARCH 12, 2001
STEVE SMITH

INTRODUCTION

Napster, a peer-to-peer (P2P) sharing facility, takes its name from its creator, 18-year-old Shawn Fanning, whose nappy hairstyle earned him the nickname "the napster." From August 1999 Napster offered free software to Internet users, enabling them to search the hard drives of other users for MP3 files via Napster's own central directory. MP3 is a format that allows music tracks to be compressed into sound files. Napster users then downloaded MP3s to their own hard drives.

Napster quickly ran into trouble. Several musicians such as Metallica, companies such as EMI and AOL-Time/Warner, and the Recording Industry Association of America (RIAA) have all sued the organization, citing the abuse of copyright and loss of income as reason to close the site.

In October 2000 Napster joined forces with the German media giant Bertelsmann AG BMG, one of the five large record labels that had originally sued it over allegations of copyright infringement (BMG withdrew its original lawsuit.) In June 2001 Napster made a further deal with MusicNet, a collaboration between BMG, EMI Group, and AOL-Time/Warner. This new union led Napster's transformation into a paid-subscription-only service in late summer 2001. Meanwhile, Napster suspended its service from July 2, 2001, as it struggled to redesign its software in line with court orders to block copyrighted songs from its lists. User numbers plummeted from some 57 million in January 2001 to thousands as people sought music from other sites.

The Napster case has raised questions about the protection of intellectual property, or copyright, in the digital age, as well as the right for people to record and share music. Record companies say that Napster and similar sites encourage copyright theft, since people download tracks for free. This denies the songwriter and record company their rightful revenue from royalties. What Napster refers to as "sharing" the record companies would simply call stealing. The RIAA accused Napster of "facilitating piracy" and "building on the backs of artists and copyright owners" after randomly sampling songs on Napster and finding that the vast majority were of pirated origin. The RIAA asserts that Napster's role is far from passive and that it is well aware that it aids the transfer of pirated or copyrighted songs. The companies state that they themselves eagerly embrace new technology and have already taken steps to post legally downloadable songs on their own sites.

> *"We believe that the Internet and Napster should not be ignored by the music industry as tools to promote awareness for bands and market music."*
>
> —FRED DURST, LIMP BIZKIT

Part of Napster's defense rested on claims that its site was protected by the 1998 Digital Millennium Copyright Act. The DMCA prevents an Internet Service Provider (ISP) from liability if copyright laws are thwarted by its users. There is even a clear notice regarding copyright law on the Napster site that states: "As a condition to your account with Napster, you agree that you will not use the service to infringe the intellectual property rights of others in any way."

Napster's site does not actually hold any MP3 files itself and only gives users the ability to exchange them. Therefore, it denies that it encourages copyright violation. Napster also points out that it is not illegal for a user to swap music with another on a nonprofit basis.

Fanning has pointed out to record companies that they are dealing with many other similar services, such as Gnutella, FreeNet, and CuteMX, which can provide the same availability of access to files as can Napster. Defenders of such systems argue that the pricing of CDs and the profits made by the record companies are excessive. In fact, the manufacturing costs of CDs are tiny in comparison to their final retail price. People begrudge paying high prices for the product, so they seek other, cheaper methods of obtaining music.

Counter to claims by the RIAA, Fanning also claims that CD sales have not been affected by Napster and that the service, if anything, acts as a showcase for music. People can hear new music or sample tracks before they buy a CD; a survey showed that 70 percent of polled Napster members used the service this way. Defenders of Napster, including musicians like Chuck D from Public Enemy, are very vocal. They believe that since the technology already exists to facilitate P2P sharing of digital files, the record companies must either embrace it positively and charge fairly for their music or lose out.

In the following two articles "Facing the Music" supports the music industry's claims that Napster's so-called "sharing" is really just theft. Conversely, Steve Smith levels criticism at the music industry, predicting a dire future for the new digital formats if their growth is hindered in the manner of Napster.

FACING THE MUSIC
Current Events

☑ Most people wouldn't walk into a music store and steal armloads of CDs. But millions of people have downloaded free tunes with the help of Napster, a popular Internet site that allows users to swap computer files of recorded music at no charge. Is that stealing?

Do you think that downloading free music using Napster constitutes stealing? If not, why not?

A federal appeals court here thinks so. On February 12, a three-judge panel of the Ninth U.S. Circuit Court of Appeals upheld a lower court's ruling that Napster "knowingly encourages and assists" its users in violating U.S. copyright law. Copyright law makes it illegal to copy without permission "works of authorship," such as recordings, writings, and drawings.

The decision was music to the ears of the Recording Industry Association of America (RIAA), a trade group that brought suit against Napster in December 1999 on behalf of five major record labels. Napster, however, is singing a different tune. On February 20, Napster offered to pay record companies a $1 billion settlement over five years for the right to use their music in a new fee-based song-swapping Internet service. If its offer is rejected, Napster said it will ask all the ninth circuit judges to reconsider the panel's decision. And if necessary, Napster plans to appeal the ruling to the U.S. Supreme Court. In the meantime, the lower court judge, Marilyn H. Patel, is rewriting her injunction, which is an order requiring someone to stop doing something, that could shut the site down during the legal wrangle.

Stop the music!

Is it right that artists and record companies do not profit from song swaps on the Internet?

Since Napster was founded in May 1999, more than 64 million people have shared songs on the site free of charge—which means there have been no royalties or payments based on sales for artists or profits for record companies from the song swaps. Users downloaded more than 3 billion copies of songs in January. In the weekend after the three judges' decision against Napster, fans of the site made 250 million copies of songs, fearing Napster's imminent shutdown.

The February 12 ruling estimates that more than 87 percent of the music traded on Napster is copyrighted, much of it by the record companies suing the site.

"The court's decision is a victory for all creators," said RIAA president Hilary Rosen. "To say that taking music without compensation is not stealing is to suggest that music has no value," added Rosen. Many musicians agree. Rapper Dr. Dre and heavy metal band Metallica filed their own suit against Napster last April. Metallica insists that recording artists must be "able to control how, when, and in what form their creativity is distributed." Jerry Rosen, a violinist who earns much of his income from royalties, is bewildered by what he sees as Napster fans' sense that they are entitled to free music just because it is available on the Net. "There's a sense among young people that [using Napster] is their God-given right."

Napster's defense

Nineteen-year-old Shawn Fanning developed Napster to make it easier to find digital music files on the Internet. Napster claims it isn't in violation of copyright law because it doesn't actually copy music or store songs itself. Instead, Napster software searches the computers of a network of users who have uploaded music files and helps people find the songs they're looking for. Napster said its users "share" songs and that no money is exchanged among users.

Napster also argues that it should be protected by the 1992 Home Audio Recording Act, which allows people to record music or videotape movies so long as it's for their personal, not commercial, use. That right should be extended to using personal computers, say Napster attorneys.

Napster users claim the site wouldn't be so popular if CDs weren't so expensive. "Iget really angry when I hear [the recording industry] complaining about Napster, because they've aided and abetted this whole process by jacking up CD prices," said music store owner Chris Zingg. Not all musicians are anti-Napster. Rapper Chuck D. thinks recording artists should welcome Napster. "We should think of it as a new kind of radio-promotional tool," he said. Fred Durst of Limp Bizkit said his band plans to participate in concerts to generate support for Napster.

Gene Kan, who developed Gnutella, a site similar to Napster, says the recording industry has itself to blame for the popularity of song-swapping on the Internet. "The music industry hasn't come forward with its own version of Napster to allow people to swap files online, which is something people obviously want to do." Have you or your friends ever used free music-swapping sites like Napster? Now that the court has ruled using these sites is illegal, will you stop? Why or why not?

Strictly speaking, it is legally permissible to distribute such music recordings free of charge. The same is not true of copied literature or photographs.

It can be effective to close an argument with a thought-provoking question. How would you answer this question?

RANTS ABOUT FREE DOWNLOADS
Steve Smith

Last week [March 12, 2001] the Consumer Electronics Association sponsored a one-day seminar in Washington, D.C., called "Digital Download: Public Access to Content in a Digital World." As part of the drumbeat for the seminar, CEA issued in February a survey of more than 1,800 people that revealed two interesting results the entertainment industry should consider:

- 89 percent of Internet users download multimedia content and information;
- 61 percent oppose laws that prevent the usage of file-sharing software such as Napster.

In releasing the report CEA president Gary Shapiro said: "We must protect the ability of technologies to evolve, especially those that allow personal, noncommercial recording. These new technologies vastly expand our collective knowledge base and ultimately benefit those most concerned—copyright owners."

DivX is a technology that enables digital-format movies to be compressed to a size at which they can be transferred via the Internet.

We couldn't agree more. The entertainment industry, if it completely gets its way, will charge everyone every time you access one of its products. The public won't stand for it. Remember DivX? You had to buy the disk to watch a movie twice and then had to pay over and over again when you wanted to watch it later. That format certainly broadened the entertainment industry's profits, didn't it?

What next—DVD-Audio?

With Napster losing its case against the recording industry quickly and dramatically, the Divx strategy still hasn't died. Prior to the case's settlement, our staff talked with several industry executives who theorized that if Napster won even a partial victory the music industry would move quickly to DVD-Audio for all new releases. Why? Well, as part of the spec there is copy protection that could allow a choice of the following: unlimited DVD-Audio copies from the original disc; one or a limited amount of DVD-Audio copies; two-channel CD copies; MP3- or FM-radio-quality copies; or zippo. Nada. Nothing. (Gee, unfettered by law, which selection would record companies prefer?) Even with the Napster win in its back pocket, the recording industry may just follow that

COMMENTARY: Meet Mr. Napster

The Napster software was developed in mid-1999 by Shawn Fanning, then an 18-year-old freshman at Northeastern University in Boston. He was the illegitimate outcome of a liaison between his 14-year-old mother, Colleen Fanning, and a rock-musician scion of a rich Massachusetts family. She later married and gave Shawn four siblings, and her brother John helped with Shawn's upbringing.

The youngster instantly showed promise at school. Not only intelligent, he was also good at sports. John gave him a computer in his high school sophomore year, and Shawn soon became absorbed in the Internet. He also taught himself Unix programming. Studies at Northeastern bored him, and he eventually skipped classes to stay at his uncle's office, where he focused single-mindedly on his dream: to create a file-sharing music application for the Internet. His plan was to combine the instant-messaging capabilities of Internet Relay Chat (a net chat application), the effectiveness of existing search engines, and the file-sharing functionality of Microsoft Windows.

Fanning circulated a test version of Napster among friends in June 1999 on condition that they keep the project secret. But within days thousands knew of it. Sensing an urgent need to launch Napster before competitors outdid him, Fanning launched the full version later that year. Though it rapidly ran into trouble, Fanning's legacy goes beyond his transformation of the music business. He also revitalized the Internet, spawning a generation of so-called peer-to-peer systems; they have great potential in business and science applications.

Napster creator Shawn Fanning at a press conference in San Francisco in 2001.

How Napster works

1 The user sends a request for a song to the Napster server

2 Napster searches its database to see if the song is available on another user's pc

Napster server

4 The song is downloaded directly from the selected pc

3 The song is located and listed on the original user's pc

The fact that Napster did not itself hold copyrighted material on its database, but enabled users to locate such material on others' hard drives, gave credence to its claim that it was merely an Internet service provider and was not in clear breach of copyright law.

strategy anyway. The "collective knowledge base" Shapiro talks about would shrink drastically ... as would sales of other home audio and portable audio products.

This paper, and others, have called the past few years the "digital revolution" for all the new digital products that have been developed. But the truth is that due to the foot-dragging the entertainment industry, broadcast, and cable TV moguls have wrought during this time, full-blown HDTV is years away. These same forces are also trying to curb any digital home recording of copyrighted music and video. Thanks to the entertainment industry, this "revolution" is taking longer to evolve than the Hundred Years war....

Is it reasonable to curb digital home recording, or is the music industry merely exploiting the technology to maximize profits?

Now, this is a serious issue, one that should be vigorously monitored by the public and the consumer electronics industry. But I have a transcript of a monologue by

---

"Napster: It is the future, in my opinion. That's the way music is going to be communicated around the world."

—DAVE MATTHEWS,

DAVE MATTHEWS BAND

---

comedian/*Monday Night Football* gadfly Dennis Miller from his HBO show, and I pass along his rant [with obscenities deleted], one because it is dead-on funny, and two, because I feel Miller echoes the feelings of many consumers:

"Pop music has a rich legacy of ripping people off. First, the white musicians stole from the blacks. Then, the producers stole from the performers. Then, the performers and the producers formed an alliance to steal from us by charging $19 for a CD with only one halfway decent song on it. So I for one salute Napster because it's high time the public had the opportunity to horn in on a piece of the action.

A clear consumer benefit of Napster was that it enabled users to take one or two good songs from an album of "filler" tracks.

"Now, industry people will tell you that Napster is unfair. But musicians are going to waste their hard-earned cash anyway, OK? ... Hey, the bottom line on Napster is, it means no more paying for overpriced CDs and putting money into the pockets of the bloated, corrupt media conglomerates. All you need is a high-speed modem, extra memory, a CD-ROM attachment, an extra phone line, Internet access, a CD burner, blank CDs, a how-to manual and NO LIFE.

Summary

Both articles center on the argument of whether downloading copyrighted music equals theft. In "Facing the Music" the author asks a hypothetical question at the beginning of the article. You wouldn't go into a store and try to steal an armful of CDs, so why would you steal the same music online? Your answer will depend on your moral viewpoint. But if you were the artist and you thought that there was a decline in the sales of your CD because large numbers of people were downloading your work for free, how would you feel?

For Steve Smith, in the second article, popular practice and opinion count for much. He quotes from a Consumer Electronics Association survey that details wide support for Napster and warns the music industry to take note. In the fallout from the Napster case what does the future hold for digital media? Smith predicts the start of a wholesale clampdown on home-recording freedoms and quotes comedian Dennis Miller. Truths surface among Miller's humor; for example, it's a time-honored tradition in the music industry to rip people off. Why stop now?

FURTHER INFORMATION:

Useful websites:

www.metallicavsnapster.com/
Charts battle between rock band Metallica and Napster. Metallica's drummer, Lars Ulrich, led a legal campaign against the service and its founder, Shawn Fanning.
www.boycottmetallica.org/
A website taking the side of Napster, and its policy of sharing music, in the legal battle with Metallica.
www.macworld.com/2000/05/12/chuckd.html
Rapper Chuck D explains his support of Napster and sharing music.
www.freebiesforever.com/music.html
Website of a Napster support group calling for a boycott of CDs.
www.salon.com/tech/feature/2000/06/14/love/
Singer Courtney Love speaks in support of Napster and against record companies in a self-written article for Salon.com.
speakout.napster.com/
A link from the official Napster site allows supporters of the service to contact their Congressional representatives by giving them a toll-free number to call.
www.usatoday.com/life/cyber/tech/review/crh452.htm
A USA Today article discusses support for Napster.

www.howstuffworks.com/question392.htm
How Stuff Works describes how Napster functions and discusses the ethics of file sharing.
www.cnn.com/interactive/computing/0003/napster/frameset.exclude.html
Describes in a simple way how Napster works.
www.cbsnews.com/now/story/0,1597,196609-412,00.shtml
"How Napster Works—and How It Doesn't." A CBS news story that lists the pros and cons of the file-sharing service.
www.templetons.com/brad/copymyths.html
A brief introduction to copyright law.

The following debates in the Pro/Con series may also be of interest:

In this volume:

Topic 12 Should the Internet be policed?

DOES NAPSTER ENCOURAGE COPYRIGHT INFRINGEMENT?

YES: Most people would not steal CDs and tapes from a record store, so why should they download files from Napster?

YES: Napster actively encourages millions of people to steal from musicians and record companies. It is therefore wrong.

THEFT
Is downloading files from Napster theft?

NO: If this were the case, successful musicians, such as Public Enemy, would not support Napster

COPYRIGHT
Does Napster by its very being encourage its users to breach musician's copyright?

NO: Napster is a peer-to-peer network on which users download music for personal use, not for sale

NO: Most people use the service to hear new music by favorite bands or music by new bands, after which they may go out and buy the CD or tape

DOES NAPSTER ENCOURAGE COPYRIGHT INFRINGEMENT?

KEY POINTS

YES: Record companies are notorious for making huge profits at the expense of their customers; thus if CDs were less expensive, fewer people would take music from Napster or equivalent sites

RECORD COMPANIES
If record companies charged reasonable prices for CDs, would fewer people use Napster?

NO: If record companies were sensible, though, they would use Napster and equivalent services to promote new music, much in the way that users do themselves

NO: People would still use Napster since it's a way of sampling new music without shelling out money for a legitimate CD

COPYRIGHT IN THE UNITED STATES

Copyright is a body of legal rights that protects creative works from being reproduced, performed, or disseminated by other people without the owner's permission. The first true copyright law was enacted in Britain in 1710. The Statute of Anne made unauthorized printing and reprinting illegal and provided an author's copyright. Since then copyright law has undergone substantial revision. The onset of the Internet has brought the issue of copyright to the fore again. The United States and Canada are currently looking at revising their laws to work within the framework of new media.

1790 The first U.S. copyright law is passed after the Founders recognize the need to protect authors. Article I, Section 8, of the Constitution states that Congress shall have the power to "promote the progress of science and useful arts, by securing for limited times to authors and inventors the exclusive right to their respective writings and discoveries."

1886 The Berne Convention provides the basis for mutual recognition of copyright for foreign works between sovereign states.

1908 The Berlin Act sets the duration of copyright at life of the author plus 50 years.

1909 The U.S. Copyright Act is substantially revised. Changes include a broadening of the range of categories protected to include all works of authorship. This remains the basic framework for U.S. copyright law until January 1, 1978, when the Copyright Act of 1976 actually goes into effect.

1973 Medical publishers Williams & Wilkins sue the National Library of Medicine and National Institute of Health, claiming infringement of copyright due to making unauthorized photocopies. The court decides that medical research would be harmed by finding in their favor.

1976 A new copyright act establishes a single system of federal statutory protection for all eligible works, both published and unpublished. It decides that work created after January 1, 1978, will become the property of the author for his or her life plus 50 years. However, work created by an employee during work hours becomes the copyright of the employer from publication and lasts for 75 years from publication or for 100 years from creation. For works created before 1978 under the old act, copyright lasts 28 years, but this can be extended for another 28 years. The National Commission on New Technological Uses of Copyrighted Works (CONTU) is set up to establish guidelines for "minimum standards of educational fair use."

1983 Encyclopedia Britannica (EB) sues the Board of Cooperative Educational Services. BoCES is a consortium of public school districts that have taped educational programs from public television stations and made copies for member schools. The court finds in EB's favor.

1988 The United States becomes a Berne Convention signatory. Some of the resulting changes include: greater protection for proprietors and new copyright relationships with 24 other countries.

1990 The Copyright Act is extended to prevent commercial lending of computer software. Libraries can lend software as long as a copyright warning appears on the packaging.

1992 An amendment to Section 304 of Title 17 of the Copyright Act makes copyright renewal automatic.

1993 President Clinton's administration create a Working Group on Intellectual Property Rights to examine how well copyright laws work.

1994 The Supreme Court rules in *Campbell v. Acuff-Rose Music, Inc.* that a rap song based on Roy Orbison's song "Pretty Woman" was in fair use. It found that a commercial usage of artistic work could be fair use, especially if the end markets for the original and new work were different.

July 1994 The Working Group issues a preliminary draft report on Intellectual Property and the National Information Infrastructure (NII). It decides that for the NII to achieve its full potential as a channel for distribution of a wide range of creative works, authors and publishers of those works would need reasonable assurance that their intellectual property rights would be respected. It also recommends lots of legislative changes to copyright law.

September 1994 Conference on Fair Use (CONFU) is set up. CONFU looks at development guidelines for fair use in the electronic/new media arena, including electronic reserves and visual images.

1995 Legislation to extend the copyright protection term is proposed. It would extend the copyright period by 20 years for all published work and bring U.S. legislation into line with other Berne signatories.

September 1995 The Working Group releases a White Paper. It recommends amendments to the 1976 Copyright Act and provides an analysis of current copyright law.

January 1996 The Trade Related Aspects of Intellectual Property Rights agreement forms part of the Final Act of the Uruguay Round of the General Agreement on Tariffs and Trade (GATT). This means that foreign-originated works currently in the public domain in the United States are returned to copyright on January 1, 1996.

May 23, 1996 The Database Investment and Intellectual Property Antipiracy Act (H.R. 3531) is passed. It "seeks to promote investment and prevent intellectual property piracy" in databases.

October 27, 1998 The Sonny Bono Copyright Term Extension Act is introduced. The statute amends the Copyright Act by adding 20 years to the term of copyright protection. An important amendment allows nonprofit libraries and archives (and educational institutions acting as such) to reproduce, distribute, display, or perform works or portions of the work for purposes of preservation, scholarship, or research. See www.arl.cni.org/info/frn/copy/comments.html for more information on this act.

October 28, 1998 President Clinton introduces the Digital Millennium Copyright Act.

December 2, 1998 On-Line Copyright Liability Limitation Act (H.R. 2180) is introduced to provide limitations on online material use.

Late 2000 The Working Group's White Paper recommendations are introduced formally in the NII Copyright Protection Act of 1995 (S.1284 and H.R. 2441).

Topic 15
WILL E-PUBLISHING REPLACE THE TRADITIONAL BOOK?

YES
"THE DEMISE OF WRITING"
THE FUTURIST, VOL. 33, ISSUE 8, OCTOBER 1999
GEOFFREY E. MEREDITH

NO
"ELECTRONIC BOOKS: TO 'E' OR NOT TO 'E': THAT IS THE QUESTION"
SEARCHER, VOL. 8, ISSUE 4, APRIL 2000
STEPHANIE ARDITO

INTRODUCTION

As the Internet becomes increasingly popular as a mass medium, commentators question its possible effect on existing media. Already, consumers can turn to online services for news headlines, rather than traditional TV, radio, or press news organizations. Many of the most reliable news websites, however, are created and published by traditional news-gathering organizations, such as ABC or NBC, the BBC in Britain, or the *New York Times* or *Washington Post*. Only such established organizations have sufficient resources, on-the-ground reporters, and editorial credibility to maintain up-to-the-minute news sites.

One medium in which many observers see more potential for the Internet to have a revolutionary effect is book publishing. Not only will traditional publishers create products in electronic forms; the relative ease, speed, and low cost of publishing online will lead to the emergence of

new types of publishers and encourage authors to publish themselves. The same technology that makes it easier for publishers and authors to get into print will also make it easier for readers to access what they need. Some experts believe that eventually books themselves will be replaced by e-texts, electronic means of storing and retrieving information, either arranged in pages in a way that resembles traditional books or in other ways.

E-publishing has already started to affect the book business. Some directory or encyclopedia publishers, including Encyclopedia Britannica, will now only publish in electronic formats, partly because it is cheaper than producing large sets of printed books, and partly because it makes it easier to keep a product permanently up to date. But whether or not e-publishing finally does away with the traditional book depends on factors that are not only practical, technological, or economic.

For the majority of people books and the act of reading also have great emotional significance.

In terms of practicality and technology e-publishing is already possible. Growing numbers of newspapers and publishing houses are creating websites, a process made easier by the fact that their traditional products are already created digitally. Newspapers started making the transition to electronic product in the late 1970s with the introduction of word processors. Today newspapers are designed on computers and sent to a machine that makes the casts for the printing press. Since these pages are already digital, storage and retrieval of information become easy. Books, too, are created and stored electronically. This book was written and edited by authors who live on two continents.

The technology already exists for readers to access electronic publications. The ability to search easily for keywords makes e-publications particularly well suited to reference needs. For other sorts of publishing, however, such as children's books or novels, does e-publishing promise such demonstrable benefits?

Supporters of traditional books argue that the physical feel of a book satisfies an almost innate need for people. They argue that reading is an intensely private and sensual pleasure. For them, being able to hold, smell, or touch a book is an important part of the experience of reading that cannot be replicated by reading from a bookpad or other electronic device. Other observers, however, see new electronic books as being much more flexible than traditional books. Children's books, for example, could include sound effects, music, or animations that will make the story come alive. To some traditionalists even this addition to the written text undermines the whole imaginative experience of reading.

Former *Time-Life* editor-in-chief John Papanek thinks that portability and multimedia capability are the keys to the transformation of today's paper-based products. For instance, electronic bookmarks will allow readers to call up favorite passages instantly. Author Michael Wolf argues in his book *The Entertainment Economy* that it is the continually rising costs of paper publishing that will be decisive in making publishers turn toward electronic books.

"The loss [of traditional books] will be important, but it's elusive to specify. We'll miss the culture of the book, the envelope of associations."

—SVEN BIRKERTS,
THE GUTENBERG ELEGIES

The following two articles discuss this issue. In "The Demise in Writing" Geoffrey Meredith claims, like Papanek and Wolf, that books are dying. Conversely, Stephanie Ardito discusses some of the specific problems that technology has to overcome to gain widespread acceptance. Copyright and usage are additional concerns for publishers and authors (see pages 188–189); but although digital formatting makes illegal copying and distribution much easier, it also promises long-term cost benefits.

THE DEMISE OF WRITING
Geoffrey E. Meredith

YES

It may seem curious at a time when Amazon.com has a market value approximately that of New Zealand, but books as we know them are a dying breed. Indeed, there are unmistakable signs that text will atrophy by the end of the next century; it will be used mainly for instructional purposes and be accessible only to the technological elite.

It may seem inconceivable that text will have mostly disappeared within the lifetime of anyone alive today, but remember, the rate of change is accelerating. If the World Wide Web can go from an obscure geekish curiosity to the driving economic force of the developed world in about five years, what will 50 or 70 or 100 years bring?

Technology drives future book formats

Moveable type is already gone, replaced by the digital font. Ink on paper will be next, replaced by the electronic tablet. Already, commercial versions of the digital book are available: thin LCD panels with text stored in RAM [random access memory]. The Rocket eBook has a 4 1/2" by 3" screen, weighs about a pound-and-a-half, and can store 4,000 pages of text and graphics. Today's typical novel can be downloaded in about three minutes from a transportable medium (like CD-ROM) or downloaded from a computer or the Internet. The "textport" will become the checkout desk of the virtual library of 2010.

Would you rather read a book on paper or on a computer screen? Would you like a choice in the matter?

Currently, the technology is clunky (bulky batteries that last only four to nine hours), inelegant (the text is hard to read unless conditions are perfect), and expensive (about $500 for the eBook, plus $20 per book). However, all that will change very soon. By 2005, the bookpad will cost about $20, weigh no more than six ounces, reproduce text with greater clarity than ink-on-paper, and be able to store an encyclopedia (or 500 novels) on a single chip. Of particular appeal to an aging population, the type size will be variable—you'll make it as large as your eyesight requires.

But that's the short-term, mechanical aspect. Over the longer term, the printed word will vanish as a medium of expression. By 2070, the only people using text as literature (as opposed to information transmission) will be an elite and mostly very elderly priesthood, for whom it will be an arcane art form—sort of like the sonnet or haiku today. The demise of text for literature will result from several developments.

A "haiku" is a poem with three lines and 17 syllables in total.

Increasing use of pictures and sound

Today, expressive and instructional communications are increasingly transmitted either orally or visually. An example is the so-called "graphic novel," a fusion of comicbook illustration and serious prose. The cartoon strip that preceded it was an attempt to circumvent illiteracy during the first half of this century, and it became firmly established in the United States during the low-education days of the Depression. Comic strips became so popular with those who otherwise had great difficulty reading newspapers that a weeks' worth were bundled into one place, and the comic book was born. Its current transmogrification into the graphic novel (for example, *Maus* by Art Spiegelman or *Tantrum* by Jules Feiffer) further diminishes text.

Some of the first illustrated books made more than 500 years ago were religious tracts for the illiterate.

"The transportable book brought the world of the dead into the space of the gentleman's library; the telegraph brought the entire world of the living to the workman's breakfast table."

—MARSHALL MCLUHAN, MEDIA SCHOLAR, 1969

If the graphic novel works as ink on paper, imagine how much better it will work on an eBook. The images, which are cartoonlike stills now, will be digital photo images and moving 3-D holograms by 2010. And machine-gun fire won't be written out as "Braaaaaakkk!" on paper, we'll hear it from a sound chip and built-in speakers. The proliferation of aural and visual expression will continue to be driven by technological advances, specifically voice-recognition capability and the removal of bandwidth limitations on full-motion video.

Do you agree with the author that the addition of sound effects, photo images, and 3-D animations will enhance the reader's enjoyment?

Voice recognition

Microprocessors' ability to understand and respond to verbal instructions and communicate via voice output is poised on the edge of a great leap forward, one that will finally fulfill the promise of the microchip as an indispensable tool and helpmate of the masses. Voice chips are going to change our world sooner than we expect. No longer will we interact with devices via text and keyboard, we'll talk to them, perhaps even giving them names:

"Sven," we'll say to our computer, "make reservations for me to fly to Denver today. I want to arrive about 7 p.m. and stay at the Brown Palace. Charge it to my business Visa."

"VCR, record the World Cup satellite feed from Brazil this afternoon and the Pavarotti concert tomorrow night, and remind me about them when I get home from Denver."

"Toaster, a little bit darker on the next piece, please."

And even as Microsoft gets into the business of telling us how to write, it's hedging its bet by preparing to bring the Audible, Inc., audiobook technology to Windows CE devices. Dick I. Brass, Microsoft vice president for technology development, says in *Forbes*, "You're going to be able to play a book on every platform Microsoft makes."

Realistic video

"A picture is worth a thousand words" isn't just a saying. The cerebral cortex can process 1,000 times as much information, 1,000 times faster visually than verbally. The reason is that the optic nerve has a bandwidth—or data-transmission rate—a trillion times larger than a standard telephone line, so sending moving images over phone lines is insufferably slow.

> The cerebral cortex is the part of the human brain that processes sensory information.

Why? Because the slowest speed that even approximates full-motion video is 20 frames per second. Movies operate at 24. TV flickers at 30. Traditionally, every pixel—or picture element—must be repainted every frame. So a standard 720-by-480 pixel television screen has to be repainted a minimum of 20 times a second. That's 720 by 480 multiplied 20 times each second, multiplied by 60 for one minute of motion, which is a lot of pixels per minute and a lot of information whether you transmit it in digital or analog form. A coaxial cable can handle this amount of data, but not a phone line. That's why picturephones have never worked. Compression algorithms can cut the transmission flow somewhat, but not enough for anything better than a freeze-frame image every 10 seconds or so.

> Is the author justified in making such ambitious forecasts of larger bandwidth (data transmission speeds) in the future?

But the bandwidth barrier is about to be broken. The nature of the technology that will ultimately do it doesn't matter—it could be satellite transmission or fiber or something totally new. Bandwidth limitations are too critical not to be overcome, and, as soon as they are, text will take another giant leap backward. Why spend a lot of time typing in a memo when you can simply speak it and send it? You'll be able to communicate 1,000 times more information visually and verbally than with text alone.

For the receiver, the information will be much easier to assimilate and the impact many times greater. Already we see how hard it is to use traditional methods to teach kids who have been raised in the fastpaced, visual world of MTV—lecturing doesn't begin to cut it, let alone a textbook.

And as for the sender, after a decade or two with this vastly enhanced visual capability, who will bother to learn how to write well? We write to communicate linear thinking, which does extraordinarily well in part because it causes linear thinking—the way we express thought impacts the way we think. And as we increasingly communicate with multilayered, asynchronous images, our thinking will become increasingly nonlinear as well.

The topics in this book are presented in a linear format: an introduction is followed by two articles, a summary, and a key map. In what other formats might the topics be presented?

Baseball versus football provides a simple but instructive example. Baseball—linear and sequential, ordered, one-thing-at-a-time-was our national pastime until the advent of television. Television is images, multilayered, where instant replay can even (momentarily) reverse the arrow of time. This is a medium made for football, where many things happen at once—and it's a medium that helps make football the new national pastime, as the 30-frame-per-second image begins to transform our past mode of linear, sequential, one-batter-at-a-time thinking.

The implications of this are profound. As the image replaces text as the main form of communication, our collective thought processes will move from being linear and single and sequential to simultaneous and multilayered and holistic. Society will become less "left-brained" and analytical and more "right-brained" and intuitive. The more we think nonlinearly, the less we will communicate with text, which will cause even more nonlinear thinking, which will lead to less text, and so forth in a continuously self-reinforcing cycle.

When you put all these trends together, you may begin to see how 50 years from now books, newspapers, and magazines will be but quaint relics of the past. In 100 years, few people will want to read at all, and fewer still will know how to write. Text will be outmoded, except for instruction booklets and the aptly named textbooks containing technical information. Communication, both factual and expressive, will be through sound and pictures. We will have returned to the troubadour, the cave painter, the oral tradition, come full circle back to the age of Homer.

What might the implications be for information technology, linguistics, or literature in such a textless world?

ELECTRONIC BOOKS
Stephanie Ardito

I am a Star Trek fan. My favorite out of the [five] television series is *Star Trek: The Next Generation* or *TNG*, as we Trekkers would say (never "Trekkies"). I believe the key attraction for Trekkers working in the information industry would be the leading character, Captain Jean-Luc Picard. We can relate to Picard's ease in blending nontechnical uses of the world's body of knowledge with the bells and whistles of 24th-century technology. In many episodes, a crew member will barge into the Captain's quarters or ready-room to report on the latest crisis. In these scenes, Picard can usually be found … reading an old classic. Considering that the episodes take place 400 years from now, the crew member will question Picard about why he reads printed publication. After all, the crew member will say, the world's literature, going back to Gutenberg, has been captured on computer. Since computers have emerged as hand-held devices that provide the reader with the look and feel of printed counterparts, most crew members can not understand Picard's fetish with an antiquated medium.

Picard always smiles at his crew's bewilderment and, with great patience, tells them that there is nothing like the feel of running his finger down a printed page; there is nothing like hearing the sound of the pages turning; there is nothing like seeing how the author originally intended his words to be recorded and displayed. The crew members shake their heads in bafflement, but Picard continues to read his printed volumes of Shakespeare, his detective novels, and his books on ancient cultures and civilizations.

The author devotes a page to discussing an emotional issue: the sheer pleasure of holding and reading a book. How important is this to you?

A Trekker's lament

I cannot imagine a time when there are no printed books to curl up with in bed or in a window seat, no vacation tomes suitable for readers lying on a beach, and, truth be told, no bubble-bath books. Like Picard, I am saddened by the thought of future generations who may never know the incredible pleasure of holding a book in their hands. At the same time, I am realistic enough to know that making books available in electronic form opens enormous possibilities for research and library acquisitions. I do look forward to the time when publishers in all disciplines make their titles electronically accessible to researchers and consumers.

Although the availability of electronic books across industries is growing, at this time, publishers of literary and government titles seem the primary advocates of the genre. Works written by authors dead for 70 or more years and federal documents supported by tax dollars exist in the public domain. Because publishers and database producers do not have to contend with author contract disputes, the costs of compensating rights-holders, or other potential copyright violations, literary and government print titles are the logical choices for digitalization and electronic availability. However, in the nonacademic world, corporate researchers, marketing professionals, and consumers also have a vested interest in accessing and paying reasonable transaction fees for electronic materials.

U.S. copyright law protects the rights of living artists and writers or those who have died within the last 70 years.

Traditional publishers, particularly those producing medical and scientific texts, have yet to fully embrace this new technology. Such publishers continue to charge high institutional licensing fees for electronic texts, either insisting that print sales are the mainstay of their livelihoods or contending that encoding and other electronic development costs involve major expenses that must be passed onto their users.

Benefits of e-publishing

Without doubt, the purchase of electronic books has advantages for the academic and public library communities and their users. A single copy of a work can be loaded onto a server and made accessible to an unlimited number of users, technologically at least, if not contractually. Searching for specific information in large volumes of text can save time and turn texts into reference books. Links, graphics, and sound embedded in texts can provide additional resources of information. Electronic archives can preserve historical print texts in jeopardy of disintegrating. Because there is no physical inventory, electronic books can be printed or downloaded on demand; consequently, a publisher never has to worry about running out of stock.

Over a year ago, I read *The Professor and the Mad Man*, the history of the making of the Oxford English Dictionary. It occurred to me then that if the worldwide literature from the time of Gutenberg forward had been stored electronically, the quest to understand the origin and history of every English word that ever existed would have become much easier. The nearly 100 years needed to create the

The 12-volume Oxford English Dictionary was completed in 1933. It became available on CD-ROM in 1992.

original OED would have been cut dramatically, not to mention the possible increased accuracy of determining how words developed over time. This demonstrates another advantage of electronic texts—conducting word searches for computer-counted occurrences can help track the history of language and cultures.

> *"The most common question I get is, 'Why, Mr. Digital Fancypants, did you write a book?' Books are the province of romantics and humanists, not heartless nerds. The existence of books is solace to those who think the world is turning into a digital dump. The act of writing a book is evidence, you see, that all is not lost for those who read Shakespeare, go to church, play baseball, enjoy ballet, or like a good long walk in the woods."*
>
> —NICHOLAS NEGROPONTE, AUTHOR, *BEING DIGITAL*

Stephen King started e-publishing his new novel The Plant, *chapter by chapter, in July 2000. Thousands downloaded it, but King found that too few were prepared to pay for doing so.*

Publishing electronic books has special appeal to authors. Ultimately, it could give authors greater control over their content and how their works are marketed and distributed. Authors could retain copyright ownership and directly manage the financial aspects of their publishing endeavors. In time, authors could even use the Web as a direct publishing medium and eliminate the need for commercial publishers.

Digital drawbacks

However, publishing e-books has its potential disadvantages, too. Obvious ones include the size and weight of portable computers designed to display pages on a screen, the expense of purchasing portable devices, and the difficulty in reading digitized print. The transformation from linear text to hypertext may change the authoritative nature and understanding of the original works. Users of electronic text need to know the specific edition they have received and how well the publisher or database producer has maintained the accuracy of the electronic text. For example, marginal notes may become lost or placed out of context in electronic copies. Publishers and research editors may manipulate and change text. Value-added hypertext links may be added at the whim of a questionable source.

As for licensing and copyright, several issues for concern arise. If electronic books are "borrowed" from an electronic library, accompanied by encoding designed to prevent unauthorized copying and printing, will these measures invade the privacy of individual readers? When we buy hardcopies or receive printed books as gifts, no one knows how or whether we read the material or what we copy for friends or colleagues. In an electronic book world, it is quite possible that individuals will be monitored for their use of specific sections within the complete text.

Would you welcome a system that monitored what you read?

On the other hand, this monitoring does have its advantages. It promotes compensation for authors and other rights-holders by the number of hits or reads, a model of pricing that may lead traditional publishers who are presently resisting the electronic changes currently underway to open their archives.

The future of electronic books

According to the writers of *Star Trek*, electronic books of the 24th century will not reflect the feel and sound of printed works as we have experienced them since Gutenberg invented the printing press in 1455.

The Gutenberg Bible was the first book printed on a movable-type press, the printing system that was invented by the German craftsman Johannes Gutenberg and remained the industry standard until the 20th century.

Based on my review of the industry to date, I'm not so sure. No matter what future direction the industry takes, I must admit that I admire the efforts of entrepreneurs outside the traditional publishing industry who have taken initiatives to design portable devices that one day just might give us print equivalents. Martin Eberhard, [more than two years ago], echoed my own intuition about this burgeoning e-book industry when he wrote that traditional publishers will "lose relevance in a world of primarily electronic formats."

Satisfying print book lovers

E-publishers have a long way to go before they completely satisfy print book lovers and prove Captain Picard wrong. We need sufficient content to make the industry appealing. Pricing has to be attractive. Portability and comfort are necessary (including screens that emulate the feel of books, not to mention the wonderful pleasure of hearing pages turn). And most important, we must be reassured that our privacy will not be invaded.

Summary

Geoffrey Meredith infuses his article with the enthusiasm of a convert to the possibilities of e-publishing. The future, he claims, is already here: E-books are available. Meredith investigates the potential, over the next few decades, for revolutionizing the way we use books. E-books may include sound and movie files; e-cartoons will eventually incorporate holograms. At the time of writing the technology is, however, still in its infancy. The major limiting factor today is a small bandwidth (data transmission rate), but even this stumbling block will be resolved in due course. Given the logical advancement of e-publishing, Meredith then questions what sociological and cultural effects it will have on readers. The new format of the e-book will transform communication and drive new patterns of thinking. He predicts no less than a return to a post-literate acoustic age.

In the second article Stephanie Ardito does not resist the advent of e-publishing, but issues some cautionary words. On an emotional level people will miss the physical qualities of a traditional book. More practically, there are copyright and usage fees to consider. Beneficiaries of e-publishing will include schools and libraries, in which readers can use terminals to access a centralized resource. Rare tomes can be preserved while their contents are digitized for study by bibliophiles or researchers. Authors can retain greater control over rights and distribution. Ardito's final warning concerns privacy; the new technology may enable "Big Brother" to snoop into people's reading habits.

FURTHER INFORMATION:

Books:

Birkerts, Sven, *The Gutenberg Elegies: The Fate of Reading in an Electronic Age.* Boston, MA: Faber and Faber, 1994.

Lanham, Richard A., *The Electronic Word: Democracy, Technology, and the Arts.* Chicago: University of Chicago Press, 1995.

McLuhan, Marshall, *Counterblast.* New York: Harcourt, Brace & World, Inc., 1969.

Nunberg, Geoffrey (ed.), *The Future of the Book.* Berkeley, CA: University of California Press, 1996.

Useful websites:

www.geocities.com/anzlove/e-publish.html
A directory of e-books, e-novels, and e-publishing in general.
www.loc.gov/global/etext/etext.html
A Library of Congress directory of e-publishing resources.

www.archives.obs-us.com/obs/english/books/nn/bdintro.htm
A discussion of Nicholas Negroponte's *Being Digital.*

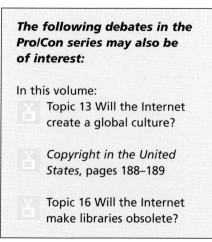

The following debates in the Pro/Con series may also be of interest:

In this volume:
Topic 13 Will the Internet create a global culture?

Copyright in the United States, pages 188–189

Topic 16 Will the Internet make libraries obsolete?

WILL E-PUBLISHING REPLACE THE TRADITIONAL BOOK?

YES: E-books bring their own new features to the book: sound effects, speech and video clips, etc.

YES: Computer links and cross-referencing systems make research much faster and easier

A "REAL" READ
Can e-books replicate the qualities of a real book?

REFERENCE WORKS
Will e-reference works be easier to use than the traditional format?

NO: Readers of e-books will miss the pleasure of using a real book; e-books will lack collectability and esthetic qualities

NO: E-books may suffer from inaccurate transcription or unsuitable modification; there is not yet a standard format that supports end-user distribution

WILL E-PUBLISHING REPLACE THE TRADITIONAL BOOK?

KEY POINTS

YES: "Stealth" monitoring can trace how much of a text is used by a reader

YES: Libraries can deploy a single source copy that several readers can access at one time; booksellers can always rely on stock

RIGHTS
Will the electronic publishing revolution make things easier for authors, booksellers, and librarians?

NO: It will be easy for readers to pirate or even to adulterate e-books

NO: Digital text is not portable or legible enough to have a major positive effect; it's healthier to read from a book than from a screen

Topic 16
WILL THE INTERNET MAKE LIBRARIES OBSOLETE?

YES
"JOINING THE 21ST CENTURY"
WWW.SIZEMORE.CO.UK
FAY MERRYFIELD

NO
"FILE THIS UNDER SHOCK, FUTURE"
U.S. NEWS & WORLD REPORT, WASHINGTON, JULY 12, 1999
DAVID L. MARCUS

INTRODUCTION

The 1950s were a time of growth, optimism, and cheap gas. Not only did the United States emerge victorious from World War II, but two vast oceans had protected its factories and cities from attack. Society had become prosperous, with an affluent new middle class; and as men came back from the war and settled down to start new families, they moved with their families out to suburbia. On their heels came strip malls with supermarkets, drive-in theaters—and branch libraries. The branch library reflected a different place and time as well as serving a different need. Prior to the end of World War II few Americans graduated from high school and entered college. As the 1950s began, large cities looked for ways to expand services to meet the needs of these new, growing families. There was no cable television, no such thing as a personal computer, and certainly no Internet. Branch libraries served very real needs.

Many established Eastern and Midwestern cities expanded social services, including bringing libraries into new metropolitan areas. Baltimore, Maryland, is a perfect illustration. With a population of more than a million, the City of Baltimore ran a large public library system with more than 28 branches scattered throughout the region. Twenty-five years later, in the 1970s, many manufacturing jobs had moved overseas, large population shifts caused cities in the East and Midwest to lose large portions of their population, and inner cities were on the verge of collapse. Baltimore was no different. Its population had shrunk to about 600,000 people, and that much smaller tax base made it difficult for city officials to offer the same services they had when the city was growing.

Today Baltimore is faced with a $21 million deficit, which is forcing city leaders to close fire departments, schools, and neighborhood libraries.

Carla Hayden, director of Baltimore's Enoch Pratt Free Library, said, "The city has serious financial problems, and Mayor Martin O'Malley is devoting a majority of resources to police, so the rest of us suffer." Baltimore's plan calls for closing up to 13 branch libraries over the next three years.

While many libraries are searching for funding, communications and computer technologies are providing librarians with "a mixture of excitement, nervous anxiety, and paranoia" according to *Buildings, Books and Bytes*, a new study that looks at the evolving nature of America's libraries. According to the report, while the number of books sold each year is still increasing, the quantity and quality of electronic devices are advancing more rapidly. Eventually, there will be enough lightweight, high-resolution displays available, and electronic publishing will take over from traditional publishing.

Current libraries are the outgrowth of the value and volume of information that existed in society. Funding for public libraries began with philanthropist Andrew Carnegie in the second half of the 19th century. Today there are different types of libraries. Research libraries, particularly those with large holdings of scientific information, already contain high volumes of digital information in specialized databases. Public libraries have a different mission; they are primarily providers of entertainment.

In recent years public library collections of electronic materials, such as CDs and videotapes, have grown much more rapidly than collections of books. A Benton Foundation study found that the public is supportive of libraries installing electronic materials. More and more libraries offer computer terminals with Internet access, and research suggests that Internet access is stimulating additional book traffic.

"The role of e-books in academic libraries is still not clear, and there is considerable development of standards, technologies, and pricing models needed to make the market for e-books viable and sustainable."
—LUCIA SNOWHILL, UNIVERSITY OF CALIFORNIA, SANTA BARBARA

However, libraries face competition from a variety of sources. Today more than half of all homes have personal computers, most of them with Internet connections. Large book chains such as Barnes and Noble and Borders, with their attached coffee shops, provide a friendly atmosphere conducive to browsing. Many public school systems provide "virtual library databases" as student resources to help with homework assignments, and the recent introduction of e-books has caused a stir in the publishing business.

The following articles tackle the problems related to libraries and the services they provide. Fay Merryfield argues that the traditional library is redundant unless it moves with the times; David Marcus, however, argues that libraries have already changed to meet the demands of their customers.

JOINING THE 21ST CENTURY
Fay Merryfield

Beginning an argument with a definition from an authoritative source is a popular way to clarify your topic from the outset.

LIBRARY [dictionary definition]—**a** : a place in which literary, musical, artistic, or reference materials (as books, manuscripts, recordings, or films) are kept for use but not for sale **b** : a collection of such materials.

Terminal decline

What can a physical library, and by that I mean a bricks and mortar building, offer that the Internet can not? The answer is, sadly, very little indeed.

Many library buildings are poorly maintained and funding for their renovation is limited. Further monetary problems have caused the buildings to be understocked and as such they do not provide a wide and comprehensive service to their customers—a fact reflected in a survey carried out by U.S. News and World Reports/Gallup in 1995 which showed that only 17 percent of Americans had visited a library in the last year. The Internet, however, provides a wealth of information at the press of a button, and the fact that many libraries simply ignore material published online makes them incomplete and outdated.

Back up your argument with statistics. That will help give your case credibility.

To put it plainly libraries are in a terminal state of decline, their acquisition programs are out of date, their staff are undertrained, and they are hampered by lack of space and outdated resources. They are out of step with what the customer wants and the situation for the future quite frankly looks bleak. The Internet, on the other hand, has no such problems and remains a popular source of intellectual growth and stimulus.

Myth v. reality

Establishing a fact and then disproving it is a good way to make your argument.

There are, however, a few myths surrounding libraries that need to be dispelled.

First, many people argue that libraries are warm and comforting places, staffed by people who love books and know about everything. This is not true. A recent poll revealed that young adults between the ages of 18 and 24 preferred superbook stores such as Borders and Barnes and Noble to their local libraries, as the bookshops were more comfortable, had up-to-date books, provided coffee, and played good music. Some of the stores also have access to the Internet.

Second, library staff, far from being the "font of all knowledge," are now finding themselves obsolete. A report by the Benton Foundation showed that most people surveyed believed that librarians could be replaced by community volunteers, such as retired people. This shows that librarians are not perceived as essential trained members of the educational community.

Librarianship has long been an accepted academic and professional field. Do you think it is possible for professions to become redundant over time? Can you think of any examples?

Third, libraries are traditionally seen as the centre of a community, where young and old meet. However, this might have been true once in small communities, but not any longer. Today, Internet users can achieve a much better sense of community online than in a library building and, what's more, can interact not only with local people. but with users from all over the world—the global community. Online it is now possible to start a dialogue with someone who shares your interests at a safe distance. Thus, the Internet offers more services than just a library—indeed in one morning a user could research several different subjects, chat with several different people in opposite corners of the world, buy music from Japan, listen to the radio in Britain, read/watch the latest news … all from his or her own desk.

> *"Public libraries can pretty much start digging their graves. Without government initiative, the public library will face an onslaught of negative pressures from publishers to disappear in the digital age."*
> —DAVID S. BENNAHUM,
> *MEME* E-ZINE, 1995

What advantages might a traditional, ordered public library have over the free-for-all, unlicensed information superhighway?

Globalization is leading to the death of conventional libraries. Users are more globally aware and it is not enough for them to read about an issue, for example, relating to Hong Kong written by a Harvard academic when they can access native newspapers online for on the spot information or look at the homepage of a student living in Hong Kong and get all the contrasting viewpoints they need. Users cannot simply get that kind of contact or information in a public library.

COMMENTARY: Building the digital library

The concept of an online text resource, or digital library, is not new. Several digital libraries already exist. Many of them are collections of research papers maintained by, and largely for, major universities and institutes. They are often specialized collections—in scientific, technical, or medical subjects, for example—and are accessible only to students or scholars.

The Digital Library Initiative

The recent rapid developments in information technology and its applications spurred U.S. government research into digital libraries. The first reseach project, known as the Digital Library Initiative (DLI) Phase I, was undertaken during 1994–1998 by six universities. A collective of government agencies—the National Science Foundation (NSF), National Aeronautics and Space Administration (NASA), and the Defense Advanced Research Projects Agency (DARPA)—put forward funds of $24 million, which were matched by corporate sponsors such as IBM and Microsoft. Each of the universities selected a "testbed" application for its digital library: The University of California at Berkeley launched its Environmental Planning and Geographic Information Systems, Carnegie Mellon University created an Informedia Digital Video Library, and so on. Launched in February 1998, Phase II took the DLI project further still; in the words of the NSF, it was to investigate "next-generation operational systems in such areas as education, engineering and design, earth and space sciences, biosciences, geography, economics, and the arts and humanities," and to "address the digital libraries life cycle from information creation, access and use, to archiving and preservation." The eventual application of the findings from DLI are certain to enrich the academic life of students.

Project Gutenberg

Some digital libraries offer more popular titles. One of the best-known is Project Gutenberg (www.gutenberg.net), named after Johannes Gutenberg, the inventor of the movable-type printing press. Project Gutenberg offers classic works of literature that can be downloaded for free over the Internet. Gutenberg was conceived in 1971 by Michael Hart at the University of Illinois. It was Hart's aim to reach the lowest common denominator—to provide as much popular literature as possible for "99 percent of the general public." This meant selecting works by such authors as Shakespeare and Walt Whitman, and supplying the texts in the simplest available format, namely ASCII (American Standard Code for Information Exchange). All Gutenberg texts are in the public domain (though a few have specific copyright restrictions), so they can be retrieved, stored, printed, or forwarded free of charge by the end user. By the start of the 21st century Project Gutenberg was just short of completing its 10,000th book.

Beat writer Richard Brautigan once conceived of a library that existed to give a home for all the pieces of work never published. In many ways Brautigan's idea can be applied to the Internet—anyone can publish on it and access it, it provides a wealth of information—that no one library could ever store, and as such has relegated conventional libraries to history. In fact focus groups referred to libraries in the future as being "information archives." Although this fact will sadden some of the population it is still a fact; but thanks to the Internet, subsequent generations will be able to read about the history of libraries and how they become obsolete.

> Richard Brautigan was a U.S. writer (?1935–1984), who achieved cult status in the 1960s as one of the San Francisco poets. See www.riza.com/richard/samples.shtml for examples of his work.

Libraries become gateways

Technology is becoming more and more widely available; many public places now offer internet access. In fact, a future role for library buildings might be to host the technology needed to access the Internet—they could become gateways to the net rather than simple book depositories. Thus customers could have immediate access to the very latest information on their given subject. This could include breaking news that could be "flashed" to them via email—they would thus have access not only to traditionally published texts but also to original work that is only available online.

So what chance is there for libraries?

All in all, what chance do libraries have of survival? Very little in our increasingly technocentric world. The Internet provides far more wide ranging and wide reaching sources than a conventional library ever could. Thus, the government should face facts and listen to what its citizens really want. Stop funding outmoded libraries and direct those funds instead toward new media.

FILE THIS UNDER SHOCK, FUTURE
David L. Marcus

NO

Stop by the corner of Taylor Street and Southwest 10th Avenue in downtown Portland, Ore., and you can sip a cup of Starbucks latte, take a personal finance workshop, surf the Web, view an art show, listen to a jazz concert, pet a potbellied pig, buy a book—and oh, yes, borrow a book. This is the Multnomah County public library, after all.

The author instantly challenges popular notions about libraries and their services.

The American public library, that dowdy dowager of the 70s and homeless shelter of the 80s, is now a full-fledged urban "destination." In New York City, libraries host 30,000 children's puppet shows, readings, and magic acts a year. San Francisco's main library has 220 public computer terminals. Chicago's 78 libraries loan museum passes; Louisville, Ky., has offered cooking classes.

And voters who used to routinely shortchange libraries are now supporting multimillion-dollar renovation projects. "Libraries have to meet the demands of their customers, just like any good retail operation, and the demands are changing," says Susan Kent, head librarian in Los Angeles, where the restored main branch drew 10,000 visitors on a single weekend for a "Teen Comic Art and Animation Festival" and Diane Keaton is curating a photo exhibit.

Still here

For years, it was predicted that libraries would become superfluous—mausoleums for books—when so much was available online. Instead, library visits now far exceed annual attendance at sporting events, concerts, and museums combined. It turns out that the very electronic revolution that was supposed to make libraries obsolete has made them indispensable. "Computers have attracted all kinds of people who had never been in libraries before but want to research what camera to buy or just see what's for sale on ebay," says

Ebay is an Internet auction site.

Marilyn Mason, who oversaw the five-year $90-million renovation and expansion of the Cleveland Public Library, which reopened this spring with Internet ports every five feet, a drive-up window for pickups and returns, and 30 miles of bookshelves.

"There's a coming together of demographic and cultural factors that benefit libraries," says Phyllis Dain, coauthor of the new *Civic Space/Cyberspace: The American Public Library in the Information Age*. Latchkey kids need a safe place to go after school, senior citizens want to read quietly but not alone, and babyboomer parents devour children's books by the shelfload.

> The public library can provide a range of social, as well as cultural, functions.

A place in society

Libraries have always had a special place in American culture; the very first meeting of the Continental Congress, in 1774, was held at one in Philadelphia. But those who run libraries have long been wary of the people they served. The nation's first municipal library, in Boston, had a typical view. Predicting an onslaught of Irish immigrants who would misuse its resources, the library's 1852 report to City Council sniffed, "They think little of moral and intellectual culture." At the turn of the century, steel baron Andrew Carnegie began his project of building more than 1,650 public libraries across the country, in a campaign to ensure the "education & improvement of the poorer classes." Several of his libraries had auditoriums and even boxing rings, the better to attract patrons and distract them from trade unionism.

> Andrew Carnegie (1835–1919) was a philanthropist as well as godfather of the U.S. steel industry. He gave away some $350 million of his wealth, declaring that "A man who dies rich, dies disgraced."

As city budgets dried up after World War II, libraries became the musty relics Philip Roth described in *Goodbye, Columbus*, where "bums off Mulberry Street slept over *Popular Mechanics*." These days, however, palatial libraries are opening or have opened in Seattle; New Haven, Conn.; Denver; San Antonio; Savannah; Grand Rapids, Mich.; and Rochester, N.Y. Having just rejected measures to improve police and firefighting services, Los Angeles voters recently approved a $178-million bond to renovate 28 library branches and build four new ones.

New arrivals

Carnegie wanted immigrant visitors to his libraries to do what he felt he'd done: pull themselves up through study and hard work. Indeed, a touchstone of the immigrant experience in 20th-century America has been the library, where newcomers have taught themselves English and learned about their adopted culture. That trend is still alive and well, though today they are as likely to use a computer as read a book. In New Haven, librarians teach Central American laborers to use the Internet and write resumes on computers. At the library in East Hampton, N.Y., nonresidents are allowed only 15 minutes online on busy days, but Eoghan O'Dwyer, 21, a golf caddy from Tipperary, Ireland, has developed a routine: "I check my email, I read

> Do you feel that the Internet promotes "study and hard work"?

The Library of Congress, founded in 1800, is the nation's oldest federal cultural institution. It has offices worldwide, and many of its collections can be viewed over the Internet.

the Gaelic football and hurling results on the sports pages
of the papers at home, and then I just flick around and start
the *Irish Times* crossword."

New problems

While heartening, these increasing demands have stretched
budgets and crowded older libraries. Twenty years ago, L.A.
offered books in Romance languages, German, and Greek.
Last year, the city library system bought books, videos,
cassettes, and software in 100 languages. In San Jose,
Calif., where circulation has soared 55 percent in three
years, library director Jane Light struggles to choose among
requests for computer how-to books in a dozen languages;
English tapes for Vietnamese speakers; and bilingual
children's books that Russian parents can share with
their English-speaking kids.

Even as technology lightens some of this load, last week's
convention of the American Library Association showed that
it brings complications, too. Electronic books that can be
downloaded on demand will offer relief for cramped stacks,
but publishers have yet to decide how to charge libraries
for the service. And while more than 80 percent of libraries
offer Internet access, the debate over whether to install
antipornography filters has yet to be settled. Which gets at
a very old-fashioned conflict between the library's role as
caretaker of books and server of the public.

Why should these two roles conflict with one another?

Summary

The two articles present the current debate surrounding the Internet and libraries. Have new media made conventional libraries obsolete?

In "Joining the 21st Century" Fay Merryfield argues that, far from being mainstays of the community where young and old alike gather to expand their knowledge, traditional public libraries are often underfunded and have poor resources. Their staffs are normally little more than caretakers, and community volunteers could do their job. Merryfield argues that the Internet, with its vast wealth of knowledge, both previously published and unpublished, is a far better resource that can allow its users to be part of a global, international community. Thus the government should redirect funds allocated for public libraries toward new media instead.

In "File This Under Shock, Future" David Marcus paints a very different picture of modern libraries. He argues that, far from declining, libraries now benefit from big boosts from civic funds. Marcus believes that access to the Internet has allowed the tradition established by Andrew Carnegie in bringing knowledge to everyone to continue. While librarians acknowledge that e-books could take customers away from conventional books, investing in new technology will allow a future for libraries.

FURTHER INFORMATION:

Books:

Crawford, Walt, *Being Analog: Creating Tomorrow's Libraries*. Chicago: American Library Association Editions, 1999.

Lesk, Michael, *Practical Digital Libraries: Books, Bytes, and Bucks*. San Francisco: Morgan Kaufmann Publishers, 1997.

Molz, Redmond Kathleen, and Dain, Phyllis, *Civic Space/Cyberspace*. Cambridge, MA: MIT Press, 1998.

Negroponte, Nicholas, *Being Digital*. New York: Alfred A. Knopf, 1995.

Shuman, Bruce A., *Beyond the Library of the Future: More Alternative Futures for the Public Library*. Englewood, CO: Libraries Unlimited, 1997.

Useful websites:

www.dlib.org/dlib/april97/04arms.html
Arms, William Y., "The Hare and the Tortoise: Relaxing Assumptions about the Future of Digital Libraries." *D-Lib Magazine*, April 1997.

www.benton.org/Library/Kellogg/buildings.html
"Buildings, Books, and Bytes: Libraries and Communities in the Digital Age." A report, published by Benton Foundation, on what library leaders and the public have to say about the future of libraries in the digital age.

www.salonmag.com/21st/feature/1997/12/02feature.html
Corcoran, Kate, "Are We Ready for the Library of the Future?"

www.infotoday.com/cilmag/feb98/story2.htm
Noble, Cherrie, "Reflecting on Our Future: What Will the Role of Virtual Librarian Be?"

The following debates in the Pro/Con series may also be of interest:

In this volume:

Topic 15 Will e-publishing replace the traditional book?

Copyright in the United States, pages 188–189

WILL THE INTERNET MAKE LIBRARIES OBSOLETE?

YES: The Internet's capacity is theoretically limitless, and simple word searches can bring results within seconds

YES: Civic budgets cannot support the vast library networks of yesteryear, and many branches are in decline or already shut

EASE OF ACCESS
Is it easier to use the Internet than it is to use a pubic library?

USELESS BUILDINGS
Are library buildings losing their purpose?

NO: The Internet is chaotic; successful data access often depends on knowing exactly where to look (there are no librarians); the technology may have great potential but is ergonomically unsound

NO: Modern libraries have a broader role in the community, offering places to stop and shop, eat, browse books and journals, and sample music before buying

WILL THE INTERNET MAKE LIBRARIES OBSOLETE? KEY POINTS

YES: Libraries cannot fully exploit e-books because there are as yet no software and hardware standards, no consensus on licensing and rights management, and no decisions on long-term access

YES: Publishers are reluctant to devolve control to libraries; the former want to make money, the latter have a public duty to offer texts for free

E-BOOKS
Will increasing access to online books favor the Internet rather than the public library?

NO: Technical problems will soon be overcome and allow libraries to stock "master copies" that can be accessed by several users at once

NO: Libraries could play a key role in providing access to copyrighted material that is not in the public domain

GLOSSARY

blocking programs computer programs that enable parents and corporations to prevent their children and employees respectively from accessing unsuitable or time-wasting material via computers. *See also* censorship, Internet.

body image the perception that a person has about how his or her body should look.

brand image the association of a certain lifestyle, for example, with a certain brand of product.

censorship the act of checking books, magazines, broadcasts, etc., to remove unsuitable or inappropriate material; also the act of removing such material. *See also* blocking programs, prior restraint.

commercial speech written or spoken material—for example, advertising—purely concerned with profit-making activities.

consumerism a term describing a strong desire to buy and own goods; also the theory that an increasing consumption of consumer goods is economically desirable.

copyright laws laws that protect the owner of a piece of written, musical, or artistic work in the event of someone else reproducing or performing the work without permission. *See also* intellectual property, pirated, royalty.

cyberspace the term for the theoretical zone through which information passes when the Internet (see below) is used. *See also* virtual, World Wide Web.

database a large amount of information stored on a computer in such a way that it can be accessed quickly and selectively.

developed country any one of the world's industrialized, wealthier countries, for example, Britain, Japan, or the U.S.

developing country any one of a range of countries that are primarily agricultural or partly industrialized or rely on a single product, such as oil. Most, but not all, are poor. Examples include Ethiopia and India.

dot com a term derived from the familiar suffix to numerous website addresses—.com—that is often applied to companies that trade via the Internet (see below). *See also* e-, electronic media, media.

download to copy material from one computer to another or from a computer to a removable disk. *See also* MP3.

e- a short form of "electronic." It is placed at the start of a word to show that an activity is carried out by computer, for example, e-mail, e-publishing, and e-commerce. *See also* dot com, electronic media, media.

electronic media a term describing new media—media organizations that pass on information or provide entertainment by electronic means, for example, radio, television, or the Internet (see below). *See also* dot com, e-, media, online.

freedom of speech the right to freedom of expression of one's views and opinions, and freedom of the press, protected by the First Amendment.

global village a term coined by Canadian scholar and writer Marshall McLuhan. It refers to the ability of television and other electronic media to reach many people over great distances, making the world effectively smaller and at the same time less diverse. *See also* electronic media.

globalization the expansion worldwide of private corporations and of the culture of the countries they come from.

high-resolution a term that describes an image—for example, on a computer or TV screen—that is of a clarity that permits a large amount of detail to be seen.

intellectual property a term for any creative work, such as the text of a book, a design, or an invention, the ownership of which may be protected under copyright laws. *See also* copyright laws, pirated, royalty.

Internet the international network of computers that permits the passage of information and conduct of business between companies, instititutions, and individuals all over the world. The word is sometimes shortened to the "Net." *See also* cyberspace, dot com, e-, electronic media, Internet Service Provider, media, media violence, multimedia, online, tabloid media, virtual, World Wide Web.

Internet Service Provider (ISP) the generic name for a company that connects people to the Internet (see above).

media the plural form of the word "medium." The media are any of the organizations that pass information or supply entertainment to people, for example, newspapers, radio, television, and dot coms. *See also* dot com, e-, electronic media, multimedia.

media violence a term describing violence represented in movies and fictional TV shows. *See also* media, social violence.

MP3 a computer format that compresses audio signals—for example, music tracks— so that they can be more quickly copied from computer to computer via the Internet (see above). *See also* download.

multimedia the name for the concept that allows a computer user to access and switch between text, video, audio, and illustrative material. *See also* electronic media, Internet, media.

multinationals a term for large corporations that operate in several countries.

nationalized a word describing an industry that is run or owned by the government.

negative advertising a form of advertising used in politics that focuses on the alleged shortcomings of a political opponent, for example, perceived character flaws or alleged mistakes made while in office.

new media *see* electronic media.

online a term describing an activity carried out via a computer network such as the Internet (see above), for example, online banking. *See also* dot com, e-, electronic media, World Wide Web.

paparazzi the plural form of the Italian word *paparazzo*, which is now widely used to describe freelance photographers who specialize in taking pictures of celebrities.

pirated a term describing video or audio material that has been copied without the permission of the creator or owner of the original work. *See also* copyright laws, intellectual property, royalty.

prior restraint an order issued by a government forbidding in advance the utterance, publication, or broadcasting of material that is, for example, deemed to be defamatory or against the interests of national security. *See also* censorship.

ratings system a system that grades the suitability of television programs for various kinds of audiences.

regulate to impose a formal set of rules governing the conduct of an industry or activity; the term "deregulate" refers to the removal of such rules.

royalty a payment made to the creator of a piece of written or musical work by those who have permission to reproduce or perform it. *See also* copyright laws, intellectual property, pirated.

social violence the term for acts of violence that take place in a society during the course of the overall day-to-day life of that society, for example, wife beatings, rapes, murders, or gang fights. *See also* media violence.

tabloid media a term for newspapers that are produced in a compact size and in which the content and treatment of news are typically sensationalist. *See also* media.

virtual a term used to describe a computer-generated scenario or environment that seeks to mimic reality and may seem real or very close to it, for example, virtual pet, virtual reality. *See also* cyberspace.

World Wide Web (WWW) the name for a vast quantity of cross-referenced electronic pages and sites that is accessed by connecting to the Internet (see above).

Acknowledgments

Topic 1 Should the Media Be Subject to Censorship?

Yes: From "The Matter of the Plague/Die Sache Mit Der Leichenpest" by Joseph Goebbels in *Das eherne Herz*, Munich: Zentralverlag der NSDAP. Copyright © 1943 by Calvin University. Used by permission of the translator, Dr. Randall Bytwerk.

No: From "Freedom of Expression in the Arts and the Media," ACLU Report 14, by the American Civil Liberties Union. Copyright © 1997 by American Civil Liberties Union. Used by permission

Topic 2 Do Newsmakers Have a Right to Privacy?

Yes: From "The Media: Sinking Ever Deeper" by Judy Mann in *The Washington Post*, December 2, 1998. Copyright © 1998 by *The Washington Post*. Reprinted with permission of *The Washington Post*, Washington, D.C.

No: From "If it's *OK!* for Stars to Cash in on Weddings … Then They Must Accept It Is *Hello!* to Loss of Privacy" by Mark Lawson in "Opinions and Letters," *The Guardian*, December 23, 2000. Copyright © 2000 by Mark Lawson. Used by permission.

Topic 3 Do People Watch Too Much Television?

Yes: From "Warning: Too Much TV is Hazardous to Your Health" by TV Turnoff Network Newsletter (www.TV-Turnoff.org/hazardous.pdf). Copyright © 2001 by TV-Turnoff Network. Reprinted by permission of TV-Turnoff Network, 2001 (www.tvturnoff.org).

No: From "Television Heals" by Jib Fowles in *Why Viewers Watch: A Reappraisal of Television's Effects*. Copyright © 1992 by Sage Publications. Reprinted with permission of Sage Publications, Thousand Oaks, CA.

Topic 4 Does the V-chip Work?

Yes: From "The V-chip: Where Do We Go From Here? The Reality of Television Ratings in the United States" by Children Now (www.childrennow.org/media/vchip/v-chip_transcript. html). Copyright © by Children Now. Used by permission.

No: From "'V' is for Virtually Ignored: Few Americans Have Bothered to Learn How to Use the Child-Protecting V-chip" by Aaron Barnhaart in *The Kansas City Star*, April 27, 2000. Copyright © by *The Kansas City Star*.

Topic 5 Does Movie and Television Violence Cause Social Violence?

Yes: From "Impact of Televised Violence" by John P. Murray, Ph.D., School of Family Studies and Human Services, Kansas State University (www.ksu.edu/humec/impact.htm). Copyright © 1994 by John P. Murray. Used by permission.

No: From "Ten Things Wrong with the 'Effects Model'" by David Gauntlett in *Approaches to Audiences—A Reader*, edited by Roger Dickinson, Ramaswani Harindranath & Olga Linné. Copyright © 1998 by David Gauntlett. Reproduced by permission of Arnold Publishers.

Topic 6 Do the Media Encourage a Distorted Body Image?

Yes: From "Body Image and Advertising" in *Issue Briefs*, April 25, 2000, Mediascope Press. Copyright © 2000 by Mediascope Press. Used by permission.

No: From "Weighty Matters: The British Government Plans to Take on Heroin Chic in a Body Image Summit This Month" by William Underhill, June 7, 2000, (Salon.com). Copyright © 2000 by William Underhill. Used by permission.

Topic 7 Is Advertising Too Powerful in American Society?

Yes: From "Rise of the Image Culture: Reimagining the American Dream" by Elizabeth Thoman in *Media and Values*, Issue 57, Winter 1992. Copyright © 1992. Reprinted by permission of the Center for Media Literacy, 3101 Ocean Park Blvd., Ste. 200, Santa Monica, CA 90405 (www.medialit.org).

No: From "In Defense of Advertising: Arguments from Reason, Ethical Egoism, and Laissez-Faire Capitalism" by Geoffrey P. Lantos in *The Journal of Consumer Affairs*, Vol. 29, No. 1, Summer 1995. Copyright © 1995 by Journal of Consumer Affairs. Reprinted by permission of the University of Wisconsin Press.

Topic 8 Is Advertising to Children Morally Wrong?

Yes: "Children and Advertising in U.S. Society" by A. Vasudevan. Copyright © 2001 by A. Vasudevan. Used by permission.

No: From "Pester Power: A Report on Attitudes in Spain and Sweden." Research by NOP Solutions for the Children's Program, December 1999. Copyright © 1999 by the Children's Program of the UK Advertising Association. Used by permission.

Topic 9 Should Tobacco Advertising Be Banned?

Yes: From "Tobacco Advertising" by Marc C. Willemsen, Dutch Foundation on Smoking and Health, The Hague, Netherlands, and Boudewijn de Blij, Netherlands Heart Foundation, The Hague,

Netherlands. Copyright © Marc C. Willemsen and Boudewijn de Blij. Used by permission.

No: From "More Taxes and Less Free Speech" by Linda Gorman, The Independence Institute (i2i.org/SuptDocs/PersonalFreedom/CensoringTobaccoAdvertising.htm). Copyright © 1999 by Linda Gorman. Used by permission.

Topic 10 Does Advertising Threaten Objective Journalism?
Yes: From "The Power of the Press Has a Price" by Lawrence Soley, in *Extra!*, July/August 1997. Copyright © 1997 by Lawrence Soley.

No: From "The Wall" by David Shaw in the *Los Angeles Times*, December 20, 1999. Copyright © 1999 Times Mirror Company. Used by permission.

Topic 11 Is There Too Much Political Advertising?
Yes: From "Gouging Democracy: How the Television Industry Profiteered on Election 2000" by the Alliance for Better Campaigns (www.bettercampaigns.org). Used by permission.

No: From "Political Advertising Regulation: An Unconstitutional Menace"? by Stephen Bates in Policy Analysis No. 112, September 22, 1988. Used by permission.

Topic 12 Should the Internet Be Policed?
Yes: From "Against Racial Discrimination on the Internet," Department of Housing and Urban Development press release, July 20, 2000. Courtesy of Department of Housing and Urban Development.

No: From "Censorship in a Box" by the American Civil Liberties Union (www.aclu.org/issues/cyber/box.html#censorship). Copyright © 1998 by American Civil Liberties Union. Used by permission.

Topic 13 Will the Internet Create a Global Economy?
Yes: From "Globalizing the Internet" by Sunder Katwala. Copyright © 2001 by Sunder Katwala. Used by permission.

No: From "Electronic Empire" by Anthony M. Townsend and James T. Bennett in *Communications of the ACM*, Vol. 44, Issue 3, March 2001. Copyright © 2001 by Anthony M. Townsend and James T. Bennett. Used by permission.

Topic 14 Does Napster Encourage Copyright Infringement?
Yes: From "Facing the Music" in *Current Events*, March 16, 2001. *Current Events* copyright © 2001 by Weekly Reader Corporation. All rights reserved. Used by permission.

No: From "Rants about Free Downloads" by Steve Smith, in *Twice*, March 12, 2001, New York. Copyright © 2001 Cahners Business Information, a division of Reed Elsevier, Inc. Used by permission.

Topic 15 Will E-publishing Replace the Traditional Book?
Yes: From "The Demise of Writing" by Geoffrey E. Meredith, *The Futurist Magazine*, October 1999. Copyright © 1999 by World Future Society. Used by permission of the World Future Society, 7910 Woodmont Ave., Suite 450, Bethesda, MA.

No: From "Electronic Books: To 'E' or Not to 'E': That Is the Question" by Stephanie Ardito, *Searcher Magazine*, Vol. 8, April 2000. Copyright © 2000 by Stephanie Ardito. Used by permission.

Topic 16 Will the Internet Make Libraries Obsolete?
Yes: From "Joining the 21st Century" by Fay Merryfield. Copyright © 2001 by Mike Atherton. Used by permission.

No: From "File This under Shock, Future" by David L. Marcus in *U.S. News & World Report*, from the July 12, 1999 issue, pages 48–49, Text Only. Used by permission.

Brown Partworks Limited has made every effort to contact and acknowledge the creators and copyright holders of all extracts reproduced in this volume. We apologize for any omissions. Any person who wishes to be credited in further volumes should contact Brown Partworks Limited in writing: Brown Partworks Limited, 8 Chapel Place, Rivington Street, London EC2A 3DQ, U.K.

Picture credits

Cover: Hulton/Archive; Corbis: 210; Bettmann 41, 170; Michael Gerber 80, 84–85; The Purcell Team 124–125; **Hulton/Archive:** Central Press 150–151; Keystone 14; **Image Bank:** B. Busco 158; Vicky Kasala 22–23; **PA Photos:** 27; European Press Agency 146, 183; EPA Photo ANSA/Giorgio Benvenuti 33

SET INDEX